Henry Baker Tristram, James Fergusson, William Amherst Hayne

The land of Moab; travels and discoveries on the east side of the Dead sea and the Jordan

Henry Baker Tristram, James Fergusson, William Amherst Hayne

The land of Moab; travels and discoveries on the east side of the Dead sea and the Jordan

ISBN/EAN: 9783337208103

Printed in Europe, USA, Canada, Australia, Japan

Cover: Foto ©Andreas Hilbeck / pixelio.de

More available books at **www.hansebooks.com**

THE
LAND OF MOAB:

TRAVELS AND DISCOVERIES
ON THE EAST SIDE
OF THE DEAD SEA AND THE JORDAN.

BY

H. B. TRISTRAM, M.A., LL.D., F.R.S.,
HON. CANON OF DURHAM.

WITH A CHAPTER ON THE PERSIAN PALACE OF MASHITA,
BY JAS. FERGUSON, F.R.S.

WITH MAP, AND
ILLUSTRATIONS BY C. L. BUXTON AND R. C. JOHNSON.

NEW YORK:
HARPER & BROTHERS, PUBLISHERS.
FRANKLIN SQUARE.
1873.

PREFACE.

The circumstances under which the expedition, the results of which are narrated in the following pages, was undertaken, are sufficiently explained in the first chapter.

The object was a careful examination of the present state of a country frequently referred to in the Old Testament Scriptures, and intimately connected with Jewish history, but which has not been traversed at leisure by any explorer since the fall of the Roman empire.

That the journey has produced some results which may justify us for having disregarded the advice so earnestly given by the Palestine Exploration Fund to persons about to explore—Don't! "To those who propose to raise any private expedition, we would say, Wait!"*—it is hoped will be admitted on a perusal of the narrative.

The recovery of several ancient sites; the careful verification of Machærus, the scene of John the Baptist's imprisonment and martyrdom; the very interesting discovery of Zoar, with the valuable illustration it affords of the careful accuracy of the Scriptural narrative in the minutest details; the finding of a palace of Chosroes, with its sumptuous architecture, and the ray of light it casts upon one of the most obscure periods of later Roman history—these certainly were enough to reward the most sanguine explorer.

Even apart from these principal discoveries, there is scarcely a passage in Holy Writ, in which Moab is mentioned, which was not in some degree illustrated

---

* "Our Work in Palestine," p. 328.

during the journey; and the glowing prophecies of Isaiah and Jeremiah, the allusions of Amos and Zephaniah, the story of the wars of Sihon, of Jephthah, and of Joab, must ever be read with deepened interest by those who have noted their marvelous coincidences with the state of the country as we now see it.

Arab society also is in a more primitive and simple state than where affected by intercourse with other nationalities in the rest of Syria. The Beni Sakk'r are true Midianites in all their habits: the minor tribes reproduce, perhaps, the nearest parallel to the state of Canaan at the time of the Israelitish conquest which can be found existing at the present day.

I must take this opportunity of expressing my deep sense of my obligations to the friends who have assisted me in the work:—to Mr. Fergusson, for his solution of the problem of the Persian palace, and for the valuable contributions, both by pen and pencil, to its architectural history, which enrich the volume; to my friend and fellow-traveler, Mr. Klein, for the sagacity and forethought which insured the success of our journey; and to my zealous and indefatigable young brothers of the tent, whose enthusiasm and happy tempers lightened every labor, and whose only rivalry was in promoting the objects of our expedition. To Messrs. Buxton and Johnson I owe all the illustrations of the volume, selected from the splendid series of one hundred and eighty photographs which they secured and generously placed at my disposal.

One of our party is now beyond the reach of my thanks—William Amherst Hayne, of saintly memory, suddenly, within the last few days, removed, at what seemed to be the dawn of a career of rare promise. He lived in his Bible, and clung to its promises; and now in a foreign land his body rests, awaiting in Christ a glorious resurrection.

GREATHAM VICARAGE, *February*, 1873.

CONTENTS.

CHAPTER I.

View of the Mountains of Moab from Jerusalem.—Previous Expediditions.—Messrs. Palmer and Tyrwhitt Drake.—British Association.—Companions.—Mr. Klein.—Preliminary Negotiations.—The Adwân.—Preparations at Jerusalem.—The Ta'amirah.—Arab Chicanery.—Muleteer in Prison.—Start for the South.—Bethlehem.—Volunteer Escort of Ta'amirah.—Hebron.—Our first Bivouac.—Old Friends.—Sheik Hamzi, an Arab Attorney.—Fruitless Negotiations.—Mosque and Bazars at Hebron.—A Jewish Interior.—Abou da Houk and the Jehalin.—Diplomatic Difficulties.—A Kerak Guide.—Signature of a Contract.—Payment of Deposit.—Storm under Canvas.—Route from Hebron................Page 17

CHAPTER II.

Route from Hebron to Engedi.—Yakin.—Forest of Ziph.—Kirbet Zadoud.—Ka'abineh Camp.—Hospitality.—Arab Coffee.—Unexpected Flood in the Night.—Effect of sudden Rains.—Change of Flora.—Wady el Ghâr.—El Husasah, *Hazziz*.—Cliff of Ziz.—Steep Pass.—Descent to Engedi.—Rich Botany.—Rashâyideh Arabs.—A Bedouin Fantasia.—Ornithology of Engedi.—Camp under Sebbeh (*Masada*) Wady Seyal.—Lifeless Desolation.—Wady Makheras.—Visit to the Fortress of Masada.—Ancient Jewish Synagogue.—Contrast with the Synagogues of Galilee.—Acoustic Phenomenon.—Remarkable Aurora.—Route to Jebel Usdum.—Ford to the Lisan.—View of Mount Hor.—Curious Arab Custom.—Oasis of Zuweirah.—Lateness of the Season........................ 35

CHAPTER III.

An early Start.—Effect of the Sun on the Mountains.—Sudden Thunder-storm.—A Salt Cavern.—Marl Deposit on the Salt Mountain.

—Its Origin.—Elevation of the New Red Sandstone.—Position of the Salt Rock.—Crossing the Sebkha.—Alarm of Marauders.—Frontier of Moab.—Sudden Apparition of Enemies.—A threatened Skirmish.—Naked Warriors.—Our Guide stripped.—The Beni Atiyeh.—A Treaty made.—March through the Wood.—Difficulties of Exploration.—A costly Guard.—Vegetation of the Sáfieh.—Ancient Remains.—Kasr el Bushariyeh.—Old Mill.—Moslem Burying-ground.—Remains exposed.—Boundary of Moab.—Brook Zered.—Suphah.—Variety in the Vegetation of the Safieh.—Horsemen from Kerak.—Son of the Mudjelli.—Petty Thefts.—A Mule on its Trial.—Return of the Jehalin..................................Page 53

CHAPTER IV.

From the Sáfieh to Kerak.—Wady Gra'hhi.—Ford of the Stinking River.—Nemeirah.—The Waters of Nimrim: their real Position.—Not identical with Nemeirah.—Poor Ruins.—The Brook of the Willows.—Wady Asal.—The Shoulder of the Lisan.—Wady Dra'a.—View of the Lisan.—Contrast of the Geology of the east and west Sides of the Dead Sea.—A charming Glen.—Mezra'ah, Zoar.—Disputed Identity with Dra'a.—A turbulent Guard.—Nocturnal Alarms.—Splendid Sunrise.—Attempted Robbery.—Successful Extortion.—Ascent to Kerak.—Magnificent Gorge.—Geological Studies.—Basaltic Streams.—El Kubboh.—Crusading Traditions.—Raynald of Chatillon.—Panoramic View of the Dead Sea.—Bedouin Camps and Shepherds.—Wady R'seir.—Wady of Kerak.—Rugged Ascent.—Strange Access to a City.—Tunnel in the Rock.—Arrival at Kerak... 70

CHAPTER V.

Kerak.—A natural Fortress: its Height, Position, Form, Area, Fortifications.—Accessible only by Tunnels.—The Castle of Bybars.—The great Castle: its Shape, Moat, Cistern, Crypt, Chapel, Gateways.—Occupation of Castle by Ibrahim Pasha.—Water Supply.—Mosque.—Ancient Basilica.—Our Camp in the Castle of Bybars.—Greek School-master.—A Friend in need.—Kerak Interior.—Roman Pavement.—Ancient Bath.—Antiques and Coins.—Christian Quarter.—Greek Church.—School and Bibles.—Threats of the

Chiefs.—Ransom demanded.—Find ourselves Prisoners.—Messenger to Jerusalem.—Every Man his own Thief-catcher.—Value of Pork.—Daoud's Stratagem.—Midnight Interview.—Welcome Aid.—Arrival of the Beni Sakk'r, Sheik Zadam.—The Tables turned.—A Sunday under Arrest.—Arabic Service.—Greek Christians.—Demands on the Hakim.—View from the Castle Wall.—Relations of Kerak and the Beni Sakk'r.—Excursion under Guard.—Our Letter discovered.—Renewed Threats........................... Page 85

CHAPTER VI.

Excursion to the south of Kerak.—Kureitun.—The twin Towns.—*Kiriathaim*.—The Highlands of Moab.—Ruined Cities.—Azizah.—Wine-presses.—M'hheileh.—Jubah.—Roman Road.—Mahk'henah.—Cisterns.—Modeh.—Roman Mile-stones.—Mesh'had.—Madin.—Theniyeh.—Arabic Names.—Kerak, *Kir-moab*, or *Kir-hareseth*.—Obstinacy of the Mudjelli.—Visit to the Council.—Diplomacy about Ransom.—Arab Manœuvres.—Off at last.—Tremendous Storm.—Road to Rabba.—Rakim.—Roman Road.—Arrival at Rabba.—Camp in a Tank.—Description of Rabba.—Roman Temples.—Basaltic Stones.—The Kerak Men again.—Daoud's Ingenuity for the Horse's Corn.—Robbery of the Letter-carrier.—Bad News.—Mr. Klein recalled.. 113

CHAPTER VII.

From Rabba to the Arnon.—Visit from the Hamideh.—Characters of Zadam and Sahan.—Ibn Tarif.—Present from Mr. Drake.—Ibn Tarif's Attention.—Roman Way-side Temple.—Missdehh.—Hameitât, the ancient Ham.—Kasr Rabba.—Beit el Kurm.—Large Temple.—Ar and Areopolis.—A pillar Letter-box in the Waste.—News from Jerusalem.—Troops on the move for our Rescue.—The Mudjelli returns.—Restoration of Mr. Klein's Letter.—Shihan.—Curious Inclosure of Basalt.—Sihon and the Amorites.—The View from Jebel Shihan.—Mnhatet el Haj.—Jahaz.—Descent to the Arnon.—Basaltic Dike.—Traces of Roman Road.—Ruined Forts.—"The City in the midst of the River."—Rugged Ascent.—A Mountain Pass in the Darkness.—Dreary Camp on the Uplands.—Mr. Klein's Departure.—Aroer.—Topography of the Arnon.—Ride to

Dhiban.—Its Ruins.—The Moabite Stone.—Conjectures as to its original Position.—Means of its Preservation.—An Oil-press.—Identity of Dhiban with Dibon..................Page 130

CHAPTER VIII.

From Dibon eastward.—Beni Sakk'r Flocks and Herds.—The Plain of the Vineyards.—Rhibuych.—The Ruins of Um Rasas.—Its Walls.—Abundance of Game.—Wild-cats.—Beni Sakk'r Camp.—Considerate Neighbors.—Deep Tank.—The Raven's Home.—Um Rasas, within the Walls and without.—Three ruined Churches.—Apses still remaining.—Arches and Streets.—Amphitheatre.—Isolated mortuary Tower.—Church in the Plain.—Quaint Tradition and Legend.—Freedom of the Desert.—Intense Cold.—Animal Life of the Plains.— M'Seitbeh.—Ancient Block-houses.—Wady Butm.—Letters from the Brigade.—A long Sunday's Ride.—Crossing the Themed.—Visit to Zadam's Tent.—Westward ho!—Rumors of the Troops.—Ajermeh Camp.—Ride in the Dark.—A Turcoman Guide.—The Camp.—Reception by the Pasha.—Depositions taken down.—A bitter Night.—Beiram.—Grand Salute.—Speculations on Kerak... 153

CHAPTER IX.

Return from the Wady Na'ur to Um Rasas.—Royal Entertainment by the Ajermeh.—Our Horses keep Beiram.—Coffee-drinking.—Sherouau's many Calls.—Wandering Tramps.—A Beggar's Hospitality.—Return to our Tents.—Reports of a buried Stone.—Zadam's Account of the black, or basalt, Country eastward.—El Hharreh.—Stone Cities.—Eastward ho!—Mirage on the Plains.—Gazelle Hunt.—The Hadj Road.—Khan Zebib.—Description of the ruined Khan.—Traces of earlier Buildings.—Remains of a Doric Temple.—Labyrinth of Cisterns.—Prehistoric Remains.—Cairns.—A vain Pursuit after the Stone of Rasas............................ 175

CHAPTER X.

Departure from Um Rasas.—Dhra'a.—The Themed.—R'mail.—A riverside Camp.—Zafaran.—A military Keep.—Supplies running short.—Start for the North-east.—Kasr el Herri.—Surveying.—

Roman Road.—Um Weleed.—Extent of Um Weleed.—Saracenic Khan.—Roman City.—Streets.—Large Court, or Pretorium Gateway.—Doric Temple.—Date of these Cities.—No Clues to the ancient Name.—Um el Kuseir.—Large Caverns.—Ziza.—Interesting Remains.—Roman military Station.—Magnificent Tank.—Elaborate System of Irrigation in olden Time.—Large vaulted Fort.—Burial-place aloft.—Ibrahim Pasha's Garrison.—Other Forts destroyed.—Remains of Cuphic Inscriptions.—Fine Christian Church.—Variety of wild Animals and Birds.—Return of Convoy from Jerusalem.—Evening Bells.—A Fugitive.—Stripped by the Anizeh.—The Ibex-hunter.—Honesty of our Men and of the Turkish Soldiers.—Sunday's Rest.—Mohammedan Criticism on Christian Inconsistency..Page 190

CHAPTER XI.

The Palace of Mâshitâ.—Ride from Ziza.—Limestone Knolls rising above the Plain.—Their geological Origin.—Gradual Formation of the Table-land.—Hadj Road.—Palace suddenly in Sight.—First Impressions.—Description of the Palace.—Outer Wall.—Bastions.—Gorgeous Façade.—Octagonal Bastions.—Gate-way.—Delineations of Animals and Birds.—Inner Area.—Inhabited Portion.—Its Plan. — Rich Gate-way.—Corinthian Capitals.—Arch overthrown by Earthquake.—Long Inscriptions.—Nabathæan or Pelvic?—Peculiar Bricks.—Large open Hall.—Vaulted Roof.—Inner Doorway.—Peculiar Capitals.—Large inner domed Hall with alcoved Recesses.—Inner Chambers.—Construction of the outer Wall.—Hollow Bastion.—The Palace never finished.—The Builders interrupted.—No local Tradition of its Origin.—Probably Chosroes II., of Persia, its Builder, A.D. 614.—Campaign of Chosroes.—Conquest of Syria.—Capture of Jerusalem.—Sudden Reverse.—Advance of Heraclius, A.D. 624.—The whole East reconquered by Rome, A.D. 632.—Irruption of the Saracens.—Final Devastation of the Country.—Its Disappearance from History.—Sassanian Origin of the Palace confirmed by its Architecture.—Mr. Fergusson's Opinion.—El Ah'la.. 210

CHAPTER XII.

Second Visit to Mâshitâ.—Expedition to Kustul.—Imperial Eagle.—Interesting Character of the Remains of Kustul.—Castellated Temple.—Corinthian Pilasters.—Nabathæan Inscriptions.—Larger Castle.—Vaulted Chambers and massive Bastions.—A Greek Altar exhumed.—Walls for collecting Water.—Kustul-Castellum.—Thenib.—Rujum Hamam.—Views of the Belka.—Southward Migration of the Beni Sakk'r.—Move Camp toward the West.—Azabarah.—Jebel Jelul.—Magnificent Panorama.—Sufa.—Trained Falcons.—Women Water-drawers.—Arrival at our Camp.—Visit from Fendi y Faiz.—Entertainment of the great Sheik.—Photographing of the Princes.—Escort of the Hadj.—Parting with the Suhan.—Delay at Habis.—Descent of the Wady Habis.—Junction with the Zerka Ma'in.—Contrast between the Highlands of Moab and the Mountains .... Page 231

CHAPTER XIII.

Change from the Highlands.—The Hamideh.—Lords of high and low Degree.—Septs and political Divisions of the Hamideh.—Their Habits and Character.—Ornithology of the Glens.—The Callirrhoe.—An Evening's Fishing.—Geology of the Zerka Ma'in.—Basaltic Streams.—Descent to the hot Springs.—The Baths of Herod.—Hamideh Camp.—Nubian Slave.—A Sulphur Hot-bath.—Descriptions of Josephus and Pliny.—Ptolemy's Geography.—Sulphur Terraces.—Rapid Deposits.—Basalt and Limestone.—Palm-groves.—Temperature of the Springs.—Natural Formation of Tunnels.—Primitive Vapor-bath.—Arab Traditions.—Legend of King Solomon.—Sacrificial Rites.—Strange Plants.—The Shrub of Josephus.—The Sulphur Plant.—Orobanches.—Butterflies and rare Birds.—Ibex.—Sunday at Callirrhoe.—Amateur Physician.—Venison and Butter.—Hamideh horned Cattle................................. 245

CHAPTER XIV.

Visit to Machærus.—Delays at Starting.—Superstitions and Obstinacy of Muleteers.—Wady Z'gara.—Deep Gorge.—Fine Landscape.—Ruins of Machærus.—The Town.—Roman Road.—Fortress.—Citadel.—Dungeons.—The Baptist's Prison.—Pliny's Account.—History of Machaerus.—Josephus's Description.—The Maccabees.—Herod the Great.—Fabled Plant.—Siege by L. Bassus.—Identity of the Castle with the Baptist's Prison.—Hamideh Hospitality.—Fresh Butter.—Grand Panorama.—Stone Circles.—Expedition to Attarus.—Horses lost and found.—A wooded District.—View.—Jebel Attarus.—Kureiyat.—Identity with Kiriathaim.—Attarus and Ataroth..Page 267

CHAPTER XV.

Visit to Zara, the ancient Zareth-shahar.—Volcanic Soil.—Rich Botany.—Descent to Dead Sea.—Ancient Road.—Scouts ahead.—False Alarm.—Beni Sakk'r and their Camels.—Vegetation and Springs of Zara.—Hebrew City.—Baths, hot and cold.—Birds.—Along the Shore.—Rugged Path.—Mouth of the Callirrhoe.—Romantic Glen.—The Ibex-hunter.—A rough Scramble.—Water-fall.—Home at last.—Sunday in the Gorge.—The Ibex and its Habits.—Unsuccessful Hunt.—The Hakim.—Medical Cases.—Ornithology of the Callirrhoe.—Our Postman robbed.—Topography of the District... 291

CHAPTER XVI.

Departure from Callirrhoe.—Night Alarm.—Horses stolen.—Pursuit.—Camp Fires.—Wild Seclusion.—Ascent to the Highlands.—Primeval Remains.—Dolmens.—Corn-fields.—Gazelle.—Ma'in, *Baal-Meon*.—Balaam's Progress with Balak.—His Stations.—Medeba.—Pigeons.—Alarm of Shepherds.—Farewell to the Hamideh.—A Beni Sakk'r Farmer.—Tenure of Land.—History of Medeba.—Its Citadel.—Isolated Columns.—Inscriptions.—Colonnaded Square.—Churches.—Immense Reservoir.—Richness of the Soil.—Part with old Friends.—Letter from the Adwân.—A Jericho Naturalist.—Endless Villages... 310

CHAPTER XVII.

The north-west Corner of Moab.—Its many Ravines.—Wheat Cultivation.—Belka Arabs.—Maslubeiyeh.—Splendid Panorama.—Dolmens.—Jedeid.—Nebbeh.—Its Identity with Nebo.—View of

Moses.—Ancient Authorities.—Zi'ara.—Interesting Ruins.—Balaam's Views.—Identity of Zi'ara and Zoar.—Position of the Cities of the Plain.—Arguments for placing them north of the Dead Sea.—Mr. Grove's Inference.—Ayun Moussa.—Springs of Moses.—Picturesque Glen.—Cascades.—M'Shuggar.—Ajermeh.—Heshbon.—Adwân Camp.—Elealeh.—Night Search for Camp.—Goblan's Welcome.—His Character.—Tragic Crime..................Page 331

CHAPTER XVIII.

The Wady Heshban.—Goblan's Affection.—Married beneath him.—Botany of North-west Moab.—Ancient Tablets and Tombs.—Changed Features of Scenery.—Circle of Dolmens.—Cairn.—Descent to the Ghor.—Ghawarineh Camp.—Old Acquaintances.—Beth-haran.—Night-watch.—Excursion down the Coast.—Beth-jeshimoth.—Camp of Israel.—Wady Jerifeh.—Ain Suwaineh.—Vegetation of the Shore.—Wady Ghadeimeh.—Clear Atmosphere.—Rich Coloring.—Wady Ghuweir.—Arab Battle-field.—Falcons.—Our Path blocked.—Palm-groves.—A Halt.—Ornithology.—An Arab Collector.—Gale of Wind.—The Tents carried off.—A sound Sleeper.—Ride to the Jordan.—Ferry-boat.—Return to Civilization.—Jericho.—Our old Camping-ground.—Bethany in Spring.—Entry into Jerusalem.—Our Wanderings ended.................. 355

CHAPTER

ON THE PERSIAN PALACE OF MASHITA.

By JAMES FERGUSSON, F.R.S.................. 378

APPENDIX A.—Aurora at Sebbeh. By R. C. JOHNSON.......... 397

APPENDIX B.—Account of a curious Physical Phenomenon witnessed at Ziza. By R. C. JOHNSON.................. 398

APPENDIX C.—On the Flora of Moab. By the late W. AMHERST HAYNE, B.A., Trinity College, Cambridge........................ 400

LIST OF ILLUSTRATIONS.

EXTERNAL FACADE, PALACE OF MASHITA.................*Frontispiece.*

No.		PAGE
1.	SEBBEH, AND DEAD SEA...	47
2.	ARAB SKIRMISH.......................................*to face*	58
3.	TUNNEL ENTRANCE, KERAK......................................	83
4.	CASTLE WALLS, KERAK...	87
5.	OUR CAMP, KERAK..................................*to face*	89
6.	CRUSADERS' FORT, KERAK...	90
7.	KERAK HOUSE-TOPS...	95
8.	ANCIENT LAMP FOUND AT KERAK...............................	110
9.	RUINS OF DHIBAN...	148
10.	OIL-PRESS..	151
11.	SKETCH OF UM RASAS...............................*to face*	158
12.	CHRISTIAN TOWER, UM RASAS....................*to face*	160
13.	KHAN ZEBIB...	186
14.	SCULPTURED ENTABLATURES, KHAN ZEBIB....................	188
15.	PLAN OF TEMPLE, UM WELEED...................................	195
16.	ZIZA, FROM THE DISTANCE...	198
17.	TANK AT ZIZA...	199
18.	PIGEON-HOLE STONES, ZIZA.......................................	203
19.	CUFIC INSCRIPTIONS, ZIZA...	204
20.	INTERIOR OF RUINED PALACE.....................................	213
21.	GATE-WAY OF PALACE..	214
22.	OCTAGON TOWER...	215
23.	FALLEN ARCH..	216
24.	PLAN OF PALACE, MASHITA.......................*to face*	219
25.	EL KUSTUL..	233
26.	PANORAMA, UPPER ZERKA MA'IN...............*to face*	245
27.	ROCKS AT ENTRANCE OF ZERKA MA'IN........................	250
28.	PLAN OF MACHÆRUS..	274

LIST OF ILLUSTRATIONS.

No.		Page
29.	Terebinth-tree on Attarus	286
30.	The Zerka Ma'in	288
31.	Zara	296
32.	Mouth of the Callirrhoe	299
33.	Dolmen	314
34.	Columns at Medeba	323
35.	Temple at Medeba	325
36.	Palm-trees by the Dead Sea	to face 368
37.	Inner Palace of Mashita, from within the outer Gate-way	to face 379
38.	Elevation of West Wing Wall of external Facade of Palace at Mashita	to face 382
39.	Elevation of one Compartment of Western Octagon Tower at Mashita	to face 384
40.	Tak Kesra	385
41.	Church at Tourmanin	392

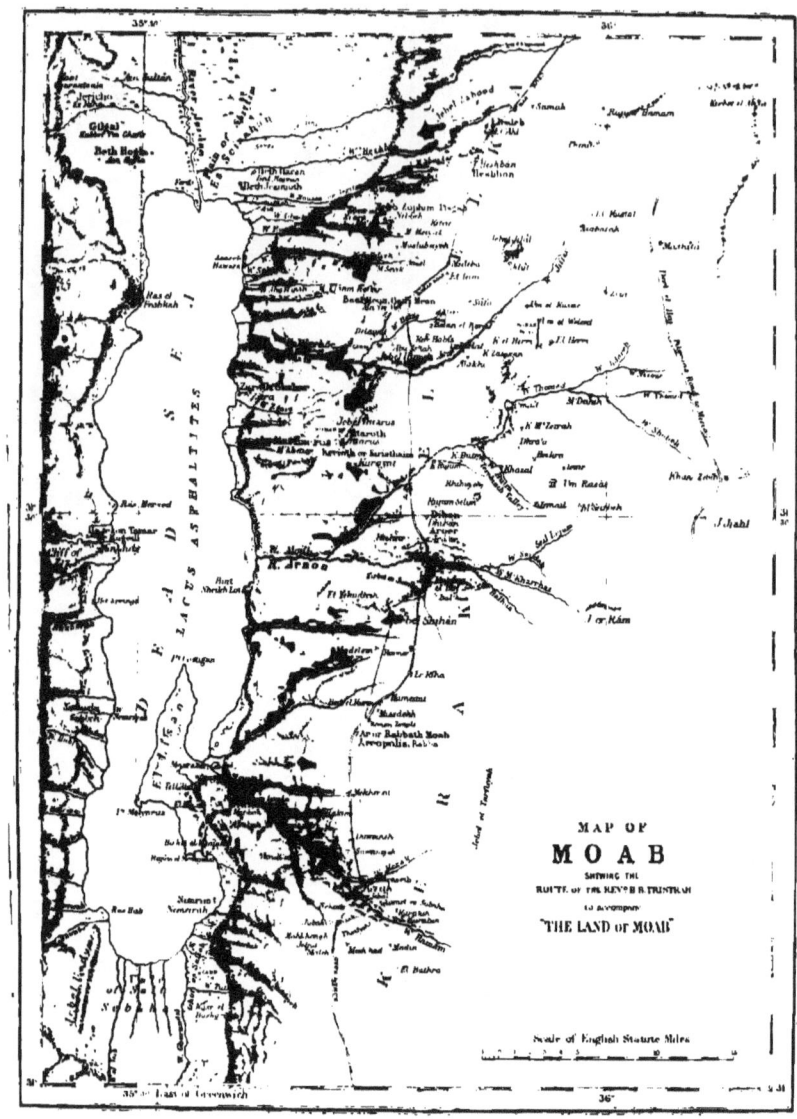

THE LAND OF MOAB.

CHAPTER I.

View of the Mountains of Moab from Jerusalem.—Previous Expeditions.—Messrs. Palmer and Tyrwhitt Drake.—British Association.—Companions.—Mr. Klein.—Preliminary Negotiations.—The Adwân.—Preparations at Jerusalem.—The Ta'amirah.—Arab Chicanery.—Muleteer in Prison.—Start for the South.—Bethlehem.—Volunteer Escort of Ta'amirah.—Hebron.—Our first Bivouac.—Old Friends.—Sheik Hamzi, an Arab Attorney.—Fruitless Negotiations.—Mosque and Bazars at Hebron.—A Jewish Interior.—Abou da Houk and the Jehalin.—Diplomatic Difficulties.—A Kerak Guide.—Signature of a Contract.—Payment of Deposit.—Storm under Canvas.—Route from Hebron.

WHO that has stood outside the walls of Jerusalem, or on the Mount of Olives, has not gazed with wistful interest on those blue hills rising with clear outline beyond the thin haze which overhangs the deep hidden lake of salt, nor wondered what the land of Moab might reveal? Those hills, which look so near, yet are in reality so inaccessible, have whetted the curiosity of many a traveler.

When, fourteen years ago, the writer first visited the Holy Land, he almost registered the vow that, sometime or other, he would make the attempt to explore what then was practically a sealed region. On his second visit he was only partially successful. His first attempt, by the southern route, was baffled by the feuds of the Arab tribes, and a later effort from the north enabled him only to touch the fringe of the country, as far as Heshbon and Nebo.

At length the discovery of the famous Moabite Stone drew more attention to the exploration of Moab than the country had hitherto received. Dr. Porter had only ventured to hint that research among its bleak highlands and lawless tribes might reward the adventurous explorer; but the almost accidental discovery of the monolith was a pledge that the antiquities of Moab must certainly repay investigation.

Accordingly, after Professor Palmer and Mr. Tyrwhitt Drake had, under the auspices of the Palestine Exploration Fund, completed their daring and perilous examination of the desert of the Tíh, they continued their researches, in the spring and summer of 1870, into the Land of Moab, from the northern border of Edom, or Petra. Their attention was chiefly directed to the search after Phœnician inscriptions. Owing partly to the lateness of the season and the extreme heat of the weather, and partly to difficulties among the tribes, they did not attempt to examine the highlands south of the Arnon, the true country of the ancient Moabites, and never included in the allotment of Israel; but skirting the coast of the Dead Sea till they passed the shoulder of the peninsula of the Lisan, they then turned up the country under the protection of the Hamideh, crossed the ravine of the

PREVIOUS EXPEDITIONS. 19

Arno at the usual spot, and made a bold dash eastward, as far as Um Rasas. Then returning hastily, they made their way to the low-lying fertile plain of the Seisaban, at the north-east end of the Dead Sea, where they crossed the Jordan and re-entered western Palestine. This journey was comparatively barren of results, though it added something to our topographical knowledge. Professor Palmer reported his sojourn in Moab expensive and unsatisfactory. He examined every known " written stone " in the country, and the conclusion at last forced itself upon him that, above ground at least, there does not exist another Moabitish stone.

Still it was felt that, apart from the question of inscriptions, a careful survey might probably add much to our topographical knowledge, and at least decide the position of many ancient sites marked at random on the present maps.

The British Association, at its meeting in Edinburgh in 1871, renewed a former grant of £100, and doubled it, appointing a committee "for the purpose of undertaking a *geographical* exploration of the country of Moab." Stimulated by this grant, an expedition was organized in the autumn of 1871, which sailed from England on the 10th January, 1872, *viâ* Brindisi and Alexandria, and landed at Jaffa, January 22d. The party was ably re-enforced by Mr. C. Louis Buxton, Trinity College, Cambridge, whose camera illustrated the results of the expedition with about eighty excellent photographs, and whose gun did good service; Mr. R. C. Johnson, of Liverpool, experienced as astronomer, surveyor, and photographer, to whose camera we are also indebted for upward of one hundred admirable stereoscopic views, and to whom I owe almost the whole of the map which accompanies this journal; Mr. W. A. Hayne, Trinity College, Cambridge, our indefatigable botanist, who has supplied the chapter on the Botany of Moab; and Mr. Mowbray Trotter, Trinity College, Cambridge, to whose prowess we were indebted for many a meal. At Jerusalem we were joined by our invaluable friend Mr. Klein.

Negotiations had been carried on, through the kind assistance of the Rev. F. A. Klein, Church Missionary Society's representative at Jerusalem, with the sheiks of the transjordanic tribes, before our arrival, and especially with Fendi y Faiz, the sheik of the Beni Sakk'r; but his son, Sheik Zadam, on whose escort the party relied for the north of Moab, did not arrive during our detention of a few days at Jerusalem. The Adwân, who claim the exclusive convoy of travelers north of Heshbon, but whose inability to introduce any one into the Highlands of Moab I had experienced in my former journey, having heard of our plans, sent us a very polite letter expressing their anxiety to see their old friend again, denouncing the treachery of the Beni Sakk'r; and wound up with the assurance that if they caught Zadam attempting to cross the Jordan to meet us, his blood should flow for the trespass. We were not a little amused after-

ARAB NEGOTIATIONS.

ward to find that while indulging in those grandiloquent threats, Sheik Goblan was actually negotiating a matrimonial alliance between his daughter and the son of his rival, a scheme prompted, as we were gravely assured, far more by personal admiration than by the contingent prospect of political advantages.

We replied politely, by a special messenger to our friends of the Adwân, that we intended to enter the country not by the north, through their territory, but from the south; that our intention was merely to meet the Beni Sakk'r near Kerak; and that we should with pleasure call at the Adwân's encampments in the spring.

But still, to go round by the south end of the Dead Sea demanded an escort. Messengers were dispatched to find the sheik, either of the Ta'amirah or the Jehalin, the tribes who claim the suzerainty of the district west of the Dead Sea, and waiting their arrival various preparations had to be made. Through Mr. Klein's aid, dragoman, servants, horses, and mules had been provisionally engaged; but these had to be seen and tried, and many a trick was attempted, both with regard to bipeds and quadrupeds. Groceries and provisions of every kind had to be be laid in for two months, since Moab itself is absolutely destitute of supplies, even of corn, and only kid and game could be counted on as procurable. on the spot. We were not quite prepared to follow the advice of a would-be explorer, whose experience had never gone beyond his study or a railway station, and who suggested that we were needlessly encumbering ourselves, for that sugar, coffee, and rice might be procured more easily in the villages of Moab!

At length, after a delay of three days, a delegate from the Ta'amirah presented himself, and volunteered a guard of his tribe round the south end of the Dead Sea. The contract was drawn out and approved at the consulate; but we waited in vain for the sheik to put in his appearance and seal it, and on the 29th January we started for Hebron free from the annoyance of an escort. In a safe country like that between Jerusalem and the south end of the Dead Sea, any company more troublesome than that of a backsheesh-craving escort, such as those corrupted by intercourse with Europeans, it is impossible to conceive. You halt for a moment to examine some desolate heap, and the ragged crowd surround you, jabbering and producing pieces of pottery or smooth pebbles, and demanding backsheesh as for some newly-discovered treasure. You turn aside after a covey of wild partridges running up the hill, and your nimble guard rushes wildly in front, yelling and shrieking, and puts up the birds far out of shot. You are attracted by some bright flower in a cranny, and before you can dismount, your Arabs, ever alert at the wrong time, have cropped the petals, and hand you the fragments of the plant, amazed at your want of gratitude as you despairingly throw down the worthless handful.

At the very moment of starting we narrowly escaped another vexatious delay. The animals of our convoy belonged to various owners, who accompany their property, and at the last moment our best riding horses and their masters were missing. We soon discovered that our chief muleteer had been suddenly pounced upon by the soldiers, and taken to prison for an alleged debt. The creditor had taken no steps to enforce his claim until the last moment, when, astutely guessing that we would not willingly be detained, but would rather pay ourselves than incur further loss of time, he had timed his arrest as cleverly as though he had been a Whitby electioneerer. Off I had to tramp to the consulate at the other end of Jerusalem, whence, fortified by a letter from the consul, and the company of a cavass in full accoutrements, I proceeded to the Cadi, showed that the debt was disputed, and having signed a bond that I would not pay the man his wages until the case was decided, presented myself at the prison, the doors of which at once opened and the man was set free. The matter in litigation proved to be a case of horse warranty, as perplexing to a Turkish Cadi as to an English jury, and eventually nothing came of it.

Unlike the road to Jaffa, that to Bethlehem has undergone no improvement of late years; nor has the extension of suburb, so marked on the former road, extended to the southward of Jerusalem. A Bethlehem Christian Bedouin, who had attached himself to us as a sort of intermediator in various negotiations, was our companion, and we cantered onward to Bethlehem, only drawing rein for a short time to pause at Rachel's tomb. We could not pass Bethlehem without revisiting the grand old Church of the Nativity, the shrine, the so-called manger, St. Jerome's cell and shrine. Every thing we found in much better repair than eight years ago, chiefly owing to liberal Russian expenditure. The Church Missionary Schools have been abandoned, and handed over to the Berlin mission, which has a large establishment here.

After a hasty inspection of the sights, and running the gauntlet of the sellers of beads and scallop shells, and other backsheesh-hunters, more importunate in Bethlehem than anywhere else, we pushed on southward, and overtook our party at the Pools of Solomon, where they had halted. These vast cisterns were not nearly so full of water as when I had visited them before, in the rainy season. The lower one was all but empty, revealing the perfect cement on its sides and bottom, and the staircase by which, when the water was let out, the workmen could descend to repair the plaster. Various inlets into the pool, to receive the drainage on either side, were shown, and the cement was all as smooth and unchipped as on the day when it was laid on. The second pool, as well as the first, was still full of water, and a little flock of teal was paddling unconcerned on its surface.

Just before descending the hill to the Pools, the mounted chief of the Ta'amirah suddenly accosted us. In vain we assured him that an escort was needless, that we were well armed, and intended to find the Jehalin south of Hebron.

Our determination to dispense with the services of Falstaff's ragged regiment was in vain. No sooner had we started from the Pools than the wild fellows were thrown out on all sides, and formed a skirmishing front all the way to Hebron. Even when we pushed at a canter across the little plains, the footmen, without an apparent effort, were always in advance, and effectually precluded the chance of a shot at a partridge, or the sight of a gazelle.

Well as I knew the road, I think the pleasure of revisiting these sacred scenes, imprinted on the memory, is more intense than that of the first sight as a stranger. Bethshur, Halhul, Ramah of Judah, and other desolate sites, sustained our interest as we rode through them. At Mamre, by the ruins of Constantine's massive Basilica, we made a detour to the right, in order to show to the younger members of the party the great terebinth-tree, which now does duty for Abraham's oak, long since perished. The hills looked bare and bleak as a winter without rain could make them, for the spring flowers had not yet begun to show; but the last two miles of our road led us by narrow paths through vineyards with their vines carefully trained, each fenced with a low stone wall surrounding it; and in many of them the watch-tower often referred to in Scripture, at the upper end, a heap of brush-wood on the top of it, the bedding of the sentry during the grape season. Near the wicket-gates we might see the ass that was to carry the laborer home, tied up to a vine, "Binding his ass's colt unto the choice vine."

We had passed our convoy of mules some miles before, and it was dark before they arrived at the camping-ground. Now the inexperienced critic who remonstrates at the number of followers in an Eastern journey might find the use of having twenty men to picket, set up tents, and prepare for the night. It was past eight o'clock before we sat down, under a lovely, moonlit sky, to dine. Picturesque and bright was our first bivouac; to the majority of the party, their first night under canvas. We dwelt among the tombs in the Moslem cemetery, on the slope rising to the south of Hebron. The lights glimmered fitfully among the houses of the city on the opposite slope, and occasional bursts of rough music and firing of guns told of a marriage being celebrated.

Our arrival had brought many new and old acquaintances around us. One man constituted himself water-bearer to the camp; another, running messenger; while the governor politely sent a soldier to offer us a guard for the night. We thanked his excellency for his kind consideration, but assured his envoy we were well able to provide for our own safety—a reply which sent him back not a little crestfallen, since a guard meant, of course, a backsheesh suited for the acceptance of a governor. The Ta'amirah volunteers, determined not to lose sight of us, quietly sat down for the night by our camp-fire, with their matchlocks across their knees, listening incredulously to the assurance that we were not their brothers, nor in their keeping.

Among our earliest visitors was Sheik Hamzi, the Arab lawyer of Hebron, and who had been my companion for many weeks on my former visit, unchanged, save that his beard was more blanched; oppressive in his attentions, and palpable, as of old, in his intrigues. He did us good service, however, and sent at once to the camp of the Jehalin, on the way to Beersheba, to request the attendance of the sheik Abou da Houk, the son and namesake of our former guardian, now deceased, to come and make an arrangement with us for an escort to Kerak. Various other old companions in travel came to claim acquaintance. One after another, either a great man or his henchman, appeared at the tent door, and sat down, dropping their slippers, and sometimes venturing beyond the threshold, in the hope of a cup of coffee or a pipe. It was not easy to get rid of our friends, and midnight was approaching, when we were compelled to call in the aid of our servants to tell them, what we could not, according to the rules of politeness, say for ourselves, that we must be left alone for prayers, and to retire to bed. At length we retired, with the mule-bells tinkling incessantly, and the horses, asses, and muleteers, inside their pickets, mingled in a confused circle round our three tents. The night was cold enough, with the thermometer at 35° Fahr.

The next morning dawned brightly, with Venus peeping down through a crevice by the tent door, and before daylight all was astir, and a crowd surrounded us. The day was given to diplomacy, and a weary one it was. Scenes, strange and unwonted to western eyes, fascinate everywhere the novice in Eastern travel; but the various events of this day far exceeded in humor and quaintness the ordinary episodes of tent life. Hamzi was early afoot, and in the door-way before we were dressed. Some new intrigue we were quite sure to have from the clever Arab attorney and money-lender, who holds half the sheiks of Judea under his thumb. He is very cautious, however, in negotiating about Moab. He remembers how, for once in his life, he was outwitted there, when accompanying Palmer and Drake: they had intrusted to him all their cash; and the old man had allowed himself (for he is an arrant coward) to be bullied out of every piastre of it by the Moabite Bedouin, and afterward had to refund. He came now to recommend the Ta'amirah as joint guides with the Jehalin, which meant double backsheesh from us, and a liberal percentage on both for himself; but, in spite of his oppressive politeness, I was stupid, and Mr. Klein imperturbable.

After breakfast we set out with a Moslem Hebronite to visit the outside of Machpelah, and the other lions of the place. There has certainly been a marvelous improvement in the manners of Hebron since our last visit. The visits of the Prince of Wales and of Mr. Fergusson, and their admission within the very sacred building itself without any heaven-sent calamity as the result of the profanation, have, perhaps, checked fanaticism; but at least they have found that Europeans are profitable visitors. We were admitted a few steps up the mosque stairs, and this without any of the scowls and curses which met me on my former visit. We were afterward very civilly conducted round the outer walls, made their circuit, and on the high ground on the north side were allowed to get on to the roof of a side chapel, and to peer through an opening in the dome into the mosque below, where we could only see one tomb, with a lamp suspended over it.

Wandering afterward in the bazar, we invested in some jars of native quince jam, and were accosted by a Jew, who offered us wine for sale, and invited us to his house, curiously concealed, up alleys and dark entries. Rude, but scrupulously clean, was the *menage*. The upper part of the large room, which formed the dwelling, was raised five steps above the rest, and here we were entertained. The host's fair wife, for the family were Russian Jews, spread a clean white tablecloth, and produced glasses and a bottle of wine. The only more private part of the house was a portion above the dais, partially partitioned off, where sat the daughter, a pretty Jewess, at her needle-work, and showing by her glances her interest and curiosity.

When we had completed our purchase of excellent wine of Eshcol, and returned to our tents, another diplomatic scene occurred. Abou da Houk and some Jehalin had arrived; but the Ta'amirah spearmen still sat impassive round our camp, in silent array, loath to lose the charge of such golden travelers. Sternly Mr. Klein told them they were not engaged; still they sat imperturbable and motionless. The sun was shining brightly, and, without their knowledge, some capital photographs of the groups were secured.

Later in the day we attempted a walk toward Debir and the "Upper and Nether Springs" (Judg. i., 15), but after some hours were fain to hurry back on the threatening appearance of the sky, the wind having gone round to the west, and clouds rapidly banking up. We had scarcely returned before we had to encounter one of the least agreeable experiences of tent life, in a storm of wind and rain such as southern latitudes only know. Every thing was made snug and taut as speedily as possible; trenches dug round the tents, boxes piled one on another under canvas, mules and horses, with corn-sacks and chaff, hastily hurried off to the shelter of the khan; but still the motley crowd of Hebronites hung around us, wet to the skin, but with curiosity not yet damped.

Intrigue meantime had been hard at work. We had offered Abou da Houk 2500 piastres to take us safe to Kerak. He felt inclined to accept it, but the Hebron Bismarck, Hamzi, withdrew him, and got him into conference with the Ta'amirah sheik.

He soon returns with Hamzi and the others, says it must be £50 (6000 piastres); Mr. Klein throws back his hands in horror; Daoud, our head man, vociferates his orders to the muleteers to pack up for Jerusalem. Hamzi turns affectionately to kiss me; I sternly turn aside, and will not even look at him, as I sit on my bedding. Another sederunt of the groups aside, under the lee of another tent, though it is now pouring with rain. At length they come back and announce to Mr. Klein "*tayib*," "very well," without the slightest movement of a muscle. He quietly raises his head from his book, and asks for the seal of the sheik, which is handed to him.

Daoud, meantime, has been playing *his* little game, telling the Jehalin that if they get a high price, he, as dragoman, must tax it for his share; but if they accept a smaller sum, he should let them off, and look to us for his percentage. But Abou da Houk has taken fright at the threat that we should cross the Jordan by the north route, and so save him all further trouble. Knowing the fickleness of the Arab mind, Mr. Klein had demanded his seal as a pledge till the contract could be drawn up. The other chiefs of the Jehalin also draw their rings from their fingers, in obedience to his example.

At once a messenger is dispatched for a professional scribe, and a sheet of paper duly stamped with the imperial monogram, on which the important deed is to be drawn; for even the Turks have learned the value of stamp duties to the exchequer. The pair (Abou and his uncle Selameh) retire, meanwhile, to take counsel with Hamzi, and return to say they repent of their bargain, and must have 1200 piastres additional. But the crafty Hamzi has outwitted himself, and Mr.

Klein is large in indignation, and firmly refuses to surrender the pledged seals. They grumble, but remain seated in the tent door-way. The scribe soon arrives—an intelligent, pleasant-looking, well-dressed Turk—drops his red shoes, and seats himself just inside the tent, with his inkhorn and reed-pen. We are all inside, sitting on the carpets in a circle round the walls, Mr. Klein alone on a camp-stool in front, while the other high contracting parties sit unconcernedly under their hoods outside. Daoud, standing behind the scribe, keenly watches every word as he writes it down on the paper spread on his knee. The Jehalin outside look, under the rain, their wildest and their dirtiest, and most uncomfortable ruffians to meet in an unfriendly way. Hamzi, cunning and well-dressed as ever, has by his side the disappointed Ta'amirah sheik. Every word of the contract is discussed and pertinaciously wrangled over, the young sheik alone feeling it dignified to maintain silence. Hamzi pertinaciously suggests amendments, which Mr. Klein as determinedly resists. Finally, the document is finished; but meantime the sun has set in a lurid glare, and a tremendous thunder-storm bursts forth. It is by the light of the incessant flashes that the last sentences are written; but the imperturbable Arabs move not. And now for the sealing. Mr. Klein hands the rings to Daoud, who carefully moistens them in the inkhorn, and applies them to the paper. One of the chiefs has forgotten his seal; so Daoud takes the man's forefinger, wets it in the inkhorn, and gravely presses it on the document. Then come the attesting witnesses, and finally, during a terrific peal of thunder, the final solemn words are added, "God is the best witness." Then come appeals for backsheesh, food, and other customary encroachments on the strict letter. We finally conclude a codicil that a sum of 250 piastres is to be paid by us to the sheik of the Beni Atiyeh, a tribe of very bad repute, said to be on a marauding expedition from the frontiers of Egypt, in the south, in case we, unfortunately, fall in with them in the Ghor es Safieh; and it is understood we start in the morning for Engedi. And now we think we see our way clear to Moab.

After agreeing on the contract, some amusing precautions had to be taken. Half the money was to be paid in advance; and before the solemn sealing the napoleons were delivered by me to our dragoman, counted out by him, then placed, one by one, by him in the palm of Abou da Houk, while our representative held the said palm open, and then turned the gold pieces on to the ground, in the centre of the circle, where they had to remain till all was completed.

The storm cleared before sunrise, and, after dispatching a crowd of medical consultees, we could enjoy a bath, *al fresco*, in the pools left by the last night's rain.

Our road to Engedi was the next question. There are two known routes, one the northerly, joining the track from Bethlehem to Tekoa, Wolcott's route; the other, taken by Robinson and Smith, going south to

Kurmul (Carmel) and Maon, and thence turning due east. Finding the district between these two a blank on the maps, we determined to try to cut across this wilderness. All declared there was no such road; but we determined to make one; and our muleteers and guides at length gave way.

CHAPTER II.

Route from Hebron to Engedi.— Yakin.— Forest of Ziph.— Kirbet Zadoud.—Ka'abineh Camp.— Hospitality.—Arab Coffee.—Unexpected Flood in the Night.—Effect of sudden Rains.—Change of Flora.—Wady el Ghâr.—El Husasah, *Hazziz*.—Cliff of Ziz.—Steep Pass.—Descent to Engedi.—Rich Botany.—Rashâyideh Arabs.— A Bedouin Fantasia.—Ornithology of Engedi.—Camp under Sebbeh (*Masada*) Wady Seyal.—Lifeless Desolation.—Wady Makheras.— Visit to the Fortress of Masada.— Ancient Jewish Synagogue.— Contrast with the Synagogues of Galilee.— Acoustic Phenomenon.— Remarkable Aurora.— Route to Jebel Usdum.—Ford to the Lisan.— View of Mount Hor.— Curious Arab Custom.— Oasis of Zuweirah.—Lateness of the Season.

AT length we quit Hebron, and turn our backs on the outskirts of civilization. We found our new route perfectly practicable, though very rough, and without much to interest. The first part of it lay across the wilderness of Ziph. The ground was very hilly, with narrow valleys of rich loam, which were all rudely cultivated for wheat, without fences. These open fields are the property partly of the Hebronites, but chiefly of the Ta'amirah, who, with a ready market at Jerusalem, have begun to find agriculture profitable, and are condescending to till the soil. We left Kurmul on our right, near enough to reconnoitre its fine old castle through our glasses. On the left we saw, here and there in the distance, a few straggling trees, lonely witnesses of the forest that once existed there, and continued as late as the time of the crusades. Here and there a covey of rock-partridges ran up the rugged sides of the hills; and twice we espied gazelle browsing on the young wheat in the valleys. The sportsmen were at once in pursuit; but we were not destined to have venison for supper that night.

After leaving the remains of *Yukin*, none of the places, or rather sites and desolate heaps, which we passed are marked in any of the maps, and only one wady, *Wady el Ghâr*. We proceeded nearly due east, sighting *Beni Na'ur* on our left, to the north, where were a few scattered trees, and visiting the castle called *Kirbet Yakin*, a curious ruin, with a cistern, and a well long since dry. Within was a sort of square inner chamber, over the door-way of which was let in an old quoin, on which was cut an Arabic inscription.

On this spot we found ourselves exactly on the water-shed of the Mediterranean and Dead seas; and now ended all cultivation in the bottoms of the wadys, and the traces of the olden terraces which had hitherto uninterruptedly furrowed their sides. We had entered the true wilderness. How far the forest of Ziph extended it is not easy to say; but there are traces of it in an occasional tree; and there seems no reason, from the nature of the soil, why the woods may not have stretched nearly to the barren sandy marl which overlies the limestone for a few miles west of the Dead Sea.

We passed but few ruins—Um Halassah, nothing more than a small village, and Kirbet Zadoud. Up and down the bare, rocky hills we passed, till, just before sunset, in a little grassy hollow, we came, much to our surprise, on an encampment of Ka'abineh Arabs, the tribe whose home is between the south end of the Dead Sea and Petra, and with whom I recalled a not very agreeable rencontre, when, in my former visit, we had to capture several of them as they attempted to plunder our camp. Now all their flocks and herds were with them, and they were, of course, pacifically disposed. Here, therefore, we at once determined to camp, on the slope a few hundred yards above them. As hospitality demanded, we rode down straight to the Ka'abineh camp. The sheik was away, but a head man promptly invited us into his tent. We dismounted, left our arms piled outside, and stooped, or rather almost crept, under the black camel's-hair roof.

The description of our entertainment may serve for that of many a subsequent one during our expedition. Picture a parallelogram of canvas quite black, and with a roof only three or four feet above the ground, one side turned lengthways against the wind, the other opening into a sort of square surrounded by similar abodes, a fire of broomsticks in the centre, with the smoke and ashes blowing into every one's face; all our party squatted on their hams, or sitting on their heels with spurs on, and their costumes diversified by those of their Arab hosts; the tent full to overflowing. An ancient in the centre holds a little flat pan with coffee berries over the flame, and stirs them with a stick, then with great care pounds the roasted coffee in a mortar, turns it with his hand into a little tin pot of boiling water; then letting it simmer for a minute or two, turns it over into a second, and lets that simmer in turn, and when it threatens to boil over, pours the beverage into three handleless, saucerless blue china cups, which form the company store of the household. He carefully inquires from an Arabic-speaking howadji which is the sheik of the party, sips his cup to show that its contents are not of a baneful nature, and then courteously hands it and its fellows to the chief guests; the rank and file being supplied in their turn as the cups become empty. Dusk is falling on us, and the little fire sends up light as well as warmth from its grateful embers, as we sit on, and gather, through our dragoman, some stories of the adventures and wanderings of our hosts from Petra, their original home.

As we left the Ka'abineh camp, a return visit was invited and promptly promised, with the hint that a little raw coffee would be an acceptable present. A more truly pastoral scene can scarcely be imagined than the trooping home of the sheep, goats, and a few camels from the hills at night-fall. Our camps were snugly ensconced in a sort of basin, toward which the hills gently sloped on all sides. From every side the flocks appeared, almost simultaneously, *led* by the shepherd, often a little boy; the goats and sheep, generally in parallel lines, gamboling after him as he sang an Arab stave, and the proud bell-wethers keeping close to his heels, making music from their tinkling necks.

The rain, which had considerately kept off all day, made up for its complaisance at night. With a simplicity not very creditable to experienced camp-men, we had neglected the trenching of our tents. The whole slope on which we had pitched became a shallow stream, and we awoke before day-break to find a river flowing through the camp, over and under our water-proofs indiscriminately.

Camp-moving in the rain is a dreary business; but it had to be done; and the party had a stock of good-humor and readiness to enjoy every thing, from coffee and stale brown bread, in the open, for breakfast, to the minor amusements of horse-catching and vain efforts with wet guns.

It rained for the greater part of the day, lifting occasionally, but never sufficiently to show the sky. At least we had the fortune to see what can have fallen to the lot of but few European travelers—the bare rugged hill-sides and the deep ravines of the wilderness of Judah covered with torrents, and rolling down tiny cascades from every rock, while each valley was a pool of water. The tremendous force of sudden rain on a thirsty, stony soil was well exemplified; and the rapidity with which the loosened stones and large fragments of rock, split by the combined action of sun and water, were hurried down the tiny glens scooped out many a channel, and gathered ever-increasing masses of débris in the course of the torrents. So easily disintegrated is the soft limestone of these wadys, that the rain of a few hours, probably the first heavy down-pour since last winter, did more to deepen and widen the channels than the storms of several years could effect on a Northumbrian hill-side. No geologist could watch the effect of this storm without being convinced that, in calculating the progress of denudation, other factors than that of time must be taken into account, and that denudation may proceed most rapidly where rains are most uncertain.

The gradual change of the flora is worthy of notice. From the moment of our crossing this water-shed the vegetable mold, which more or less scantily covers the country on the Mediterranean side, disappears— perhaps because this soil is due to the primeval forest, while the forest did not extend eastward of the crest. This I merely throw out as a conjecture; but though vegetation instantly becomes more sparse, it only gradually changes its character, until, by the time we have reached the crest of the cliffs overhanging Engedi, there is scarce a plant identical with those of the neighborhood of Hebron; and though the altitude has not diminished more than 1000 feet, the flora is strictly of the desert type, such as is found south of Beersheba, and in the Ti'h.

During our ride we crossed and followed for a short time the wadys Aboul Hayad and Mudabab-flakk'r, neither of which are laid down in the maps, and both of them insignificant ravines; then the Wady el Ghâr.

which is very deep and rugged, certainly the most important in the drainage of the district.

Finally we crossed the Wady Dal'al, not marked in the maps, a feeder of the Wady Sudeir from the south-west, and soon reached the top of the pass down to Engedi, riding across a piece of table-land called El Husasah — i. e., *Haz-ziz* — the cliff of Ziz (2 Chron. xx., 16). Our ride must have been across the wilderness of *Jeruel* (*id*), of which name we caught no trace in the Bedouin nomenclature; and some one of those desolate heaps, now nameless, which we passed before reaching it must have been "the watch-tower in the wilderness" (2 Chron. xx., 24) from which the invasion of the hordes of marauders from the south was signaled.

This pass and cliff of Ziz seems to have been, even from the days of Chedorlaomer and Abraham, the one ascent by which invaders from the south and east, after doubling the south end of the Dead Sea, entered the hill country of Judea. Up to Engedi they could march without interruption, by the shores of the sea below; and though there are several openings south of Engedi by which troops could easily make the ascent into the upper country, yet any of them would necessitate a long march across a rough and almost waterless wilderness. Practically, then, Ziz was the key of the pass. To the north of it the shore line is impracticable even for footmen, and there are no paths by which beasts could be led up. Hence the old importance of Hazazon-tamar, or Engedi, which is still the route by which the trade between Jerusalem and Kerak is carried on, and by which the former city obtains its supplies of salt.

The clouds lifted just as we reached the crest, and we looked down on the grand panorama of the sea, and the line of the Moab mountains beyond; while the steam rose up from the oasis of Engedi at our feet, literally smoking from the unwonted moisture. At the risk of being accused of suffering from "Holy Land on the brain," by those who can only measure grandeur by bigness, and who can see nothing to enjoy in Hermon or Lebanon because they are only 10,000 feet high and do not reach the Alps or the Himalayas, I must confess that few landscapes have impressed me more than the sudden unfolding of the Dead Sea basin and its eastern wall from the top of this pass.

The path is a mere zigzag, chiefly artificial, cut out of the side of the precipices, but occasionally aided by nature. We dismounted, and led our horses carefully down the rugged and winding staircase, those who were in front inwardly uneasy lest any of those behind, or rather above us, should dislodge a stone and hurl us to the bottom. The descent, by our barometer, was about 1800 feet.

The pass is just at the inner edge of the semicircular wall of cliff which, spanning a chord of about three miles from the Wady Sudeir to Wady Areych, embraces a horseshoe plain that gently slopes to the shore. Three hundred or four hundred feet from the bottom is a break in the cliff; it becomes a rugged slope; and at the base of a rock the copious, warm, fresh spring of Ain Jidy (Engedi)—*i. e.*, "the fountain of the kid"—bursts forth amidst an oasis of tropical vegetation. Here that quaint asclepiad, the osher, the jujube, the beautiful parasite *Lonicera indica*, and a host of strange semi-tropical plants, send our botanist into an ecstasy of delight. There were still three hours of daylight, which were usefully spent by the botanists and naturalists gun in hand.

The Rashâyideh, the tribe who claim and who cultivate the oasis, were encamped not far off, and busily occupied in weeding their young wheat. They have not many visitors, and I was very soon recognized and greeted by several of them as an old friend. The Rashâyideh are a very small and weak, and therefore, prudently, an unwarlike tribe, contriving to keep on good terms with both Jehalin and Ta'amirah, and occasionally rather heavily laid under tribute by both. Like the Ghawarhineh, they are partly agricultural, though not substituting the hut for the tent, and are of a decidedly different type of countenance from the Jehalin, whom they far surpass in good looks, and, as I found on my previous visit, in quick-witted intelligence. They willingly lent a hand to gather forage for our horses; and after we had bestowed on them and on our Jehalin guard a supper of rice, they rewarded us with a capital "fantasia," or Arab dance and recitative, round our camp fire, which they continued till far into night.

The entertainment was on this wise: A string of eight Bedouin of the two tribes appeared before the door of the "great," or dining tent, under the eaves of which the howadji were accommodated with camp-stools. Ranged in a line, one acted as master of the ceremonies (for band there was none), and led off in a monotonous chant, taken up by others one by one, and then joined in by all in chorus, their bodies bending to the ground, hands clapping, and feet moving half a step forward in regular time, till within a few inches of the noses of the spectators, when, with grinning rows of ivory gleaming out of the dark night, they yelled and retreated. A Chinese lantern of cloth supplied the place of gas; a railway reading-lamp did duty for foot-lights. The interlude consisted of guttural roars or growls, such as may be heard any day in the Zoological Gardens shortly before the feeding-time of the carnivora. The various acts sung the praises of the illustrious guests and their mountaineering feats, the botanist, as "the Father of Cabbage," being duly honored with special mention. The grand finale of each scene was a thrilling whoop, described by a huntsman present as a grand "view-holloa," but voted by all to be inimitable. The firing of matchlocks and illuminations of magnesium wire were prominent features in the piece, thus successfully put on the—we can not say boards, but the sand and stones which took their place, at Engedi, for the first time, on February 2, 1872.

The greater part of the next day was spent in revisiting the most interesting sites of desolate Engedi, especially the fine caves up the Wady Sudeir, with their stalagmites and luxuriant tresses of maiden-hair fern. The access is not easy, and involved so much scrambling that it was not surprising that some travelers who have been here since my first visit had failed in discovering the caves. Many small birds were making the oasis their winter-quarters, and I was fortunate enough to obtain a pair of a new or undescribed species of warbler, something like the Sardinian warbler of South Europe, and which has been named *Sylvia melanothorax*, Black-throated warbler ("Ibis," 1872, p. 296).

In the afternoon we bid farewell to the Rashâyideh, the successors of the Kenites of Engedi, and followed our mules along the shore, intending to camp and spend our Sunday under Sebbeh, the celebrated ancient fortress of Masada. With the exception of one or two sulphur hot springs close to the edge of the lake, the ride is the most uninteresting possible, utterly devoid of life, and with the cliffs and mountains rising upward of 2000 feet sheer, glaring red in the sunlight, and the soft marl deposit at their base of a monotonous, dazzling whiteness. This part of the shore more truly reaches the popular notion of the desolation of the Dead Sea than any other.

We found our tents pitched not very far from the shore, by the side of the bed, if bed it may be called, of the Wady Seyal, or "Acacia Valley," and at least two miles from the base of the hills, which could only be reached through a labyrinth of soft marl, scooped, torn, and furrowed by winter torrents into every fantastic shape in which wild fancy could have molded matter; ruins, and crumbling castles, flat-topped mamelons, square forts, cairns, pinnacles, and tide-washed rocks, all made of this crumbling white and very salt deposit, so soft that it was very difficult anywhere to climb them. Yet not a plant nor a bird could be seen, save here and there in the low bed of the wady a tuft of some salt-loving plant and a gnarled acacia. A solitary desert hare, with body not larger than a rabbit, and ears one-third longer than our hare's, was occasionally started, and was speedily lost in the labyrinth.

We soon felt the change of temperature implied in being 1300 feet below the level of the sea. The night was sultry, and more so was the day, happily the day of rest. After morning service in our tent, I had the pleasure of revisiting Sebbeh, and recalling once more on the spot the tragic history of Masada. The fortress will well repay many a visit; and I was especially interested in refreshing my memory while enjoying the sanguine hope of soon seeing the sister castle of Machærus, yet more closely bound up with both Jewish and inspired history. We did not attempt the eastern face, but felt that the quiet zigzag round to the western shoulder by the Roman causeway was more within a Sabbath-day's journey.

I am not about to describe afresh what I have already described, and what others who followed me (one of whom left for us his pocket-handkerchief, marked

C. M.) have still more accurately depicted. We corrected our barometric observations of the height of the fortress, which is 1250 instead of 1500 feet, as I had erroneously calculated it. The great cistern at the south end we found, in spite of the late rains, to be empty, doubtless from the stoppage of the conduits, which

NO. 1.   SEBBEH.   DEAD SEA FROM OUR CAMP.

can still be seen. Near the top we noticed two openings in the cliff, hewn through the native rock at the south face, and which a pair of lanner falcons and several pairs of owls had found most convenient as affording secure access to their nests in the roof, while the hyenas had been using the broken steps down which we scrambled.

The comparatively perfect building in the centre of the inclosure, and which I, in common with others, for want of a better term, have spoken of as the chapel,* seems, most probably, to have been the synagogue of the fortress. As there is no trace of any Christian occupation, historical or architectural, and as the building seems undoubtedly contemporary with the rest of the constructions, we may fairly adopt this conjecture, especially as, on close examination of the contiguous chamber to the north, there are traces of its having been fitted as a bath, doubtless for the ceremonial ablutions, while the other chamber would be for the use of students of the holy books. If this be so, this is certainly the most ancient synagogue preserved to our days, and the only one prior to the capture of Jerusalem by Titus. All those so admirably illustrated in the papers of the Palestine Exploration Fund by Captain C. W. Wilson, R.E.,† in Galilee, were presumably erected after the return of the Jews in the time of Hadrian, with, let us hope, the exception of that at Tel Hum. If this building were a synagogue, it differs from those in Galilee in being placed east and west, instead of north and south (although that at Irbid is almost *a rectangle*), and in the absence of columns. Both these variations may be simply caused by the difference of conditions between a fortress chapel, constructed for the wants of a garrison in a

---

* "Land of Israel," 2d edit., p. 313.
† "Palestine Exploration Fund Statement," 1869, p. 37.

confined space, and a house of worship in an open village or town.

While on the fortress, we descried a party of Arabs descending the gorge of Nemriych toward our camp, and our guides, keener-sighted without, than we with, our field-glasses, pronounced them to be the company of our old friend Hamzi of Hebron, on their way to re-enforce our escort; and on our return we found our old tormentor and protector overflowing as usual with poetical civilities.

The acoustic properties of these clear regions have often been spoken of. We had here a wonderful instance. Hayne had remained behind for an hour, when we started for the ascent of Masada. When at the top, we saw him, on his way to join us, at the foot of the next cliff, about 500 yards from the base of the rock of Masada, and 1250 feet below us; yet at this immense distance of over 600 yards we not only carried on a conversation with him, but, as he proved, on joining us, he could hear several of our remarks to each other. We found abundance of water in the gullies, west of Sebbeh. On our way back, I noticed a pair of the beautiful and rare wheat-ear *Saxicola monacha*, which I never found elsewhere, except on the salt mountain of Jebel Usdum, but which is also found on the dreary steppes of Nubia and Abyssinia.

We sat up rather late after evening service, attracted by a magnificent aurora borealis, a sight unwonted in these latitudes. I never remember, even in the north of England, to have seen one so brilliant, and so persistent in its coloring. It was all orange-red, with grand streaks intensifying the rays occasionally, but no green or pale rays.* The Arabs, to our great surprise, seemed very little attracted, and certainly not, as we might have expected, alarmed by it. On our questioning them, they said they had seen it sometimes before, and that the last time was when the French and Germans were going to fight. We asked them if they thought it was a portent. They said they did not know, but they believed it had to do with the north country, and not with themselves. We were interested some weeks afterward to find, by the European papers, that we, down by the Dead Sea, had not been alone in our admiration of the extraordinary northern lights of 4th February, 1872, but that they had attracted great attention not only in Europe, but even in Egypt, far up the Nile. From Sebbeh the route to Jebel Usdum is along the shore.†

---

* See Appendix A.

† I was able to correct, or at least to alter, the orthography of one or two names. There are seven wadys from Sebbeh to the south-west angle of the sea, and none of these bear names which can be referred to an earlier time than the Arabic language. They are Wady Safsaf, "the willow valley," erroneously marked "Hafhaf;" Rubt el Jamus, "the binding of the heifer;" Senin, "broom;" Um el Bedûn, "the mother of the Ibex;" Hatrura, Umbaghek, "the mother of the cow," and Mejd. These names sufficiently show that no tradition of olden time has shaped the nomenclature. I was amused at an instance of the way in which names may become interpolated. One of our party, eager to collect information, asked old Selameh the name of the headland on our right. At the same moment a pair of sand-grouse were flushed. "K'tar k'tar," exclaimed our guide, looking on game as far

When just opposite the opening of Wady Hâtrûra, Selamch pointed out to me the exact spot where he, when a youth, had forded across to the Lisan. From his age, this may have been sixty or seventy years ago. There must have been considerable changes since then in the currents of the Dead Sea, for Lynch's soundings show a maximum of three fathoms, or eighteen feet. No one, according to Arab testimony, has attempted this feat for many years; yet Selamch avows he did it on his camel, which would make the maximum depth eight feet.

Just at the crest of the headland "Mersed," which we crossed, and where there is no wady whatever, we observed a curious Arab custom. It is just at the point where Van de Velde's and my own maps show that the cliffs come quite close to the sea, leaving no beach whatever, and where we have to mount the shoulder of the headland. On reaching the crest of the shoulder, the distant mountains of Edom come in view; and among these, very distinctly, Jebel Haroun, "Mount Aaron," the Mount Hor of the Scripture, and a sacred spot of the Moslems. Every rock and boulder of the rugged steep by the track was piled with small stones. No devout Bedouin will pass that way without adding to the pile; for every traveler, when he first catches sight of the holy mountain, must, according to custom, place there his "stone of witness."

We had another instance of the tenacity of old

---

beyond names in importance, and down went Wady el Kattar in the note-book. Nor was this enough, for a second time in the same journal did Wady el Kitter, evoked under like circumstances, appear.

Scriptural customs in the way in which, as of old, names are given. One of our Jehalin guard was called Rhideir — *i. e.*, "watering-place." On Mr. Klein asking him how he came to have so strange a name, he told us he was born as his mother was going with her pitcher to the watering-place, and first saw the light at the "Rhideir."

Passing Wady Nejd, we soon reached the turn toward the east; and riding across the open scrubby plain which forms the oasis of Zuweirah, reached the north-west shoulder of Jebel Usdum, the "Salt Mountain," where we were to camp, favored by some fine acacia, or "seyal," trees. Grievous was the disappointment of our botanist. I had promised him here a rich harvest. On my former expedition we had collected here, in the very same week of the year, more than seventy species of plants in flower. The gravel was then literally carpeted with color; now scarcely a blade of green or a blossom could be seen. The lateness, or the non-arrival, of the rains had made all the difference between barrenness and fertility. On strolling along the edge of the mountain, I was struck by the change which the short period of eight years had made in several well-remembered spots— how sundry isolated fragments of salt, or "Lot's wives," had been washed away, and other pinnacles had been detached by the rains to take their places. Turning round the northern corner of Jebel Usdum by Ras Ilish (the Sodom of De Saulcy, but merely the remains of a small fort for the protection of the salt workers), we enter on the "Vale of Salt."

CHAPTER III.

An early Start.—Effect of the Sun on the Mountains.—Sudden Thunder-storm.—A Salt Cavern.—Marl Deposit on the Salt Mountain. —Its Origin.—Elevation of the New Red Sandstone.—Position of the Salt Rock.—Crossing the Sebkha.—Alarm of Marauders.— Frontier of Moab.—Sudden Apparition of Enemies.—A threatened Skirmish.—Naked Warriors.—Our Guide stripped.—The Beni Atiyeh.—A Treaty made.—March through the Wood.—Difficulties of Exploration.—A costly Guard.—Vegetation of the Sáfieh.—Ancient Remains.—Kasr el Bushariyeh.—Old Mill.—Moslem Burying-ground.—Remains exposed.—Boundary of Moab.—Brook Zered.—Suphah.—Variety in the Vegetation of the Sáfieh.—Horsemen from Kerak.—Son of the Mudjelli.—Petty Thefts.—A Mule on its Trial.—Return of the Jehalin.

It was important to have an early start, in order to get into the Sáfieh, or south-east oasis of the Dead Sea, in good time; and our people, who had not forgotten our chidings for many previous delays, determined to rouse us betimes, and, accordingly, served coffee and began to loosen tent pegs at 3.30 A.M. We would not risk a late start by sending them back to bed, but took their practical joke as a matter of course. Brightly burned our four watch-fires as we sauntered about. Mr. Johnson took the opportunity of a clear, starlit sky to make observations for latitude and longitude. A little after four o'clock the crescent moon rose over the mountains of Moab; and the sun had scarcely cast the gloaming of approaching dawn over the eastern peaks, when, before six o'clock, we were off, and began to round the north end of Jebel Usdum.

At 6.30 the sun rose, and its effect on the western face of the Moab mountains in front, and on the sea beneath them, was very wonderful. A deep, greenish mist seemed to wrap the lower parts, gradually melting into a dark red higher up, and the few fleecy clouds were gilded. Soon a change came over all, and the rolling peals and black masses in the southwest warned us of a coming storm. We could not hurry on. We were now in the most desolate and dreary corner of that desolate shore, without one trace of vegetable life, not even a stray salsola or salicornia, to relieve the flat sand-beds. The sand and loam of the shore was deep and heavy, our horses sunk at each step above the fetlocks, and not until we were wet through could we turn to the salt mountains on our right and ride into a salt cavern, or rather tunnel. The bottom was dry and dusty. We dismounted, and explored it with wax-matches, when suddenly there was a sound of waters overhead, and in a few minutes a stream of salt mud was rushing along the cavern to the sea.

The storm was not of long continuance, and grandly it rolled northward up the lake in a black mass, leaving us in sunshine. I had time here to notice and consider some points about the mountain and its formation. Some fine perpendicular sections were displayed from top to bottom, the salt having cleft perpendicularly. The whole ridge of pure rock-salt, perhaps two hundred feet high, is covered by a layer of chalky marl and natron about fifty or sixty feet thick. I have often wondered how this was formed, and used to imagine it had been uplifted on the top of the salt, and that the position of the ridge was due to local elevation. But it seems to me now, from some facts I noticed during the sudden rain, that the superincumbent mass is simply the earthy matter left on the top by the action of water, which has, in the course of ages, washed all the soluble salts into the sea, leaving only this detritus, or sediment. The process is actually going on, and may be seen on any of the detached blocks which have been disintegrated from the mass, and which, clear and transparent at first, soon became covered, but only on their top, with this earthy deposit. How many ages must have been requisite to wash away by gentle rain action salt enough to leave fifty feet of marly sediment on the ridge!

I see no signs of any upheaval of the ridge. The mass would rather appear to have been left, owing to the superior hardness of the salt, when the torrents from the south scooped out the whole southern Sebkha, and swept all its soft loam and chalk into the sea, while the torrents of the Mahawat and Zuweirah performed the same office less completely on its western side, the gravel and sand being there fifty feet higher than the mud on the eastern side.

This theory would leave the whole salt mass below

the old level of the marl deposits, which fringe the
base of the cliffs all down the western shore, and
also the shoulder of the Lisan on the eastern side.
Again, our observations in Moab showed us that the
new red sandstone can not be far beneath the surface
on the western side, because there has been a manifest
upheaval along the whole line, and the new red sandstone is uniformly displayed under the eocene limestone, which overlies it to a depth of about two hundred feet more than the whole height of the western
range. Assuming, then, the equal deposition of the
chalky limestone on either side, the rock-salt must
be lying on the new red, at a depth of more than two
hundred feet below the surface. Thus the salt deposit of the Jordan valley is similar in its nature and
geological position to the salt rocks of Cheshire and
the new red sandstone of England.

At 9 A.M., after three hours, we reached within a
mile the south end of the Salt Mountain, and finding
the bottom firmer, immediately turned due east to
cross the Sebkha, or desolate sand swamp. Heavy
work we found it after the rain, and for safety we
had to keep close to our mules, for this is "no man's
land." Great alarm was expressed by our guards on
detecting a party of men in the far distance, on the
plain south of Usdum. However, wonderful as are
their powers of vision, our field-glasses beat them for
once, and we were able to re-assure them by telling
them that of the seven one only had a gun, and that
they were driving two black cows, or donkeys. We

found afterward that they were a party of cattle lifters, who had stolen two cows from the Sáfieh in the night.

We crossed the shallow beds of the Kuseib, the Jeib, the Ghurundel, and other lesser drains from the Akabah, whose united contributions to the waters of the lake are very small; and before 11 o'clock we reached the Wady Tufileh, a mere ditch with muddy banks, without a particle of vegetation, with a strip of narrow, greasy, sandy plain beyond; and then, at the distance of 200 to 250 yards, a line of thick, dense canebrake, the commencement of the Sáfieh, the exact boundary-line between ancient Edom, where we were, and Moab. As we rode up to the deep muddy bank, ready to ford, a tall, mounted Arab, with a long spear, dashed from a narrow opening in the reeds, and in an instant about 150 wild, armed Bedouin deployed from the canebrake and spread themselves along the narrow plain on the other side, gesticulating, and wildly brandishing their weapons. They were a savage-looking lot, more like Maoris, or Fiji islanders, than any Western race, as they yelled and capered, evidently meaning mischief, and stripped for the fight; for the Bedouin, unless mounted, always go naked into battle. Some had guns, some spears, a few huge swords, and many only most formidable clubs, or maces with a round, spiked head.

We were bewildered for the moment, and I feared the Sáfieh was destined to be for the second time a turning-point for me. Suddenly our gallant old sheik, Selameh, dashed across the stream, to parley with the single mounted horseman, a fine-looking, wild fellow, clad in a sheep-skin coat with the woolly side in, and painted yellow. Several shots were fired, harmlessly, from the other side, but none in return from ours. As the old sheik mounted on the opposite bank, his horse sunk in the mud, and rolled over: in an instant he was dragged out by the ruffians, his gun and all else taken from him, and he was lost to our sight in the melée.

Some of the foe now waded across to where we were standing in line by the edge, apparently aiming at capturing some of the mules behind. One of our Jehalin foot-guard, a fine young Bedouin, who was my special companion, and had been also with me on my former expedition, tried to push them back, and was instantly felled senseless to the ground by the butt end of a gun, which cut his cheek to the bone. Another fellow came up, as if to dispatch him with his club, but was held back by his own party. Old Hamzi now came to the front on foot, assured us that it was a tribal quarrel, and that we had nothing to do with the fray, and, bare-legged, waded across in great excitement, when he too was lost in the yelling crowd.

Daoud, our dragoman, next spurred his horse across, but fell; and before he could recover his footing, his outer clothing, belt, satchel, and money-bag were stripped from him; but he still held on tenaciously to Hayne's gun, which he was carrying. In a moment

ARAB SKIRMISH.

his saddle-bags, which contained the luncheon of the party, were emptied; but he succeeded in recovering his horse, and was. the only mounted man of our side across. Another Jehalin who ventured over was felled; but Daoud, who throughout behaved with admirable coolness, had evidently by this time got the chieftain's ear, and a long and vociferous discussion ensued, which we anxiously watched. To fight would have been madness; we had no cover, no possible retreat, and were overwhelmed by numbers; so we kept back our muleteers and guards, and patiently awaited the event.

It turned out that the tribe were the dreaded Beni Atiyeh, a new tribe from Arabia, who have only recently taken to marauding in this part of the country, and have the worst possible reputation. With them were a few of the Ma'az from Orak, south of Kerak, a tribe of similar habits, and also of the Ghawarhineh, the proper inhabitants of the Safieh, and who by themselves are by no means an unmanageable or dangerous tribe, though, from their climate, more degraded than any of the highland clans to the eastward. These Beni Atiyeh had a blood feud with the Ta'amirah, whom they supposed we had taken with us, but none with the Jehalin. Well was it now for us that we had steadily refused the advances of the Ta'amirah at Hebron.

At length the yellow-coated horseman and Daoud rode back together toward us. The sheik cried out, "The Christians are my friends! the Ta'amirah only are my enemies!" Hamzi, lifting up his hands, swore loudly that not a Ta'amirah was with us; and the horseman, galloping along the line of his savage followers, ordered them back. Reluctantly, and with many a significant gesture, the naked horde, baulked of their prey, fell back a little, and we crossed. Meantime an angry debate arose between our sheik, Selameh, and theirs, doubtless as to the amount of backsheesh, which we left them to settle. We now formed in file, and slowly and cautiously proceeded, the Beni Atiyeh sheik leading the van, those who cared more for their personal safety than for the loss of the baggage, or of any stray mules, accompanying him; while the rest of the party formed a rear-guard, and kept a sharp look-out on the sumpter animals—no easy task through three miles of tangled brush-wood and thicket, with the wild and naked warriors swarming on all sides, endeavoring to scare any stray mule to the right or left, when two minutes would have sufficed for the partition of the booty.

At length we reached a small open space near the Ghawarhineh camp, where we were ordered to pitch. Carefully we formed a cordon, to keep off the wondering and still rather irritated crowd. From the treacherous character of our hosts, we took care to keep an armed guard, relieved at intervals during the night, round our camp, grateful, indeed, for the Providence which had preserved us so far in safety, and joining with heartfelt gratitude in the 23d Psalm, as we lay down for our first night within the boundaries of Moab.

The next day was devoted to a careful examination of the few traces of antiquity in the Sáfieh. This was not easily accomplished, as our wild hosts would not suffer us to move out alone, and demanded extravagant backsheesh for a guard of honor of eight horsemen, which they insisted were necessary for our safety. Time was more precious than money, and we had to submit to this extra extortion. Mounting our horses, we first of all turned south-east from our camping-ground toward the principal ruins of the Sáfieh. Our leader was the sheik of Ghawarhineh, Dabbour, who informed us he had acted in the same capacity for Messrs. Palmer and Drake. The ground is nowhere completely cleared, but cultivated in patches, hemmed in with dense and impenetrable clumps of Zizyphus, and Seyal Acacia trees, with other thorny shrubs, arranged in a natural, park-like fashion. Few other trees were to be found in this part, and no palm-tree of any kind.

We soon reached the Seil es Sáfieh, a tolerably-sized stream, with a gravelly bed, here flowing in a northerly direction, and receiving little affluents from the east. On the other side of the stream the vegetation was different, and the soil not the rich marshy loam which covers the plain from the stream to the sea, but lighter and gravelly. The thickets were not so close, and the osher-tree (*Calotropis procera*) was the feature of the tangle. All along the course of the Sáfieh the stream is tapped by little conduits on its left bank; so that the whole Ghor can be turned into a watered meadow, as is practiced by the same tribe at Jericho. The cultivators were only now beginning to turn on the water for their little patches of corn, tobacco, and indigo. There seems a well-arranged system by which the riparian proprietors exercise their rights of "water-privilege" in rotation, each being allowed to tap the Seil in turn, but only for so many days. Three days' water is sufficient to clothe a barren stubble with a rich green hue. The little streamlets are led off carefully westward, from patch to patch, until the supply is exhausted. We kept on the left bank of the Seil till we reached the ruins.

The remains, though extensive, are very poor and disappointing. On a slightly rising slope are strewn a mass of loose stones, covering several acres, with a few fragments of walls, many solid foundations, and a few portions of round columns. The name given to these ruins, Sheik 'Aisa, affords no clue whatever to any ancient name. Unlike the ruins of western Palestine, the city has been constructed of soft sandstone exclusively; and this has been much weathered, and reduced often to a state of complete disintegration. The sandstone is never found west of Jordan, as nowhere, west of the great fissure, has the eocene chalk been sufficiently elevated to show the underlying formation. The fragments of columns were all plain, none fluted; and we could find no inscriptions, and only one sculptured stone, probably of Christian origin, for the central ornament was a Greek cross. There were no traces which could indicate the date of the buildings, and certainly there was not the slightest vestige of any fortification, or even of a wall surrounding the straggling village. Fortification we could not expect to find, as the position is one peculiarly defenseless, and the very last which would have been selected in the times of ancient warfare as a frontier fortress. We have, probably, here merely the remains of a Roman village in the more peaceful days of the early empire.

A few hundred yards higher up are some far more perfect ruins, called Kasr el Bushariyeh, of a much later date, not earlier than the Crusading or earlier Saracenic times. These had been pointed out to me before as the Tawahin es Suhkar ("Sugar-mills"); but Dabbour assured us that the true Sugar-mills were north of the Lisan, in which his report agrees with Burckhardt's information. There have evidently been water-mills of some kind here, and there are two stone-lined and covered channels by which the water has been guided to turn undershot wheels. These, with the sluices, are in perfect preservation. There is a massive gate-way built of dressed stone with pointed arches. But this original building has been largely added to by mud-built walls; and it seems as though the mills had been abandoned, and the whole converted into a khan by the later additions of earthen walls. On the gate-way are many tribe marks, carved like those on the fortress of Masada, which, from their comprising the signs of Mars and Venus (δ and φ), have been imagined to be astronomical symbols. Round these ruins is the cemetery of the neighboring tribe. The bodies are merely placed in the bank of drifting sand, and so lightly covered that we saw the bleached and withered forms of two women, with their ordinary clothes on, lying exposed on the surface. Our guards had sufficient civilization to feel ashamed of this exposure, and to make apologies for it, as accidental from the high winds.

A little way above the Kasr is the third ruin, decidedly Moslem in its origin, and called El Mushnekk'r, or "the gallows;" not that any gibbet is there, though skulls dug out of the graves by the hyenas strew the ground. There appears to have been a Mohammedan wely here; but I could find no traces one could fairly assign to a Christian chapel.

About half an hour farther south the Wady Feifeh comes in; and this was the limit of our southward exploration. Beyond it is Wady Tufileh, which we had crossed before entering the Sáfieh. The Wady Feifeh, we were informed, receives the Wady el Ahsa, in which are hot springs. The wady seems to change its name more than once during its course, or, at least, several branches to have different names. It is the recognized boundary between the districts of Kerak and Petra—*i. e.*, between the ancient Moab and Edom—and has, with every probability, been suggested as the "brook (or wady) Zered" (Deut. ii., 14), or Zared (Numb. xxi., 12), the limit of the proper term of the Israelites' wanderings. Mr. Palmer, who explored

THE SÁFIEH. 65

the upper valleys of the south-east of the Sáfieh much farther than we were able to do, followed up the Wady Siddiyeh for some distance, and traced the fertilizing Seil Gerahi flowing into it. We were not able to trace the junction, but were assured that the Siddiyeh flowed into the Feifeh, which we had crossed lower down.

We found that the belt of fertile, well-watered soil extends much farther south than has usually been recognized. For about six miles south of the extremity of the Dead Sea the fertile ghor stretches, sheltered under the mountains, which feed it with sweet rivulets, and parted off by a sharp line from the desolate sand plain, without any blending belt of half desert scrub, till it contracts to a point, beyond the entrance of the Gharundel into the Sebkha. An exactly similar extension may be noted in the Seisaban, at the north-east end of the Dead Sea. It has been suggested that the Sáfieh and this boundary are alluded to in Numb. xxi., 14, where the authorized version reads. "What he did in the Red Sea, and in the brooks of Arnon ;" or, as "the Red Sea" is rendered in the margin, "Vaheb in Suphah"—*i. e.*, the Sáfieh. Whether the Hebrew בְּסוּפָה is represented by the Arabic صافيه, I must leave to Orientalists to decide; but there seems, at first sight, a probability in the conjecture.

It was evident our guards were anxious to show us all they could, as every ruin meant backsheesh: and it was equally certain that no other remains could be traced in the south of the ghor. They spoke of many farther north, by the shore, which we afterward saw, but shook their heads and waved their fingers at the idea of finding any thing but wild boar southward.

Having returned to camp, we next set out on foot to examine a section of Sáfieh from east to west—*i. e.*, from the river to the Dead Sea. It was a barren expedition for the naturalist, sportsman, and botanist. Instead of the teeming abundance of game and plants found on my last visit, there was no vegetation except the park-like wilderness of trees and shrubs, and bare clearings, hard and dry, covered with "dhurra," or millet stubble. Game there was none, except a few of the large Indian turtle-dove, for the pot (*Turtur risorius*). We roamed about, attended by a half-naked crowd of savages, who would have made short work of the property of any one they had caught out of sight of the rest of the party; yet even thus we were glad to escape from our tents, which all day long were surrounded, and often entered, by gaping crowds, perpetually raising wrangles, and stealing any thing on which they could lay their hands.

We observed that the ghor consists of several distinct zones of vegetation. First, the gravelly slope under the hills, of which the osher-tree was the characteristic feature, and which produced but scanty undergrowth. Next, the rich park-like land, the most considerable portion of all, in which are the patches of cultivation, yielding barley, wheat, millet, tobacco, and especially indigo, the wealth of the district. The sugar-cane has long since disappeared. Then comes a belt of scrub, affording only browsing for goats; after it, a thin strip of large tufts of a very tall reedy grass; parallel to this, the next belt was a mass of rushes; and from this to the water's edge was an impenetrable canebrake, of considerable width, in a deep swamp, completely barring all access to the shore, and swarming with wild boar, the tracks of which were seen in every direction, perfectly secure in their retreat.

On our return to camp we found a new excitement. The son of the Mudjelli, or Governor of Kerak, had come down with twenty horsemen, and was sitting in our tent. It seemed he had been sent for, or had come unasked, in consequence of hearing of yesterday's affair, for local news travels with strange rapidity in Arab lands, and had ridden down in one day. The chieftain was, of course, profuse in his promises —depicted in grave terms the danger of remaining here, and the impossibility of going to Kerak without a guard. He, of course, must escort us himself, and has brought a guard for the purpose—a very great nuisance, as we at once saw, precluding all hope of leisurely examining the country, and making any observations and sketching extremely difficult. But there was no help for it, and we must part with our good Jehalin men, and our oily old friend Hamzi, as the Kerak people insist on their return.

Among other amusing attempts at extortion was the following: One of our mules had kicked a boy who was tormenting it. The boy was not much the worse, as we saw; but in the evening some men came up, very angrily demanding money, in fact a deodand, for the boy's life, as they said he was dying. Mr. Klein and I offered to go and see him; but this was refused; in fact, the urchin was in the crowd at the time. Mr. Klein reasoned with them. "Who kicked the lad?" "The mule."—"Was any one riding or leading the mule at the time?" "No."—"Then it was the act of the mule alone?" "Yes."—"Well, then, we have nothing to do with it; and as the mule belongs to Jerusalem, you can not punish him here, but must send him to Jerusalem, and let the pasha put him in prison till the lad recovers." This logic at least amused and silenced them. Mr. Klein was in all such cases an inimitable Arab diplomatist, thoroughly understanding the humors of the people, and with the rare tact, patience, and self-possession that only a long experience of the East can impart.

February 8th.—In the morning, though we made an early start, it was not without an effort that we were able to escape the extortion and almost forcible plunder of the tribes. The only exceptions amidst the general onslaught were our honest Jehalin guard, from whom we had now to part, and who, satisfied with their agreement, remained by our side to keep off intruders, to the very moment of our start, when we bade them farewell, and handed to them our letters for England. I have always found the Jehalin, if not a very intelligent, at least an honest and faithful, tribe, and have never, during the weeks I have spent among them, had a single article stolen by them; and with all his faults, there are many worse friends, and less trusty in the time of need, than old Hamzi, the Hebrew money-lender and Arab attorney.

CHAPTER IV.

From the Sáfieh to Kerak.—Wady Gra'hhi.—Ford of the Stinking River.—Nemeirah.—The Waters of Nimrim: their real Position.—Not identical with Nemeirah.—Poor Ruins.—The Brook of the Willows.—Wady Asal.—The Shoulder of the Lisan.—Wady Dra'a.—View of the Lisan.—Contrast of the Geology of the east and west Sides of the Dead Sea.—A charming Glen.—Mezra'ah, *Zoar*.—Disputed Identity with Dra'a.—A turbulent Guard.—Nocturnal Alarms.—Splendid Sunrise.—Attempted Robbery.—Successful Extortion.—Ascent to Kerak.—Magnificent Gorge.—Geological Studies.—Basaltic Streams.—El Kubboh.—Crusading Traditions.—Raynald of Chatillon.—Panoramic View of the Dead Sea.—Bedouin Camps and Shepherds.—Wady R'seir.—Wady of Kerak.—Rugged Ascent.—Strange Access to a City.—Tunnel in the Rock.—Arrival at Kerak.

THE first part of the route from the Sáfieh to Kerak was not very interesting, dependent, as the district is, upon the rains and the letting in of the waters for its beauty. The scene was picturesque enough as we threaded our way through the forest. A strong escort of the Beni Atiyeh, with objects of their own, had joined our Kerak guard to see us safely to the hills; and a score of mounted spearmen, with their lances gleaming and quivering over the trees, led the van.

The ghor, or cultivatable belt, about four miles wide at our camp, rapidly contracts, and the strip, between the mountains and the sea, soon narrows to a width of two miles. Each of the different zones or belts of vegetation disappears in turn. First, we lost the rich park-like wood; then the rushes; then the canebrake; till, finally, there was only a barren salt-marsh, without vegetation, to the sea; and a gravelly dry scrub, with a few acacia-trees here and there, above it, to the foot of the mountains.

Near the north end of the Sáfieh we passed, an hour after starting, the ruins of Um el Hashib, small and insignificant, and which can never have been more than a village, without any trace of a fort. In twenty minutes more, soon after leaving the fertile land, we crossed the seil, or Wady Gra'hhi, beyond which the plain is barren. Gra'hhi has been suggested as convertible with Korcha, which name occurs on the Moabite Stone.

About half an hour farther on we forded a deep muddy ditch, Nahr Murwhashah—*i.e.*, "Stinking River"—well so named, in the fetid mud of which many of the mules stuck fast, as well as some of the horsemen, who had to be carried across on men's backs. Beyond the Stinking River begins a sebkha, or salt-marsh, far more disagreeable than that at the south end of the sea. The shore is fringed with drift-wood incrusted with salt; a thin incrustation of salt covers the plain; but here and there are shallow pools filled with vegetable matter, and the black mud under the salt-decaying crust smells horribly.

After the Seil Haneizir is the Wady N'meirah. The mountains here more closely approach the sea, and the crest facing N'meirah is called Jebel Orak. Very near the ruins, but a little above them, are the remains of an old fort, which must have commanded the road, named merely Kirbet es Sheik. The ruins of N'meirah—*i. e.*, "The Leopard"—are rugged and stony, of several acres in extent, among a set of wide torrent beds, riven by winter floods, and, till closely examined, the site looks merely a slightly elevated space.

It has usually been assumed that this N'meirah is identical with the Biblical southern Nimrim, or Nimrim of Moab ("the waters of Nimrim"), Isa. xv., 6; Jer. xlviii., 34; as the northern Beth Nimrah is with Beit N'meir, on the Jordan. But though the wady be the same, yet the expression "waters of Nimrim" would seem to refer rather to the springs or sources higher up, than to a spot in the dreary plain near the sea. In corroboration of this, Mr. Klein ascertained from an intelligent Kerak Christian, who was among our guard, that high up in the mountains, near the source of the Wady N'meirah, there are the ruins of an old city like those of the other Moabite towns of the highlands, bearing the very name of the "Springs of N'meirah," and with many watered gardens still cultivated. Not far from the course of the N'meirah, also in the mountains, another wady was pointed out to Mr. Klein, which throws light on another Scriptural site not hitherto identified.

Immediately after the mention of Nimrim, we find (Isa. xv., 7) "The brook of the willows," or, as it is in the margin, "The valley of the Arabians;" the Hebrew consonants for willows and Arabians being identical. But besides the Wady Safsaf, to the north of Kerak, noted by Irby and Mangles, and also pointed out to us when we were traveling northward, Mr. Klein had pointed out to him another wady, a little to the south of this, bearing the identical name of the "Wady of the Willows." This being toward the southern frontier, would meet all the requirements of the problem.

In four and a half hours from the time of leaving the Sáfieh we reached the Wady Asal, or "Honey River," a pleasant and sweet stream, and now began to ascend the shoulder of the peninsula of the Lisan. We climbed for more than an hour up a water-riven gorge, cut through a mass of marl and débris, the old deposit of the lake. The scene was grand, though sternly desolate and lifeless. Not a scrap of vegetation, not even a straggling salicornia, could be seen.

About the middle of the neck of the Lisan we crossed the upper stream of the Wady Weideh, which runs out on the south side of the peninsula, and in which the date-palm grows abundantly. Rising still higher, and turning nearly due east, after crossing the Weideh, we came to the Wady Dra'a, in a very deep ravine, which runs out into the north bay of the Lisan. We pitched our camp close to the ruins of Dra'a, from which the wady is named, on a platform overhanging the ravine, sloping back from which was a wide plain with scanty herbage and many gnarled acacia-trees. Our ride had occupied little more than eight hours, and our barometric readings showed that we had risen 650 feet above the Dead Sea, though we were still 650 feet below the sea level.

From the hill just behind our tents we had a splendid view over the whole peninsula of the Lisan, a scene of utter desolation, one mass of water-worn cuttings through salt-marl, without a trace of vegetation, while the nooks at the north-east and south-east angles beneath it smiled with luxuriant green. Beyond stretched the whole western edge of the Dead Sea for nearly forty miles, but far inferior in grandeur to the eastern side. Close above us towered the mountains of Moab, red and white, relieved by streaks of green.

Geologically, the east side is very different from the Judean hills. The whole range is here, excepting superficially, new red sandstone, a formation which nowhere appears on the other side. There is also a good deal of igneous superficial basalt; and in several places porphyritic dikes are shown. The bare red sandstone rocks are often worn into fantastic shapes; and in one place, on a projecting platform, as we ascended to Dra'a, the illusion of a ruined castle was complete. Near the mouth of one wady, about two hours north of the Sáfieh, I found large masses of greenstone, and huge boulders of pudding-stone, with granite pebbles embedded. The height to which the salt-marl reaches on the shoulder of the Lisan is not a little puzzling. Its elevation, as it leans against the base of the Judean hills from Jericho down to the

Akabah, never reaches more than four hundred feet. On the east side it only appears at the Lisan, and on its shoulder we find it piled to the height of nearly five hundred feet. Yet there is no other indication of the old level of the sea, during the period of its deposition, having been at this height. I can only conjecture that the upheaval of the eastern range must have continued during this period, probably while the basaltic eruptions, which occurred only on the east side, were in force; and that the marl here, on the shoulder, away from the action of the water, was raised, while it was all washed off from the sides of the precipitous sandstone ranges.

Turning to the nearer foreground, nothing could be more lovely than the glen beneath us, deep, and densely wooded with poplar, date-palms, oleanders, and semi-tropical herbage, overhanging a perennial stream swarming with fish. Truly a living fountain is a wondrous blessing in a dry and thirsty land. There was evidence here of former high cultivation, in carefully cemented channels of masonry running from higher levels of the stream, and partly excavated, partly built on the sides of the ravine, which had, like little mill-races, conveyed the stream to the higher grounds above the glen.

Another relic of a past civilization was pointed out to us in the distance, where, at about two hours' journey to the north-west, we could make out with our field-glasses Mezra'ah, or, at least, the black camp of Ghawarineh, which our guides told us was on the very spot, and where are stated to be the old Tawahin es Suhkar, or "Sugar-mills." But as Mr. Palmer visited Mezra'ah (he having taken the lower track, where we began to ascend to Dra'a), and does not mention them, they may be merely a repetition of those in the Sâfieh—ordinary water-mills.

The ruins of Dra'a itself are mean and almost obliterated, excepting some on a brow overhanging our camp, and which seem to mark the position of the keep, or citadel, for the protection of the town just below it. Little more of the town is left than a featureless heap of weathered sandstone, the artificial position of which is only proved when, turning over the exposed blocks, we find the dressed and squared blocks beneath. There are also many irregular lines of foundations leveled down to the surface of the plain, and many fragments of bricks and pottery strew the ground.

The chief interest attaching to this spot arises from its supposed identification by some writers with the Zoar of the Bible and ancient history. The mediæval writers, with one or two exceptions, place Zoar, as far as we can gather by a comparison of their accounts, on the road from the south end of the Dead Sea to Kerak, and at some little distance from the lake, in a spot abounding with palm-trees. It was an episcopal see under the Archbishop of Petra, and its bishops sat in the Council of Chalcedon (A.D. 451), and in the Synod of Constantinople (A.D. 536). It was in the province of Palestina Tertia, which included Kerak and Areopolis. No great violence is done to orthography in imagining a change from the guttural Hebrew Zoar (צוֹעַר) to the guttural Arabic Dra'a (ذرعه). It is difficult to place the Zoar of these writers anywhere else than here. But the name exists elsewhere, and we found on the plains eastward of Maïn another ruined city, with the remains of churches and other considerable buildings, also called Dra'a. This latter may more probably be the bishopric of Eusebius.

Still, admitting the identity of this Dra'a with the Christian and mediæval Zoar, it seems impossible, on any reasonable theory, also to identify it with the Zoar of Scripture. There is no imaginable situation in which we can place the cities of the plain, that will meet the conditions of the problem, if this be Bela or Zoar, as it would be too far distant from any of them. But this need not cause much difficulty, as there are very many instances, several of which have been already referred to, where the same name is applied to sites and wadys on opposite sides of the sea, and generally to those nearly in the same parallel of latitude. It would very well harmonize with ordinary usage if there were another Zoar at or near Engedi, as has been conjectured from Deut. xxxiv., 3, and other passages.

Archæological speculations were sadly interrupted by the disturbances raised by our savage guard, and which were kept up incessantly through the night. We had given them money to buy themselves a goat for supper, from a camp of Arabs near us. The two brothers of the young mudjelli kept the money, and there was a free fight over the matter at our tent doors, with knives and pistols drawn. This was at length appeased, and the chief, for security from his friends, made our servants' tent his sleeping-place. During the night our ruffian companions kept amusing themselves by firing off guns, from time to time, close to our ears. Meantime a lurking thief had cut the pickets of the horses, and was quietly leading off Hayne's steed, when he was detected and stopped by a muleteer, fortunately more on the alert than the Keraki.

With all this we had but little sleep, and before sunrise we went down to the stream, and, under the dense shade of the oleanders, had a delicious bathe. I then climbed, before the sun had overtopped the eastern mountains, to the brow of the platform above our camp, among the heaps of old Zoar. The view was magnificent in stern grandeur. The whole Lisan, in its desolate expanse, was spread at our feet, and the sun, whose rays had not yet touched us in the shadow of the mountains, was gilding the tops of the western ridge of the Dead Sea with a golden pink, and with a rich gray blue the range of the mountains of Judah behind them. As Mr. Palmer truly says, "The coloring of the Dead Sea and its neighborhood, when the atmosphere is clear, is simply magnificent." We could trace the course of the Wady Kerak to the north of us, where it rifts the shoulder of the Lisan from east to west; and then turning sharply northward, after it has been, as it appeared to us, joined by the Wady Dra'a, it opens out into a wide plain of acacia scrub with abundant pasturage. A perennial stream runs through it, fringed with a border of date-palms and oleanders, the source of life and wealth to the district, now called the Mezra'ah. There was a very large camp of Beni Atiyeh, and herds of goats, close below us; and through our glasses we could descry much more extensive camps in the Mezra'ah, which was powdered over with scattered flocks and herds.

And now began a scene. Seventy pounds was required for the expenses of the horsemen from Kerak, which must be paid and distributed at once. The spearmen and mounted gunners stood round us, and the climax came when the young mudjelli rode up threateningly to the head muleteer, and, drawing his sword, forbade a mule to be loaded till his demand had been met, intimating that, in case of further delay, he should turn upon us the Beni Atiyeh from the camp below. We were fairly in the trap; there was nothing for it but to yield; and at length, under protest, and telling them they were highwaymen, we were glad to reduce the sum to twenty-five napoleons on account.

The ascent from Dra'a to Kerak occupied five and a quarter hours' steady riding without a halt. At Dra'a we were 650 feet below the sea level, and by our barometer we measured the ascent thence to Kerak to be 3720 feet, making that city 3070 feet above the Mediterranean. Everywhere the gorges up which we climbed were deeply riven; and the prospects, wide and vast, with deep chasms and towering precipices, quite equaled Alpine scenery in their effect under a bright sun, though very different in character. The rich coloring of red, black, and white, with green patches, was exquisite; and geological formation almost effects here what snow and ice do for Alpine scenery.*

On the way-side is a ruined fort, hitherto unnoticed, and called El Kubboh. There is a pointed arch, and the character of the architecture is Crusading, corroborating the local tradition which makes it the strong-

---

* The ascent was also a good geological study. We had left the post-tertiary marl below Dra'a; and then for a little distance eastward the red sandstone is superficial, but is soon covered by the limestone, the same as that of Western Palestine. The superincumbent limestone was not conformable with the sandstone in its stratification. Another point of importance is, that for seven or eight miles from the shore eastward the strata dip to the west at an average angle of 60°; while farther east, so far as I could ascertain where the sections are shown, I noticed that the strata are nearly, or quite, horizontal. I was pleased to find my former theory of the synclinal dip of the Jordan valley thus corroborated in the only part where I had not hitherto had an opportunity of making observations, especially as the agencies which formed the valley seem to have been in more active operation in this part of it than in any other. The limestone was in many places strangely contorted, and this chiefly in the neighborhood of the basaltic outbreaks which frequently disturb the stratification on the east side, but of which no trace is found westward in the lower Jordan. When we had risen 2000 feet, the average thickness of the limestone seemed to be about 1500 feet; and from this point its denudation westward begins.

hold of a Christian sheik of the olden time. The position is admirable as a key of the pass, and well suited for a robber chieftain, for this was the only practicable route to Kerak by the south, the other path from Usdum, up the Wady Tufileh, being too rugged for baggage animals.

One could not but recall here the times of the "Talisman," and the romantic story of the wild chieftain of the Crusading outposts, Raynald of Chatillon, lord of Kerak. Doubtless some of his minions held this post, and wielded their power with as few scruples as did their lord, when, issuing from his keep of Kerak, he sacked the Damascus caravan in time of peace.

It was this act of lawless wrong which exasperated Saladin to the wars of the last Crusade, after his vain demands of redress from Raynald. Soon followed the final and fatal battle of Hattin (5th July, 1187). when the doom of the Crusades was sealed in sight of Gennesaret, and Raynald himself, with the King of Jerusalem and the Grand Master of the Templars, were among the captives. The perfidious chieftain was slain in cold blood by the conqueror, who had sworn to avenge his wrongs with his own hands; and in three months Jerusalem opened its gates to the Saracen. Still, with all his excesses, there is a halo of romance about this daring Frank, who so long held his outpost on the very frontier of Arabia, unsupported by any base for supplies nearer than Jerusalem. And this rugged pass, too, and the open desert of the Sebkha, were his only line of communication with the world behind him.

Shortly after Kubboh, we passed an outcrop of basalt through the limestone, 2050 feet above the Dead Sea, the sandstone being now far below us. Here we paused. Jebel el Haditha, a bold peak, towered to the south. We stood on the crest of a range of terraces, with a panorama of the Dead Sea before us. The whole Lisan, with Points Molyneux and Costigan, plainly marked, lay between. Jebel Usdum, Sebbeh, Engedi, and the brown ridge of Judean mountains, Hebron, and the hills about Jerusalem, were all in sight; while, on the other side, we looked down into the tremendous Wady of Kerak, some 1800 feet of nearly sheer precipice on the opposite side, the lower 500 feet being red sandstone, with the upper part white chalk and limestone, pleasantly relieved by the beading of black lines of flint. To the south was pointed out the "Wady of the Willows;" and among other names, that of Mochrath, one of the unidentified names occurring on the Moabite Stone.

Hence our road was up the south side of the Wady Kerak. We defiled in long line up a narrow pass among rocks, with many green patches, where goats seemed to be hanging to the mountain side, as they browsed in single file. A dozen resolute men behind these rocks might arrest the march of an army. The valley gradually widened above; and here and there, among the green patches, Bedouin tents, looking like black spots on the steep sides, could be detected.

TUNNEL IN THE ROCK. 83

Many of these belong to the Kerak people, a large portion of whom camp out with their herds during the summer months. Here the bottom of the wady, which was still very narrow, began to be cultivated with olives, figs, pomegranates, and a few vineyards and patches of corn.

No. 3. TUNNEL ENTRANCE TO KERAK.

We halted at a platform formed by the opening of the Wady R'seir, and in which a pretty little spring bubbles out among the grass. Close to this spot a number of men suddenly appeared, yelling and shouting on the rocks above us; but though they proved to be only shepherds, who wanted to know our business and our destination, we saw how necessary an armed guard was in such a place, to secure the baggage from plunder, as all whom we met carried firelocks.

Soon Kerak stood towering before us, with its line of wall and splendid castles, the southern one being of very great extent. We had now to descend into the valley, in order to ascend the opposite cliff to reach the city. It was almost an hour's climb from the stream to the tunnel entrance of Kerak, and this on a zigzag path along the side of a rugged slope, strewn with boulders, and so steep that in places it was scarcely possible to sit our horses. When near the top of the cone, the path abruptly turns into an arched tunnel, up which we stumble in the darkness for more than eighty yards, and then emerge into the open space or market of Kerak.

CHAPTER V.

Kerak.—A natural Fortress: its Height, Position, Form, Area, Fortifications.—Accessible only by Tunnels.—The Castle of Bybars.—The great Castle: its Shape, Moat, Cistern, Crypt, Chapel, Gateways.—Occupation of Castle by Ibrahim Pasha.—Water Supply.—Mosque.—Ancient Basilica.—Our Camp in the Castle of Bybars.—Greek School-master.—A Friend in need.—Kerak Interior.—Roman Pavement.—Ancient Bath.—Antiques and Coins.—Christian Quarter.—Greek Church.—School and Bibles.—Threats of the Chiefs.—Ransom demanded.—Find ourselves Prisoners.—Messenger to Jerusalem.—Every Man his own Thief-catcher.—Value of Pork.—Daoud's Stratagem.—Midnight Interview.—Welcome Aid.—Arrival of the Beni Sakk'r, Sheik Zadam.—The Tables turned.—A Sunday under Arrest.—Arabic Service.—Greek Christians.—Demands on the Hakim.—View from the Castle Wall.—Relations of Kerak and the Beni Sakk'r.—Excursion under Guard.—Our Letter discovered.—Renewed Threats.

BEFORE relating our adventures at Kerak, it may be well to attempt some description of this remarkable fortress, of which, until recently, the concise journal of Burckhardt, and the modest and singularly accurate narrative of Irby and Mangles, were the only easily accessible records, since both De Saulcy and Lynch have dismissed Kerak very shortly. The position is so strong by nature that it would be seized upon as a fortress from the very earliest times. A lofty brow pushes forward to the west with a flattened space on its crest, a sort of head, behind which the neck at the south-east contracts, and gives it the form of a peninsula, at the same time that the isthmus, if I may so call it, rapidly slopes down before rising to reunite to its shoulder the yet loftier hill to the east. The platform of Kerak stands 3720 feet above the sea level; yet on all sides it is commanded, some of the neighboring heights being over 4050 feet high (barometric). It is, however, severed everywhere, excepting at the neck, and also in a less degree at the northwest angle, from the encircling range. Two deep wadies, from 1000 to 1350 feet deep, with steeply scarped or else rugged sides, flank it north and south, the Wady Hammad to the south, and Wady Kerak to the north, which unite about a mile to the west of the city, and form the ravine which we ascended. The escarpment of the third side of the triangle is formed by the Wady Kobeishch, which, starting from the depression of what I have called the neck, rapidly descends to the Wady Kerak.

The platform of the city, thus surrounded, is tolerably level, by art or nature, measuring from 800 to 1000 yards on each face of the triangle, the north-east side being the longest. The whole place has formerly been surrounded by a strong wall, of which a considerable portion remains everywhere. In no place did I observe it to be entirely demolished, while in some parts it is still perfect. The wall, with its smoothly-sloped facing, fills up any irregularities in the native rock, which is scarped a considerable way down, especially at the angles, with a very well-executed revetment, wherever requisite. This lower portion of the work appears to be older than the Crusading or Saracenic times; and the wide shallow bevel suggests the Herodian, or a yet earlier epoch. The upper part of the fortress is claimed by the Mohammedans in several inscriptions, which are palpably of later date than the structures themselves.

NO. 4.   KERAK CASTLE WALLS, WEST SIDE.

There have been originally only two entrances to Kerak—one to the north-west, the other on the farther side, and both through tunnels in the side of the cliff, emerging on the platform of the town. Of late years paths have been made over the ruinous walls in two places; but these can only be scrambled over by foot passengers. They are both on the north-east face. To an enemy Kerak is utterly inaccessible, except by the winding paths at the western and north-east sides. The road from the east, by which we traveled, suddenly turns as we are under the northwest castle, and is cut to a great depth immediately under the angle, while the great castle wall, with loop-holes and parapets, towers straight up its whole width, leaving any one approaching by this great rock-hewn ditch at the mercy of the garrison.

Having passed through this cutting, we turn sharply to the left, and creep along the rugged path, completely exposed to those above, and where horsemen or footmen can only mount slowly in single file, till we enter a tunnel, the gate-way of Kerak, apparently partly natural, but with a well-built pointed arch over its entrance, above which a stone, manifestly of a later date, with an Arabic inscription, has been let into the face of the rock. The inscription is only partially defaced, but has not, I believe, been yet translated. Mr. Buxton obtained an admirable photograph of this tunnel entrance. The arch is certainly older than the Saracenic occupation, and Mr. Fergusson has expressed his decided opinion that, though slightly pointed, it is yet Roman.

The tunnel continues winding, and steeply ascending, for eighty paces, when we suddenly emerge, and find ourselves on the open platform of the town, very

near the north-west castle. This tower, which is called the Castle of Bybars, or of "El Melek," from an Arabic inscription of great size let into its wall, ascribing the erection to "El Melek" (the king) Bybars, is a massive wall forming three sides of a trapezium, the long wall stretching ninety yards, and each of the flanking or re-entering walls extending in an obtuse angle from it for fifteen yards. At the inner extremity of these walls are still more lofty towers, in which are staircases. The wall is twenty-seven feet thick in its lower stories. The upper stories are studded with long loop-holes, and an open ledge for the defenders to communicate along the whole. The arched loop-holes and chambers are now, for the most part, converted into rude store-houses, built up with rough masonry; and the ledges, some 100 feet high, are the favorite lounge of the boys and men of Kerak. Above this the wall contracts; there are loop-holes again; and a platform outside, without battlements, runs along near the top, about seven feet wide. The stones for this enormous construction have evidently been obtained from the great rock-hewn fosse below, up which we rode, and which has been a most convenient and inexhaustible quarry, thus doubly increasing the strength of the place.

The inscription running along the inner face, attributing the building to Bybars, is flanked on either side by two lions rampant, which seem part of the original structure, which the inscription is not (for the stones do not fit well, and one has been inserted by the ignorant workmen upside down). These lions, apparently older than the Arabic letters, suggested to us the idea that they are possibly part of the Crusaders' work, not removed by Saladin or Bybars.

NO. 6.   KERAK. CRUSADERS' FORT.

The fort at the north-east is comparatively insignificant, as the natural fortress was there inaccessible. But far more important and extensive is the great castle at the southern angle. This being the most exposed point, owing to the shallowness of the Wady Kobeisheh, has been the most carefully fortified. It is cut off from the shoulder of the adjoining hill by an immense scarped ditch, just as is the other castle; but there is no passage this way, and a wall of native rock has been left at each end, so as to form, in fact, a gigantic cistern. Beside this, there is an immense hewn ditch 100 feet wide. The outer wall of this castle is constructed on the same principle as the north-west tower, but of much greater thickness and height, its outer length being eighty-seven yards.

But this is, as it were, only the flanking work of a great fortress; for such this castle is, entirely independent of the town, from which it is separated on the north by a wide and deep ditch, now much filled in with rubbish. It forms an irregular quadrilateral, the northern side, toward the city, being nearly double the length of the south wall, and its width across being from 220 to 250 yards. The interior of this block is one mass of vaults, arches, and galleries, all of most massive construction, with apparently only two open court-yards.

The most interesting portion of the building, and one which tells the history of its construction, is a crypt chapel, with an eastern apse, ninety feet long. It is reached by descending a circular staircase, which lands us half-way down the side of the chapel; and there is also a staircase leading to the roof, over which have evidently been other buildings. There are four very small narrow lancet windows high up; and lamps must certainly have been required for worship here. Some fragments of columns are built sideways in the wall, and also some remains of inscriptions.

There are many patches of fresco still to be seen on the walls, but all in a state of sad decay. None of the figures can be traced entire. There was one head of a saint, with a corona, left on the plaster.

Besides the chapel, there are long ranges of buildings like casemates, magazines, and barracks, story above story, most solidly vaulted. These seem to have been four or five stories, or perhaps more, in height; but the upper parts are now much ruined. The different gate-ways, with all their appliances of defense on the side of the town, still remain, and it was necessary to pass through three of these in order to reach the central court. Under the great crypts are numerous vaulted and cemented reservoirs, capable of containing an ample supply of water for a long siege. Altogether, the great castle of Kerak is by far the grandest monument of crusading energy now existing. It was built under King Fulco, by one of the predecessors of Raynald of Chatillon, about A.D. 1131, and strengthened under the auspices of Godfrey of Boulogne; and in A.D. 1183 it baffled the assaults of Saladin.

The castle has more than once proved its invulnerability against attacks from the town; while, on the other hand, its possessors have found its defenses turned to their own defeat. Thus Ibrahim Pasha, during his conquest of Syria, in A.D. 1844, was never able to take Kerak, whose proud boast is that it yet remains a virgin city. Yet his troops occupied this castle for months, and finally, compelled by starvation to evacuate it, were for the most part slaughtered on the other side of the Wady Kobeisheh.

Between the two great fortifications of Kerak there is understood to be still an under-ground communication, and there are deep wells sunk in the castle. For the supply of water for the civil inhabitants, not only do deep wells and arched cisterns abound everywhere, but there is an enormous open reservoir very near the Castle of Bybars, apparently, from its massive masonry, of Roman work, which, at the time of our visit, was partly filled with water. There are also some fine perennial springs in the sides of the valleys close below, four of which ate near the town, and most copious. Ain Sara is used, close to its source, for turning water-mills.

Among the other antiquities of Kerak the most interesting is a ruined mosque, which has evidently been previously a basilica. The roof is gone, and the building is now used as a Moslem cemetery; but the pillars and arches remain. The door-way is pointed, or Saracenic, and the upper part of the arch is filled in with masonry, which has once been covered with Christian symbols. These have been chiseled out, and an Arabic inscription inserted; but the Moslems have left two symbols—viz., the cup sculptured on each side of their inscription—attesting the former use of the place as a Christian church.

So soon as we emerged from the tunnel into Kerak, we were directed by the chief to camp within the Castle of Bybars. The locality was certainly, in itself, a favorable one. The present inhabited part of Kerak does not extend very near it, and we were at least securely sheltered from the west, though scarcely prepared for the pitiless north wind, which afterward swept in eddies round the open court. Soon our tents were got up, while an eager crowd of men and boys watched our proceedings from the ledges of the fortress overhead, and looked curiously down as we toiled away with our men at clearing the great stones to drive in the pegs. The mules and horses were picketed for security under the wall within the line of tents. Our view toward the great castle at the other end of the place was uninterrupted, as the scattered town consists entirely of flat, mud-roofed houses, so constructed as to appear all under-ground, with no streets or lanes between them, and distributed in such a way that it is sometimes difficult to know whether we are walking on the ground or over a house.

We had scarcely arrived when a young man of pleasing countenance, in a shabby Greek ecclesiastical costume, came forward, and was affectionately greeted by Daoud and Mr. Klein. He was the master of the Greek Christian school, a native of Kerak, and had been educated at the convent of the Holy Cross at Jerusalem, where he was a frequent visitor of Mr. Klein—very well disposed, a student of his Bible, and well inclined to Protestantism. He was a youth of thought and study, in which he stands here, indeed, alone. He was accompanied by the priest, a dull, heavy-looking man, much inferior to him in every

A FRIENDLY OFFER. 95

way. He offered to lionize us, and advised our starting at once. We, having reason to suspect coming difficulties, felt no time was to be lost, left tent-pitching and unpacking to our people, and were off without delay. We walked direct to the great castle, fol-

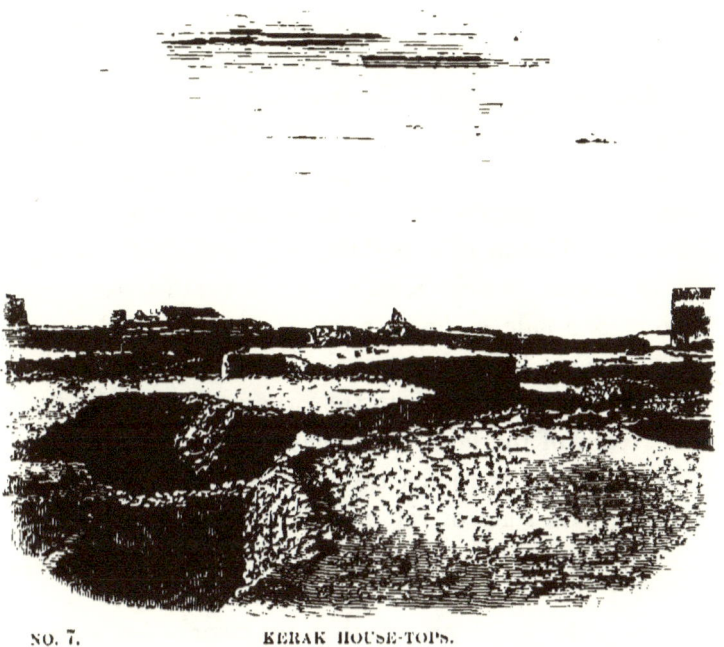

NO. 7.   KERAK HOUSE-TOPS.

lowed and jostled by scowling crowds, who repeatedly asked if we expected to be allowed to see the castle without paying for it; but several native Christians (of whom there are variously estimated to be from 800 to 1600 in Kerak) joined us, and we took no notice of our persistent tormentors.

After visiting and hastily noting down the features of the castle, the school-master pointed out to us the course of the connecting tunnel between the two castles, driven through the rock on the south side, just above the massive escarpment. We then crossed to the Moslem quarter. He beckoned us to follow him into a house. We descended a sort of sloping rubbish-heap into a narrow alley. A Kerak house is entered by a low door-way four feet high, generally arched, of dry stones, but often with a massive lintel, taken from some more ancient building. This door-way opens into a small and filthy court-yard, with numbers of projecting stones, on each of which a little conical cake of cow-dung is placed to dry—the only fuel of treeless Kerak. Underneath these runs along one side a long trough formed of dried mud, the manger for goats and donkeys. Another door, four feet high, opens into the principal room, the living room of the family. It has neither windows nor chimney, and is roofed by a succession of dry stone arches, with slabs or rafters laid across them. Exactly in the centre is a large saucer-shaped scallop of mud, the fire-place and oven, and the fumes from which have no other exit than the door. I need not say how blackened are the faces and every thing else in this smoke-trap. Opening out of this room are several dark cells, some of them evidently the crypts of the more ancient city—the store-houses of the family. Furniture there is none. All sit and sleep on the floor.

We soon found out why the school-master had brought us into this house. The floor of the hovel was a beautiful, tesselated pavement of marble, quite perfect, with the marble bases of some old columns still in their places at the edge of the pavement. Only the centre of the pattern had been broken up, to make way for the hearth. It was probably part of some Roman baths, for in the next house were the remains of the marble bath-room, which now formed the yard, with the water-pipes still protruding from the walls.

We had several other proofs of Roman occupation brought to us in the course of our stay. Mr. Klein had presented to him by one of the Christians two very fine and perfect Roman lamps, which he kindly gave me; and I purchased several imperial coins of gold and silver, besides a gold medal of Helena. The gold coins were all sold to me for rather less than their value as old gold. I also collected about fifty much-worn brass coins, from Hadrian down to the Byzantine Maurice, and two silver pennies of Baldwin, king of Jerusalem. We also obtained a few cameos, to which the finders did not attach much value, and which were all chipped.

The present Christian quarter is to the north of the town; and there we visited the Greek church, a solid, respectable building, with two aisles and an apse, and massive square pillars like an old Norman church. At the west end of the nave is a well in the floor, still used. On the rood-screen were several very creditable Byzantine pictures of saints, with little lamps burning in front of them, and smaller copies hung below for the votaries to kiss. There is a neat inclosure outside the church, and another at the west end, where are the priest's rooms and the school, a plain building with matting along one side of it—its only furniture. The Church Missionary Society had supplied some of the school-books, Psalters and Testaments; and I noticed two well-used large Arabic Bibles, with the Bible Society's stamp on their covers. The school-master much desires an Arabic Bible with marginal references, which is expensive; and we gladly promised to send him one on our return to Jerusalem.

When we returned to camp, we found our troubles begun—the people crowding round, no keeping the head men out of our tents, an intrusion for which we paid heavily in flea-bites all night—and the young mudjelli assuming a threatening tone. Other travelers had paid handsomely for going over the castle, and what right had we to start off without waiting for him and arranging terms? He must have a large sum for our assurance in going over *his* place. He roundly cursed the Greek priest and the Christians, and forbade them to come near us—an injunction he signally failed in carrying out. £600 is the lowest sum he will take, and it is very moderate. De Saulcy, the Duc de Luynes, and M. Mauss, the only visitors they have had, paid at a much higher rate. "But," we reply, "we are not princes, and will not pay like princes; indeed, we can not." "Then," said he, "the chief will shut his eyes with grief while evil men rob your baggage and horses." Meantime our mules had been, in our absence, removed to the public khan; so that, as far as they were concerned, we were at his mercy. "Then," cried Mr. Klein, "we will go to the pasha." "What can pashas do here? We are lords here, and care less than nothing for pashas or sultans." To his £600 he held firm. Even if we had had the money, we felt that payment would be no security against further demands; but we had it not. Eventually he announced that we were prisoners in our tents, and an armed guard was set to prevent our going beyond the little space between our tents and the wall.

But while the young mudjelli was playing his game in our tent, another part of the drama was enacted in the next. Mr. Klein had contrived to send a messenger for the Greek school-master, who, with a trusty native Christian, had stolen round the corner unperceived, and entered the tent. The character of the old father was discussed: "Oh, while his sons are robbers, he too has a belly as large as a tent; but then he has understanding wide as the ocean;" implying that he was too prudent ever to resort to personal violence. We were thankful to feel that, at least, these were a different class from the lawless freebooters of the Sáfieh. It was arranged that a secret messenger should be found and dispatched at once to the English consul at Jerusalem; and a sign was agreed on—that the man chosen should bring the priest's string of beads with him in the night. Long, and in undertones, did Mr. Klein and the Greeks talk, while Trotter and Johnson patrolled to see that no eavesdroppers were near, and the rest of our party kept our young jailer in parley in the other large tent. I entered, sat down, and, apparently intent on a map before me, indited on a foolscap sheet the letter to the consul, recounting our difficulty, and the tricks of the man who was eying me, and little suspecting my employment. At length Klein came in, and we understood the coast was clear. There was no further occasion to detain our keeper; so we began to talk loudly at him in English, on which he took his departure, telling us he should expect the money to be ready in the morning.

Arab experiences were the topic of the evening, when our tormentors had retired. Mr. Klein told a good story illustrative of the practice of the country, "Every man his own thief-catcher." His horse, a very valuable one, had been stolen from his stable at Jerusalem, and not a trace of it could be found, nor a shade of suspicion as to who was the thief. Some little time afterward he learned that his horse had been seen among the Beni Hassan, in Gilead. Sending across Jordan, he opened communications with Goblan, the well-known sheik of the Adwân, and the neighbor of the Beni Hassan, for its recovery, promising him a reward of £10. The Adwân reconnoitred the district secretly for some days, and at length discovered the camp, where the thief (a man of Lifta, a village near Jerusalem) had taken refuge. He then rode over with a party of armed horsemen, shortly before night-fall. They made out the tent before which the horse was picketed, and, still unseen, concealed themselves carefully for the night in the forest. The sun had not risen when, in the gloaming, the Adwân made a dash into the camp, and cut the pickets. Four of them rushed into the tent, seized the culprit, tied him across the horse, and galloped off into the forest before the Beni Hassan knew what was up. Arrived at their own camp, they stripped the man naked, beat him severely, and left him a whole day under a broiling sun, pegged to the ground. Next day they let him crawl off, and soon brought the horse to Jerusalem, where they received their reward.

"Mountain never meets mountain, but man and man may meet," was a favorite Arabic proverb of Daoud's, meaning that it is best to part friends with every body, with a view to future contingencies. Hence Daoud's unwearied civility to the most irritating schemers. He used it well in his courteous Eastern phrase, when, yesterday, he took leave of the sheik of the Beni Atiyeh, and, writing his name down in his pocket-book, assured him he should remember him, and recommend future travelers to his good offices.

Daoud was generally up to the occasion. Meanness is an especial vice of Kerak. Not only did the young sheik not send us the kid which etiquette required, when he was returned to his own land, after his dinner with us yesterday; but, after leaving our tent to-night, he condescended to go to the kitchen tent and demand a supper. Daoud baffled him by saying, "Yes, the cook is just cutting up the pork." —"Ugh; but there is some rice." "Yes, and putting the bits on the rice." This was not the first time that Hayne's flitch of bacon had done us good service; for before leaving Jerusalem, slices were cut off and distributed in the several boxes of sugar, rice, coffee, and the like, so as to defile their contents in the eyes of good Moslem thieves.

While we were together at prayers late in the evening, we heard the guard's challenge, but no reply. It was pitch dark, for the moon had set; and soon the rattle of beads was heard under the eaves at the back of the tent. Mr. Klein slipped out; and when our worship was concluded, and we had committed ourselves to a covenant Father's care in a strange land, we went to the other tent, where the two were sitting in darkness. With a careful patrol round, a candle was lighted, and I produced the letter, which the Christian carefully concealed in the lining of his garment, together with a sovereign, and, of course, an extra piece for backsheesh; with a promise of a dollar extra for every day he should be away short of ten days, the usual time for going and returning from Jerusalem. He then started unperceived—not even our Christian servants were in the secret—and went out to sleep in the mountains for a few hours, assuring us that by day-break he would be miles away from Kerak; and thus, after a day of rare interest and excitement, the party retired to their couches, or sheep-skins.

The first news of the next morning was from the Greek school-master, who arrived early to say that the messenger with the letter had got away in safety, and was supposed to have gone to his family camp in the hills; but, better still, that Zadam, son of Fendi y Faiz, the great sheik of the Beni Sakk'r, was only seven hours off. Mr. Klein at once dispatched a secret messenger, begging his immediate presence. Soon after arrived a servant of the head man, to say that he did not wish us to be close prisoners, and that, as long as we did not visit the city, we might ride out under proper guard, and see whatever part of the country we wished. But Mr. Klein knew the Arab character too well to allow this to pass. "No," exclaimed he, in energetic tones in Arabic, in the hearing of all the men that sat on the wall; "they know they have committed a crime in confining us here, and insulting us; they are afraid, and so they send a message: let them come and fetch us out." It reminded one of St. Paul's experience at Philippi (Acts xvi., 37).

We remained, therefore, still under guard till noon, when the old mudjelli arrived in person to pay us a visit of state, preceded by a negro mounted herald and a troop of spearmen, and surrounded by the magnates of the place. But with them was Zadam, the

Beni Sakk'r sheik, with his young brother, a bright youth of fourteen. At once he dismounted, and greeted Mr. Klein as an old friend. It appeared he had been unavoidably detained, but had acted on our letter, and had arrived at Jerusalem only an hour after we left for Hebron. But he had made amends for his delay, and produced a contract, signed and sealed by him in the presence of the English consul, by which he had agreed to be our guard, and to take us through all the country north of Kerak for forty days, for the moderate sum of £60 sterling. He had calculated the time we should be on the road, and had come, expecting our arrival about this time. Thus all the future of our expedition was made smooth, if only we could manage the neighborhood of Kerak itself.

The old mudjelli entered, and sat down next Zadam. Now was our turn. We recapitulated, through Daoud, the indignities to which we had been exposed; how his son had acted the brigand, and how at that very moment we were prisoners. The son was meanwhile sitting in the door-way, listening to the indictment. Mr. Klein asserted his dignity with great solemnity. Appealed to by the mudjelli, he would only speak *to him* through an interpreter. The old man evidently saw matters had been carried with too high a hand, objurgated his son, offered us every apology. His land was our land, his horses were our horses, his guards were our guards. From this moment we were free. His son was a fool. "Yes," broke in Mr. Klein with an inimitable grimace, "in every country there are low, mean robbers, as well as respectable and intelligent gentlemen." This was too much for the son, who hurriedly finished his coffee and slunk out of the tent. Meantime the Beni Sakk'r, with his keen black eye, aquiline nose, and handsome face, broke in, calmly, but very strongly. He had come to meet his friends in a friendly land, and did not expect to find them under guard, and *that* for money which had not been earned. We observed that we had come prepared to make a handsome present, but not after being robbed on the road. Our servants and muleteers were standing, grinning with delight over the heads of the sitting council; and various Kerak Christians evidently enjoyed the objurgation bestowed on their dreaded ruler.

When pipes were finished, all withdrew; and the Sanhedrim of Kerak, as Daoud called them, formed in a circle on the rising ground behind our tents, in long and angry dispute. The young men came in for hard language—more for their bungling, I suspect, than for any thing else. "May Allah have mercy on the father of your beard!" was one of the severe reproaches cast on the culprits. But, at any rate, we were allowed to go out, and took the opportunity of enjoying a ramble with some guides among the barren hills and deep wadys of the neighborhood, which produced partridge, if no more important discovery.

The next day was Sunday, and not a very quiet rest-day. We were still under surveillance, and our mules at the khan. At day-break all sorts of visitors crowded the tents, and it was only through incessant proclamations by our servants that it was our prayer-day, and that we must be left alone, that we were able to get any peace. The Beni Sakk'r Zadam showed himself more of a gentleman than the others. The old mudjelli kept sitting on in our tent, admiring every article he saw, when Zadam came in, saluted us, sat down a moment, and then got up, saying, "There are too many here for your peace." At last we had our tents tied up, and enjoyed our English service and Holy Communion together (certainly the first English celebration ever held here), and claimed the promise, "Where two or three are gathered together."

Mr. Klein was not with us, as he found an opportunity of holding an Arabic service in a room in the Christian quarter, and then was detained a long time, visiting the people after it. He had thirty men and six women to form his congregation, all belonging to the Greek Church. They are very ignorant, but from Bible teaching are Protestants in heart, have some knowledge of the truth, and thirst for more. The school-master is fond of study, thoughtful, and his great desire is to go to England to complete his education. There were earnest requests for a catechist; and if the roads were safe, life and property secure, and regular communications open with Salt, in Gilead, where the Turkish government is now firmly established, a native catechist might be sent at once, were there funds for the purpose. Some of the people, even now, prefer not to have their children baptized in the Greek Church, but send them to Salt, when there is a missionary on circuit there.

The great value, however, of Kerak as a mission station would be the opportunity of free intercourse with the Bedouin, which is most difficult on the west side, where, on the complaint of the Moslem religious authorities, the Christian school established among the Ta'amirah has been broken up, and where the Turks are afraid of the Bedouin becoming more troublesome, if they become more enlightened. On the east there would be at least no official jealousy to interpose.

The afternoon was much occupied with temporal works of mercy. Looked upon as a hakim, I had a stream of visitors. I had some difficulty in screwing my courage to use a history in a surgical case, and to open an abscess in a youth's leg. Happily, there was no artery in the way, and I saved my credit, and also the young man's life, who was going on well three days afterward. There were ladies' cases. Even the old mudjelli came, and said his fifth and favorite wife was very ill since a mishap; but when I told him I could not prescribe without seeing the patient, and also parenthetically inquired how he came to have five instead of four wives, he hastily turned the subject.

We climbed to the top of the castle overhead, and on the top of the wall outside sat down and read. We looked at Jerusalem fifty miles off, as the crow flies, across the lake, but plainly visible through our glasses. The Russian buildings, the Mount of Olives, and, farther south, Bethlehem, were easily recognized. The view at sunset was splendid—a wonderful glow of red, yellow, and green, over the range of Judea, and the old moon just in the arms of the new.

Again came the mudjelli, handling and asking for inkstands, paper, opera-glasses, pistols, or whatever he could lay his fingers on, and sorely trying our patience. After his third or fourth departure, Zadam came in, and suggested an early start. We explained that we wished to explore the southern district before turning north, and suggested that he should go, and return for us in a few days. With a quiet smile and inimitable pantomime, he told us that if he did leave us, the mudjelli would "filch, filch, filch," putting out his long, slender fingers toward each of us, and then drawing them quietly together and gathering them in. It was plain that it was only the awe of Zadam's presence that gave us our present quasi-liberty. Zadam also hinted that he did not like to stay much longer in the quarters of his vassal, on whom, of course, he and his retinue had to sponge.

Mr. Klein, who had been diligently collecting typographical information, and had catalogued about sixty names of places round, and chiefly to the south of Kerak, found very few names that promised to be of scriptural or historical interest. He thought that one long day's ride might suffice to work a radius south of Kerak to the extent of fifteen or twenty miles; so we agreed to go in two days, and persuaded Zadam and his brother to be our guests for the rest of our stay here. Trotter's little spare tent was sent up for them, rough bedding found, and their horses picketed with ours.

The relations of the mudjelli and the Beni Sakk'r are curious. The former is a Turkish-appointed governor, ranks as a colonel in the Turkish army, and draws pay as such from the imperial treasury, being, of course, answerable for the taxes due from the district. The latter is also under Turkish dominion, but only as a vassal owing feudal allegiance, and may be called on to bring so many hundred horsemen into the field when required. Practically, the Beni Sakk'r are an independent tribe; yet Kerak pays to them a regular tribute annually, to protect themselves and their flocks from pillage, very much as the towns of South Judah used to send "presents" to David during his wanderings. The tribute paid is in kind—barley, wool, etc. It is felt prudent but humiliating by the Keraki, who recall the time when they were held above the proudest of the Bedouin.

In the evening Zadam and his brother dined with us. They endured the trying ordeal of a European dinner with truly Oriental patience; and Zadam showed much shrewdness in his quiet imitation of every thing he saw us do, and much skill in the handling of those, to him, novel weapons, a knife and fork. He admitted, however, that he had seen them before, as he had visited Alexandria and Cairo when taking some Arab horses as a present to the Viceroy of

Egypt, and had traveled in a railway train. He one day asked Mr. Klein whether he thought the Queen of England would give him a present, if he took her a fine Arab horse as a gift.

One day we took advantage of a lull in the storm; and finding that we might ride out with our guards where we would, Mr. Klein planned an admirable

NO. 8. ANCIENT LAMP, FOUND AT KERAK.

route with me to several of the southern cities of Moab, the topographical results of which will be given further on. The rest of the party did good work, Buxton, Hayne, and Johnson, toiling all day at measuring, sketching and photographing, among the castles and ruins of Kerak, which, for once, they were permitted to do, with no greater annoyance than an unmannerly crowd about them.

After nine hours' absence we returned, to find there was to be no more peace for us. The fact of our having sent a letter to Jerusalem had eked out, and in a storm of rage the mudjelli and his band hurried to our camp. His brother going into the tent and finding Mr. Klein alone, told him plainly, with Arabic euphemism, he would have him assassinated whenever a favorable opportunity should occur. Klein begged to refer him to those who had written the letter. I was next taxed, and replied that, as we had no money here, we were obliged to send to Jerusalem to tell our wants. Did he suppose we would carry £600 about with us? It was vain; the curses were only louder. I was obliged in turn to try a little browbeating, and through Daoud told him, with angry and scornful gestures, that if a hair of Mr. Klein's head were touched, he should pay for it to the Pasha of Nablous. As for the Greeks, to whose quarter, we learned, he had been, to curse the Greek school-master, and to vow vengeance on every Christian who had been near us, so soon as we should be gone, Daoud took care to tell him in the ears of his people that he shook like a sheep before the Moscov (Russians), and that he dared not hurt one child under the wing of the patriarch. (The Greek patriarch makes him a yearly present for his protection of his people.) Soon there was a pause, as the mudjelli ceased cursing, and stooped down to say his prayers. Scarcely calmed by his devotions, he told us he wanted no strangers in his country who could not pay like gentlemen. We told him we should leave to-morrow. He turned round to the crowd and announced that he should only permit us to leave by the way we came, and that he should turn us back into the Sáfieh. This was too much for Sahan, Zadam's boy-brother, who leaped up, snapped his fingers in the face of the old bully, and laughed at the notion of making his brother's friends go back to Sáfieh. Zadam also hinted, delicately, that any injury to us might lead to the Kerak cattle straying into Beni Sakk'r pastures.

At last they departed, leaving a guard over our tents, lest we should escape in the night.

CHAPTER VI.

Excursion to the south of Kerak.—Kureitun.—The twin Towns.—
Kiriathaim.—The Highlands of Moab.—Ruined Cities.—Azizah.
—Wine-presses.—M'hbeilch.—Jubah.—Roman Road.—Mahk'henah.—Cisterns.—Modeh.—Roman Mile-stones.—Mesh'had.—
Madin.—Theniyeh.—Arabic Names.—Kerak, *Kir-moab*, or *Kirhareseth.*—Obstinacy of the Mudjelli.—Visit to the Council.—Diplomacy about Ransom.—Arab Manœuvres.—Off at last.—Tremendous Storm.—Road to Rabba.—Rakim.—Roman Road.—Arrival at Rabba.—Camp in a Tank.—Description of Rabba.—Roman Temples.—Basaltic Stones.—The Kerak Men again.—Daoud's Ingenuity for the Horse's Corn.—Robbery of the Letter-carrier.—Bad News.—Mr. Klein recalled.

BEFORE taking our final leave of Kerak, it may be well to give shortly the results of our surveying expedition among the ruins to the southward. We left by the north-east side of the city, riding through the Christian quarter, and, scrambling over a gap in the broken wall, led our horses down a zigzag path, into the ravine of the Wady Kerak. At this point the depth of the gorge rapidly diminishes, as, making a partial circuit of the city, we come out, after twenty minutes, under the great castle, cross first a brow, and then the Wady Tziatîn, where the soldiers of Ibrahim Pasha were slaughtered in attempting to cut their way from the castle. Here Ibrahim Pasha planted his mortars and bombarded the place.

The wady of Kerak soon begins to widen from a

ravine to a more open valley. Ancient terraces are everywhere to be traced, and here and there little green, saucer-like, level halting-places, with soft, rich herbage, where the Keraki were making their summer camp, while their goats depastured the rugged hill-sides. In forty-five minutes after starting we reached the crest of the opposite hill, and could overlook Kerak, with the gorge down to the Dead Sea, up which we had ridden a week before, and a part of the sea itself, while the mountains of Judea formed the background. Even without a glass we could distinctly make out Jerusalem. The spot had a few ruins and wells, and is called Jelamet es Subbha.

It was only twenty minutes' ride from this place to the first of the twin towns of Kureitun, perhaps a Kiriathaim of Scripture, but not the Kiriathaim of Reuben. Here are the remains of two towns close together, with a gentle hollow of not more than half a mile from crest to crest between them, bearing the same name, and thus illustrating the significance of the dual termination in the Hebrew Kiriathaim. One description might suffice for all these Moabite ruins. The town seems to have been a system of concentric circles built round a central fort; and outside the buildings the rings continue as terrace walls, the gardens of the old city. The terraces are continuous between the twin hillocks, and intersect each other at the foot. There are several wells, now half-choked and dry, in each, and the ground is full of small caverns, especially under the buildings, carefully cemented, which have been the reservoirs of each house. We find here no arches standing, but the remains of many, in the buttresses from the vaults, showing that stone had been exclusively used in the domestic constructions.

We had now got on to the plateau, or highlands, of Moab, on the crest of what looks, from the other side, to be a range of mountains, but which is in reality the edge of a high table-land about 4000 feet above the Dead Sea valley, and which gently rises to the eastward for about twenty-five miles, where a barren limestone range of no great height forms another water-shed, and is the conventional frontier of Arabia. The ravines to the westward, which, as we ascended from the Dead Sea, have been so conspicuous a feature, become now, in their earlier course, mere gentle valleys, with rounded rolling hills, none of them so steep as those of Central Judea. Whenever the limestone is elevated above the rich vegetable soil, it is honey-combed with caves, all once utilized as water-cisterns. The wells are countless, and not confined to the old cities only, showing that the Israelites must have had no little labor to stop them all with stones (2 Kings iii., 25). The soil of the plains is a rich, friable loam, covered with small stones, which shield the tender roots from the sun, and which is capable of producing any thing. Every knoll is covered with shapeless ruins, while not a tree is to be seen through the whole country, except here and there a terebinth, always among the débris of some ancient site. The ruins consist merely of heaps of squared stones, with here and there the traces of an arch (while north of the Arnon the remaining arches are countless), and walls of squared and well-fitting stones, which, apparently, were erected without mortar.

From Kureitun we turned S.S.W., and in ten minutes were on the mound of ruins called Kirbet Azizah. The remains are extensive, and with very many wells. Among other traces of older and better times, I came upon a wine-press hewn in the rock — two troughs hewn out of the native rock, with a perforated partition left between them. The grapes were thrown into the upper trough, and there trodden by the feet of the wine-pressers, the juice draining through the holes into the lower receptacle. The presses are exactly similar to those so numerous in Western Palestine. For ages, however, the threat against Moab has been fulfilled: "Gladness is taken away, and joy out of the plentiful field; and in the vineyards there shall be no singing, neither shall there be shouting: the treaders shall tread out no wine in their presses; I have made their vintage shouting to cease" (Isa. xvi., 10).

To the left of Azizah runs the Wady M'hheileh, in which there is a remarkable large, open reservoir, formed out of a natural cavity. Fifteen minutes brought us from Azizah to Kirbet Nekad, with ruins like the former, on a knoll; and in eighteen minutes more we reached Hhoweiyeh, a much more extensive place, with many wells. The old walls covered a considerable space of ground; but there are no arches left standing. The herbage here was luxuriant, and close to the ruins was a camp of herdmen and their families, dependents on Kerak.

Twenty-two minutes' quick riding across a level plain brought us to Jubah, which must have been a small place, but the masonry very solid. There is here another capacious natural cistern, enlarged by art. Here we came upon the old Roman road, very distinctly marked by the lines of two parallel walls close together, unbroken as far as the eye could reach, and running over the plain due south. We cantered along the side of the old military way, in a wide, shallow valley of very rich earth.

Fourteen minutes was enough to bring us to Mahk'henah, the Mahanna of Irby and Mangles's Journal. The remains are in a better state of preservation than any of those we had yet visited in the course of our ride. The plan of many of the buildings, and especially of an old Byzantine church, can be distinctly traced. It stands on a slightly elevated mamelon, covering several acres. Not only are there the usual number of old wells, as though there had been one for every house, according to the command given by Mesha in the Moabite Stone, "Make for yourselves, every man, a cistern in his house," but there are many caves which have been used as dwellings, and several crypt-houses quite perfect. Large dressed stones were lying about in all directions. The only present inhabitants were Greek partridges; but though we found no Bedouin here, both the caves and arches had lately been inhabited by men and flocks. In many of the caves was the raised platform, or "mastaba," for sleeping on, formed of earth, at the farther end; and several fragments of sheep-skin coverlets and garments, as well as fodder, were strewn about. We could not see Kerak from Mahk'henah, but the road close to it could be distinguished with the glass. It has been suggested that Mahk'henah is the Arabic equivalent for "Mochrath," mentioned on the Moabite Stone as the place from which Mesha repeopled Ataroth after he had exterminated its former Israelitish inhabitants.

Five minutes west of this was a small ruin, apparently of a fort and a village, which we visited, called Jeljul (Djellgood of Irby and Mangles, or Djeldjoun of Burckhardt). From Mahk'henah we crossed, in a S.S.W. direction, a splendid rich plain, full of the traces of ancient inclosures and vineyards, now a waste like the rest of Moab. After a smart ride of thirty-five minutes, we reached Modeh (Monthe of Burckhardt, Harnata or Mote of Irby and Mangles). Here, on two contiguous knolls, have been two sister towns exactly like Kureitun. They were united at the bottom of the hills, and, apparently, were inclosed by a common wall. We were again on the traces of the Roman road, and came across two mile-stones, one broken, the other still *in situ*. Among the ruins were three terebinth-trees, the solitary representatives of timber we met with in our whole ride; nor is there a vestige of scrub on the hills anywhere.

Modeh was our south-western limit in this excursion. From it we turned and set out due north-east toward the ruins of Mesh'had (Machad of Irby). Near it is Abou Taleb's tomb, a tall, crumbling mass of masonry, supported on arches. Riding northward another half hour, we came on a narrow wady, into which we descended by a rugged path, and found ourselves at the deep well called Beer Mâdîn, from the city on the top of the hill beyond. The well is a natural cave, many feet down, and fed, apparently, by some subterranean spring. We descended by steps hewn in the rock, and found the water pure, cold, and delicious. We afterward scrambled down two similar wells in the same wady. A few half-broken troughs, some of them formed of old sarcophagi, were by the mouths of the wells, and contained water for our horses, kindly left there for the next traveler by some considerate, unselfish water-drawer. This was a piece of practical benevolence we could thoroughly appreciate, for we had ourselves nothing to draw with.

After resting here a few minutes, we were again in the saddle, and a steep climb of fifteen minutes brought us to the ruins of Mâdîn, on the crest of a hill—not, like the other cities, on a gentle knoll in a plain. We seemed now to have left the level plateau, which extended far east and south, while to the west we begin here to re-enter the rugged defiles of which Kerak is the key. The ruins are rather extensive, and more perfect than any others we examined in this ride—squared stones of considerable size, and many old house-walls, still standing, apparently, at their original height, built of dressed stones, without any trace of mortar. Several sarcophagi were lying about; one had been used as the lintel for an old door-way; and there were sculptured fragments of the Roman period, and broken oil-presses. Jebel Shihan stood out clearly, bounding the northern horizon.

From Mādîn to Theniyeh, the last ruin we visited, was an hour's ride, and another hour brought us back to Kerak.*

No chain of evidence, happily, can be less open to cavil than that which identifies Kerak with Kir-moab (Isa. xv., 1), or Kir-haresh, or Hareseth (Isa. xvi., 7, 11), Kir-heres (Jer. xlviii., 31), or Kir-haraseth (2 Kings iii., 25). It was the castle, "Kir," as distin-

---

* We had also noticed, during the day, Mouriyeh (Merna of Burckhardt), Hamad, Suhl, and Nachal (Netchill of Irby). From the Kerak people we obtained, through Mr. Klein, the names of many other sites known to them, some of which seem to be the Arabic representations of Hebrew names. Among them are Dimnah (*quære:* the Dimon of Isaiah?), though, for want of a known site, Dimon has been commonly held, by an ingenious but far-fetched interpretation, to be a synonym of Dibon, Lubeirah, Sumrah, Yaroud, Betér, Hadādah, Rakun, Z'erar, Ilhomoud, Azour, and others. These were given us with very definite directions. Other places of which we obtained the names without precise identification were Dadras, Um Hayh, El Ainah, Fulkhah, Dubbak, 'Izzar, Bedthan, Keriyeh, El Fityan, En Sheynesh. Misnar, 'Am'rah el Bourdan, Sahdouneh, N'assit, Gh'marein, Hhrofillat, Hadjfeh, Alayan, Tzemakiyeh, Oneim, and Ed D'lalhyeh. These all remain for some future explorer to identify.

guished from the metropolis, "Ar," of the country—*i. e.*, Rabbath-moab, the modern Rabba. The Targum translates all these names "Kerakah," identical with the modern name.* The Crusaders mistook it for Petra, and gave to its bishop that title, which the Greek Church has still retained; but the name in the vernacular has continued unchanged. No wonder, as we look down from the neighboring heights upon it, that the combined armies of Israel, Judah, and Edom could not take it, and that "in Kir-haraseth left they the stones thereof; howbeit the slingers went about it, and smote it" (2 Kings iii., 25), but to little purpose.

The population of Kerak is said to be 8000, of whom 1600 are Christian. There could not have been any thing like that population at the time of our visit; but then the greater part of the people and their families were camping in the country, with their flocks and herds.

Our patience was now exhausted. Four days under surveillance was enough, and, duly escorted, a deputation consisting of Daoud and myself paid an early visit, next day, to the mudjelli. In the centre of the town we stepped down into a court-yard, and thence into the large cavernous chamber which formed the council-chamber of the city. The whole assembly, perhaps thirty in number, were sitting in sol-

---

* As Kerak-moab it is mentioned by Ptolemy, Steph. Byz., and other writers.

emn conclave with their pipes, round the great saucer-shaped hearth, about one yard and a half wide, containing smoking embers, for it was very cold. No one rose to salute me, nor did the mudjelli even lift his eyes as I stood. Determined to take the bull by the horns, at Daoud's whisper I stepped forward, pushed one of the sitting elders aside, and strode in front of the chief in my boots and spurs. Still no one moved till I made room for myself at the upper end of the circle, and took my seat in the place of honor, by the mudjelli, on the ground. On this a box was brought from behind, and a cushion spread on it for me. Daoud stood by me, and through him I spoke many civil words; said I had come to return the state visit paid us seven days ago, as we were going to leave this morning, and wished to part friends, and to thank him for the security to our *persons* we had enjoyed under his government. Not a word in reply. Another civil speech, and still no sign. At length some of the elders broke silence, and advised their chief to part with the Christians as friends, and to let them go in peace. A long conference ensued among them in undertones. At the proper moment Daoud broke in, embraced the mudjelli on his knees, and whispered long in his ear. Still no word. At length, seeing that no coffee was coming, I rose, and said I hoped he would come soon to our tents to say farewell, and that we should wait for him there. He then actually half rose and bowed, and gave me a salaam. When we got back to camp, Daoud prognosticated success, as the old man had whispered to him, "Do not let the howadji give me money in the sight of my people."

The great man shortly appeared on horseback, with a long retinue, and, dismounting, entered our tent with some of his chief followers. He and I had a private interview in the second tent; and as he emerged, at once the word was passed to strike tents and load the mules. Never were orders more promptly obeyed. In an hour and a quarter all was packed.

The morning's lowering sky now turned to a hurricane; and before the mules were quite ready, rain followed the wind—such rain as I have seldom seen. We started a little in advance of our baggage, intending to leave by the eastern exit; but the storm of rain and hail became so fierce that our terrified horses refused to move, and wheeled round, unable to face the blast. Under the lee of the Greek church we had to sit on our trembling steeds, soaked to the skin. The elements might have combined with the people to detain us. When the violence of the squall abated, we rode back to the castle. To our relief, the site of our camp was desolate. The muleteers, for once in earnest to be off, had taken shelter in the tunnel, whence they were now winding down the steep by which we had entered. Under a succession of drenching showers we passed the mules, and a ride of four and a half hours through very heavy country brought us to our camp at Rabba, with no further inconvenience, beyond our soaking, than the ordinary difficulties of mules objecting to ford little swollen torrents. or dislodging their burdens from their backs at the most inconvenient turnings.

On the way we passed the ruins of Suweiniyeh, Duweineh, Rakim, and Mekhersit. The different aspect of the country to the south of Kerak and of this northern plain suggests a reason why the cities are so much more crowded in the former. The most especial feature of that district is the number of "tells," little hillocks, or mamelons of rocks, rising like an irregular eruption over the plain. The northern plain is without these excrescences. Their great value in the eyes of the former inhabitants would seem to have been the facility for utilizing or excavating an unlimited number of tanks. In a land where the population must have been chiefly dependent on the rains for their supply, they preferred to settle in spots where their facilities for water-storage were unlimited.

We soon came on the old Roman road running due north and south, with its pavement still there, though broken up, and often the flag-stones set on edge by time and weather, with the two parallel lines of walls flanking it. This ruined street we followed without incident until, under the drenching rain, we were glad to reach our arranged quarters for the night, at Rabba, the old Ar, or Rabbath-moab, and the Areopolis of the Greek and Roman writers, so named from the resemblance in sound between Ar and Ἄρης, or Mars. Jerome distinctly identifies them. Since Rabba is so close to the northern frontier of transarnonic Moab, and as there is no trace of any city of importance between it and the river, it is easy to understand how, in Numbers xxi., 15, Ar is spoken of as if it were the northern border.

The place selected for camp sounds a questionable one, under a deluge of rain: the bottom of an immense tank, or reservoir, some sixty yards by fifty in extent; and though largely choked up with the litter and manure of the animals which have been folded here for ages, perhaps to the depth of twenty feet, it was still, in some places, thirty feet below the upper surface. In the sides, rather high up, were large open caves, where our guards and muleteers comfortably ensconced themselves and a few of the horses. Our tents were pitched on the porous mass of goats' dung, which rapidly absorbed the water, and gave us a tolerably dry surface. Though not sheltered from the rain, we were safe from the wind, and our tents were not rocked by the storm. We were at peace at last, though bitterly cold, and my sheep-skin bed had been rolled by a mule in a torrent, and was a mere damp sponge. To sleep in a mackintosh, and damp bedding over it, is a severe trial, with the thermometer close to the freezing-point.

Rain compelled us to remain another day in the cistern. There was, however, enough to explore in the ruins of Rabba, though the weather forbade photographing. The place seems to have been square, with the Roman road almost intersecting it from north to south; and the course of the main street may be traced.

Unlike the ruins we have previously visited, Rabba bears all the marks of a city of the late Roman period, with abundant traces of an earlier epoch. The Roman town seems to have been about three-quarters of a mile each way. There are several huge grass-grown mounds, evidently the tombs of some important buildings, which might well repay excavation. One temple has two Corinthian columns standing, and portions of several others, with two arches. There are also two other large open tanks, but all else is only a mass of walls, broken-down fragments of carved work, and Corinthian capitals; broken sarcophagi here and there, blocks of basalt, vaults and arched cellars of all sizes, some being still used by the Arabs as folds, sleeping-places, and store-houses, and in some of which were myriads of rock-doves. These vaults are countless. The Romans have evidently used in their construction many carved stones from yet earlier edifices. The material of the city is limestone. But we found many blocks of basalt, which must have been brought from Shihan, several miles off, built into the walls and arches, some of them finely faced, and others carved, telling of a still more ancient Moabite city. Among the blocks of basalt thus used were fragments of architraves and entablatures. Several of the sarcophagi were of basalt also, but without sculpture. At the eastern end of the city are the remains of a large square building, which seems, by some bases left *in situ*, to have had a colonnade round a central court, probably the prætorium.

We were not yet rid of our Kerak tormentors, though out of their power. They found our coffee and tobacco good; and their camp was too near ours for our comfort. The mudjelli and his horde kept hovering about all day, sponging upon us for breakfast and every other meal, and filching the barley of our muleteers for their own horses. However, in this matter, the muleteers are not scrupulous about stealing from each other's nose-bags, for mules can tell no tales. There is, however, a mode of detecting it. Mr. Klein, who rode his own mare, asked Daoud this morning if he was quite sure she always got her allowance. "Oh yes," he replied, "the muleteers often steal from one another, and rob their friends' horses; but I can always find out if your mare has been cheated."—"How?" "I always put some pebbles in with the barley, seven or eight, and count exactly how many I put in. The mare never eats the pebbles; and if any one steals barley, he is sure to take two or three pebbles with it. If I find the pebbles short in the morning, I make hard words, and they can not tell how I know; and so they let alone cheating her."

We had another instance of Kerak villainy to-day. In the afternoon a poor fellow came in, not only half-perished with cold, hunger, and wet, but with his garments in rags, and his limbs bruised and beaten. Mr. Klein recognized him at once as a Bethlehem acquaintance. He told, trembling and quaking, how he had been sent from Jerusalem by Mrs. Klein, with letters for her husband, by way of Jericho and Heshbon.

He had left Jerusalem before our messenger could have arrived, and therefore knew nothing of our plight at Kerak.

It seems that an hour and a half north of Rabba, the son of the mudjelli and others were lying in wait for our messenger. He inquired innocently where we were, confessed to having letters for us, and, on his refusal to give them up, was severely beaten, and the packet taken from him by force. The man happened to know the chief by sight. The scoundrels had actually had their breakfast at our tents just before, and thus used our camp as a station to prevent our sending or getting news. Their violence was an utter mystery to the poor Bethlehemite, who could not understand their object, and only by chance found out where we were. He could tell no more than that he knew he was the bearer of bad news, that Mr. Klein's eldest boy was very ill, and he believed the letter was to ask him to return.

But where is the letter? The mudjelli is actually in our camp, but treats the matter with indifference, and says in a couple of days his son may turn up. Mr. Klein feels there is no time to be lost, and, consulting with Zadam. determines that we shall all cross the Arnon together to-morrow, and camp on the northern brow. We shall then be in the Beni Sakk'r land, and in perfect safety, and Mr. Klein will push on alone with a servant of Zadam's, who will be quite sufficient guard where he is known, and the Beni Sakk'r all-powerful.

To us the loss of Mr. Klein was very grievous; and most grateful must every one of the party ever feel for his kind, energetic, and invaluable aid. To his tact, patience, and skill in dealing with the natives we owed altogether our passage without loss through the Sáfieh, and our survey of Kerak for a comparatively trifling black-mail; while the whole of the more important part of the expedition—that north of the Arnon, so successfully carried out, was due to the thorough trust and friendship which Zadam had for him. Mr. Klein's perfect knowledge of the Arabic vernacular was of the greatest value in ascertaining the names of places while he was with us, and has enabled us to add so many names to the map of Southern Moab. Another of our party took advantage of Mr. Klein's escort to return home.

CHAPTER VII.

From Rabba to the Arnon.—Visit from the Hamideh.—Characters of Zadam and Sahan.—Ibn Tarif.—Present from Mr. Drake.—Ibn Tarif's Attention.—Roman Way-side Temple.—Missdehh.—Hameitât, the ancient Ham.—Kasr Rabba.—Beit el Kurm.—Large Temple.—Ar and Areopolis.—A pillar Letter-box in the Waste.—News from Jerusalem.—Troops on the move for our Rescue.—The Mudjelli returns.—Restoration of Mr. Klein's Letter.—Shihan.—Curious Inclosure of Basalt.—Sihon and the Amorites.—The View from Jebel Shihan.—Muhatet el Haj.—Jahaz.—Descent to the Arnon.—Basaltic Dike.—Traces of Roman Road.—Ruined Forts.—"The City in the midst of the River."—Rugged Ascent.—A Mountain Pass in the Darkness.—Dreary Camp on the Uplands.—Mr. Klein's Departure.—Aroer.—Topography of the Arnon.—Ride to Dhiban.—Its Ruins.—The Moabite Stone.—Conjectures as to its original Position.—Means of its Preservation.—An Oil-press.—Identity of Dhiban with Dibon.

THE journey from Rabba to the north bank of the Arnon is some eight hours, by Arab computation. Just before starting, a Beni Hamideh sheik, Ibn Tarif, appeared. He began by presenting testimonials from Palmer as his introduction; and his eye brightened when I told him that Drake, as well as Palmer, was a friend of mine, and that I was the bearer of a ring as a present from his old visitor. Mr. Drake's ring and a sovereign were amply sufficient to appease his appetite. But, in spite of the greed of the Arab character, I believe that an attested friend of these gentlemen, even without a backsheesh, would not fare badly at the hands of Ibn Tarif.

Unfortunately, as he told us, his power of serving them was not equal to his will. I am quite sure that, if he could, he would have made any number of Moabite stones to oblige them, for he remarked, with a solemn sigh, that it was not *every* written stone that would please them.

He volunteered to escort us, and to take us around before reaching the Arnon, as he knew the whole country — a suggestion which met with Zadam's prompt approval, for he himself and his men knew but little of the names of the sites in this immediate neighborhood, out of their own territory. We arranged that Ibn Tarif should accompany us on a short detour to the top of Jebel Shihan, and that we should meet the mules and the rest of the party at the brow of the Arnon ravine.

We rode out of the city of Rabba on the west side, and, turning to the right, in a few minutes struck the Roman road, which bisects the city from south to north, and stretches across the plain straight as an arrow. We followed its course by its side the greater part of the day. The space between the two parallel walls, five yards, is generally filled in by the fallen stones of the walls; but in many places the pavement remains exposed, though, for the most part, its stones have become displaced by the action of time and weather. Along this stretch of road I found three Roman mile-stones prostrate, one of them with the inscription exposed, but defaced.

A mile from Rabba, a tolerably perfect little Roman temple abuts on the road on the left. The bases of the columns of the portico remain *in situ*, and the shafts lie broken and prostrate by them. The adytum at the west end is only partially ruined, and the lower cornices are still remaining.

Half an hour farther, on the east side of the road, are the stony heaps of another ruined tower, not marked in any of the maps, called Missdehh. It bears the stamp of great antiquity, and is without any traces of remains of Greek or Roman architecture. A few minutes later, on the same side of the Roman road, are ruins of similar character, but of much greater extent, called, by Ibn Tarif, Hameitât. They are the same as those called, by Palmer, Hammat, or Animah, and are laid down in all the maps as the remains of the ancient Ham mentioned in Gen. xiv., 5, as the place where Chedorlaomer defeated the Zuzim. Schwartz is the proposer of this identification, which, although the place does not occur in after-history, is justified by several ingenious arguments. The Zuzim appear to be the same as the Zamzummim, whose seat was in the region afterward occupied by Ammon, not far from this, and separated only by a wide plain country, without any natural obstacles. Again, the Samaritan version has *Lasha* — *i. e.*, Callirrhoe, in Moab — a little to the north; and lastly, the Targums read *Hemta*, still more closely identical with the modern names given to Mr. Palmer and ourselves.

Immediately after Hamcitât, perhaps three and a half or four miles from Rabba, are very extensive later ruins, with a fine temple partly standing, the west walls and the portion toward the west forming a conspicuous object and landmark from afar. It is the one feature on the plain north of Rabba, just as one solitary terebinth-tree to the westward of the road is the single feature between Kerak and Rabba. We had seen it long before reaching Rabba, two days since. It was called by some of our guides Kasr Rabba — i. e., "the Castle of Rabba;" by others, Beit el Kurm, "the House of the Vineyards;" both which names have been given to former travelers. The latter is evidently derived from the traces of vineyards in the long naked lines of stones to the east.

Kasr Rabba has been a magnificent and massive temple, and there are very faint traces of any other buildings about it. It has apparently stood alone, with perhaps a few chambers for attendants near it— the temple of Ἄρης (Mars), with which god the Syrians confused the name of "Ar." The whole enceinte within the block of great squared stones, some of them six feet by three, is strewn with immense fragments of columns, none of them fluted, and with Corinthian capitals and friezes. From the cracks in the standing walls, it would seem to have been shattered by an earthquake, rather than overthrown by man. We measured about a dozen portions of columns; all are of the same diameter, four feet eight inches, as if the shafts had not tapered at all. There had been a few, but very few, blocks of granite employed in the building. Alas! as at Rabba, the clouds and elements combined against the photographers, and all their plates failed.

It has been suggested by Irby that this Beit Kurm is the temple of Atargatis Carnion, or Carnaim (1 Macc. v., 43; 2 Macc. xii., 21). This, however, is undoubtedly the same as Ashteroth Karnaim of Gen. xiv., 5, where Chedorlaomer smote the Rephaim. Jerome says this place was above Sodom; and again, that the name was applied in his day to two villages between Adara and Abila. The identification must remain, so far, a mere conjecture.

The top of the west wall is easily climbed, and forms a capital look-out post over the wide plain. We descried something in the distance, and the sportsmen unslung their guns for an eagle, but, on approaching, found that the object was a man's head peering above the highest angle of the temple. He recognized us at once, and came down from his perch. It was our messenger returning from Jerusalem with the consul's letter. Fortunate it was that he had concealed himself, for from this very place had issued yesterday the Kerak men who had robbed and beaten the bearer of Mr. Klein's letter, who was now with us, glad of Mr. Klein's protection on his return. Happily, they were now off the scent, and had outwitted themselves by their violence to Mr. Klein's casual messenger.

Mr. Moore's letter was most satisfactory. The telegraph had been used to Nablous, Damascus, and Beirût; the pasha had been seen at Jerusalem, and aid was by this time on the way, in the shape of troops, for our release. Our zealous consul had, indeed, taken prompt measures. He advised us not to pay the ransom, but to wait a few days, as the soldiers would be immediately dispatched from Es Salt. Fortunately, they will find their services unnecessary. Having given the messenger a good backsheesh, and charged him to keep the matter secret, we left Kasr Rabba at 10 A.M.

Our mules and some of the party now took the straight course by the Roman road to the descent of the Arnon, passing the ruins of Er Riha, "Jericho" (another instance of binomenclature, a duplicate name occurring on the east side), which we could see about two miles ahead, while we struck off to the right to ascend Jebel Shihan, the highest point of the plateau.

Our Ahimaaz must have had a very near run; for half a mile farther on we saw a distant camp of black tents; and the mudjelli and some horsemen sallied from them, and galloped toward us. They coolly told us they had Mr. Klein's letter, and would surrender it for a pound. We inquired if they had the face to ask to be paid for robbing and beating our messenger. After some parley, the letter was handed over without payment. The scoundrels had by this time calculated that the reply could not have been got so soon from Jerusalem, and that probably their booty was worthless; for they were very anxious to find out from Daoud if we had heard from the consul. Poor Mr. Klein's worst fears were confirmed. There was a note from the physician to say that his son was stricken with diphtheria, and that there was, humanly speaking, no hope for him.

Forty-five minutes after leaving Kasr Rabba we crossed the gentle depression which marks the beginning of Wady Ghurreh. We had passed the ruins of Mejdelcin—*i. e.*, "the two Migdols," or towers—close to us, on our left. The country was all a level rolling plain, very heavy after the rain, plowed and sown in patches here and there, the rest sprinkled with herbaceous plants, and tufts of grass and stones, much as a neglected fallow might be at home, for the Arabs take one crop and then leave the spot fallow for three or four years, while they scratch up the next patch. Sand-grouse, dotterel, and plover, golden and Asiatic, were in plenty, but rose wildly out of shot; and I saw some of the graceful black-winged stilt, allured by the shallow pools left here and there by the rains.

From the slope of the Wady Ghurreh, we struck on another Roman or earlier road, or rather a branch of the road before named, leading straight up to the top of Shihan. For exactly half an hour, led by Ibn Tarif, we cantered, till, by a very gentle and easy slope, we reached the summit.

For some way before reaching the foot of the hill, and all up its southern slopes, but not its northern, is a wide extent of very singular remains—countless small inclosures, which may have been fields, gardens, or yards, all formed of blocks of basalt, not squared, and no limestone, which is the native rock, employed. They reminded me of some of the so-called Cyclopean remains in the Hauran, or Bashan; and the basalt blocks have evidently been selected with great care. They cover many acres; and the city of Sihon must have been, with these suburbs, of great extent. The old road up the hill, by which we followed, has also had its two walls of basalt, carefully fitted, and parts of them still standing, in a few places. The walls are like those of the other roads, five yards apart.

The use of the basalt, unless it has been taken from the adjoining inclosures, would seem to intimate an earlier date than the military occupation of Rome. The inclosures, at least, must be of earlier date, and, if not pre-historic, at least pre-Roman. The mind is carried back to that antique warrior whose memory is preserved in the name of the hill, Sihon, king of the Amorites, the first who vainly dashed himself against the divinely-protected hosts of Israel; and as we read the tradition handed down by Josephus, of the Amorites endeavoring to escape for shelter to their walls, and then the mass of them struggling, in their thirst, to get down to the Arnon for water, and slaughtered in their confusion, we are led to fancy that perhaps this hill marks the battle-field—that it was behind that labyrinth of black stone-walls the Amorites sought to shelter themselves, and the plain between this hill and the brow of Arnon's bank is that across which they strove to escape, in their headlong rush to the river.

On the top of the hill has evidently been the keep or fortress of the town, which is spread round the central ruin. It has been built chiefly of limestone, with blocks of basalt occasionally, the débris of more ancient buildings. There are the remains of a Roman temple, some broken shafts and Ionic capitals, and several very large domed cisterns, or matamoros, which have been carefully cemented. Two of these have evidently been in great part natural caves utilized and enlarged. There were also several deep wells, all now dry and half-choked. The place is now used as a cemetery by the Hamideh; and some of the more recent burials were marked by tresses of plaited hair, votive offerings hung on sticks stretched lengthways on the grass; while others had ragged shirts, fragments of clothing, and shepherds' staves as offerings.

The view from Shiban was almost a panorama. We could see two stretches of the Dead Sea, north and south of Engedi, separated by an intervening ridge, which breaks the line of the mountains of Judah. The Mount of Olives and Bethlehem could be seen with the field-glass. Beyond Kerak stretched the range toward Petra and Mount Hor; to the east was the vast plain undulating to the Belka; while to the north the main features were two great clefts, or gorges. The nearer gorge, apparently just below us, afforded a magnificent peep—a sheer and winding cleft in the level plateau, extending to the sea on one side, and to the horizon on the other. This was the reach of the Wady Mojib, the ancient Arno. Beyond was the broken valley of the Callirrhoe, now the Zerka Maïn.

After taking angles, and exploring the ruins, we descended in a north-eastern direction by another ancient road, riding at a smart pace, and in twenty-five minutes passed through the ruins of Bal'hua, perhaps the poorest and most featureless we have seen, and all leveled with the soil. After this, seventy minutes more of slow and heavy riding through wet and unsound ground, rendered more treacherous than usual by the washing in of the burrows of the mole-rat (*Spalax typhlus*)—which does duty, at least in the making of runs and mole-hills, for the common mole, but excavates much larger tunnels — we reached Kirbet es Sum'hra, a mere castle, apparently of Saracenic origin, near Muhatet el Haj, the remains of a city of yet older date than the castle, and identified by many with the "Jahaz," or "Jahazah," of Scripture, the scene of the battle between Israel and Sihon.

This identification would harmonize very well with the name of Shihan, given to the hill, and with Josephus's tradition of the details. But there is a difficulty which seems to be insurmountable—viz., that Jahaz was in the allotment of Reuben (Josh. xiii., 18). and was one of the Levitical cities (1 Chron. vi., 78). Now few boundary-lines are more clearly laid down than that of the Arnon, dividing Reuben from Moab.

We can scarcely, therefore, suppose that a city on the south plateau was ever held by Israel. Eusebius puts it between Medeba and Dibon, a more probable location. All we can gather from Isaiah and Jeremiah is, that it was in the "Mishor," or highland plain.

Before arriving at Sum'hra, we came up with our convoy in sorry plight. Heavy ground, wet bottoms of mire and water, with little treacherous bogs, had brought down mule after mule, and a mile an hour was a good pace over what, in ordinary weather, would have been good galloping ground. Sometimes three together would be lying helpless and immovable, with their burdens in the mud. Here we bid farewell to our Hamideh guide, Ibn Tarif.

The ravine of the Arnon does not show till we are close upon it. In this treeless land a fair-sized terebinth, just at the edge where the path begins to descend, was a conspicuous guide-post; and certainly without it a stranger might search long for the track. The rolling slopes come close to the precipitous descent, the plain being perfectly level on either side, breaking away abruptly in limestone precipices to a great depth. No idea of the rift can be formed till the very edge is reached. As far as we could calculate by observation, the width is about three miles from crest to crest; the depth by our barometers 2150 feet from the south side, which runs for some distance nearly 200 feet higher than the northern edge. This may possibly be accounted for by the fact that on the south edge is a bold basaltic dike or stream overlying the limestone, while the north is destitute of basalt.

The boulders have rolled down the slopes in wild, fantastic confusion, and add much to the effect and grandeur of the southern bank. We were much struck by the contrast between the two sides; and this impression was confirmed when, next day, we viewed the southern from the northern edge. The protrusion of the basaltic dike has been subsequent to the formation of the wady, and the continued detachment of its fragments has made the slope less precipitous, giving a variety to the coloring and the vegetation, wanting on the other side. The northern bank, on the contrary, looked an almost unbroken precipice of marly limestone, faintly tinged with the green hue of a very sparse vegetation, and occasionally protruding cliffs and needles, shining pink in the sunbeams. No search could detect at this distance any path, or apparent possibility of a path, up the rugged terrace in front.

Though, indeed, not very difficult, except among the basaltic boulders, the path was not easily made out on the south side, even when upon it. Once it has been a chariot road; and as we descended the zigzag, we frequently met with its traces; and the piers of the Roman (?) bridge at the bottom still stand in the stream. An almond-tree was in full blossom near the top; tufts of asphodel and gorgeous scarlet anemones pushing out among the stones told of a different climate from that we had left, where scarce a symptom of spring could as yet be seen.

Free, now, from every annoyance, in the land of friends, careless whether we met Beni Sakk'r or Hamideh, both alike being safe allies, we enjoyed the freedom of our scramble down this wild pass. Nowhere was the path any thing like the cliff of Ziz. Only at the upper part, where the track descends among a torrent of basaltic boulders, was it prudent to dismount from our goat-like horses. Pigeons and partridges abounded, and the younger members of the party left their horses, or were left by them, to find their own way, and went on foot throughout. One of them was landed aloft with each foot on a boulder, as his horse pushed between them, and, passing from beneath him, scrambled whinnying after the leaders in front, taking his own short cut to the bottom, and leaving his rider astride.

Steep as the descent looks, yet, when in it, it proves to be rather a rugged water-worn ravine than a precipitous cliff. A faint shade of budding green tints the slopes, and in a few days will evidently clothe the whole brown surface. Three-quarters of an hour down, we passed an old fort in ruins, with broken columns strewn about. A little above this was a broken Roman mile-stone, and two others lower down. Twenty minutes after this fort, we passed another of larger size, with fragments of shafts, bases *in situ*, and many old foundations, some of them crossing the old Roman way, which here was very distinct.

In other places, what seemed to be the foundations of buildings must have been walls of masonry built across the path, to prevent the torrents from washing away its material.

In the steeper parts of the pass many piles of stones were heaped on the boulders, said, by Burckhardt, to be provided as missiles for travelers in case of attack, but more probably only placed there to guide him on his way, as we have noticed elsewhere. The arch of the bridge, which Irby describes, has now disappeared, and only the base is left.

The mules were behind us; and after a bathe, and a draught of the Arnon, we paused to enjoy the rich tropical vegetation and genial warmth of this great depth. Water never fails; the pools were full of fish; the dark green oleanders were budding for bloom. Above the Roman bridge are some faint remains of early buildings; perhaps "the city that is in the midst of the river" (Josh. xiii., 16). At least, it is scarcely possible that such exuberant vegetation, with perennial moisture, should have remained unappropriated in the time of Israel's greatness; and whether the place so vaguely spoken of were above or below the fords, "cities" or villages there were sure to be in the midst of the "river," or wady.

The ascent we calculated at 1900 feet, 250 feet lower than the other side. While daylight lasted it was a lovely ride, with the views changing at every turn, and the path comparatively easy. Partridges really swarmed; the lovely little Hey's partridge, with its delicate plumage (*Ammoperdix heyi*), on the lower and warmer part of the pass, and higher up the fine Greek partridge (*Caccabis saxatilis*), giving out his cheery "chuckor-chuckor" from the top of every rock and boulder. An abundant supply for supper was easily secured.

Nearer the top, the path, though free from the basalt boulders which encumber the south side, was perilous enough in the dusk. We could not make way as we had calculated. Dismounting, and leaving our horses to find the path, while we held on to their tails, we debouched on the bleak plain, a few hundred yards west of Ara'ar, the desolate heap which marks the Biblical Aroer. Bitter and cold swept the wind; shelter there was none; but here we must camp. The mules were an hour behind, and must get over the precipices as best they might, by the aid of a young moon, which had, happily, just risen. No water, no wood. No fear of our horses straying now; they are too tired. We left them to themselves. Out with our knives, we cut such little brush-wood as we could, scraps of *Poterium*, none of it more than three inches high, groping for it in the dark with our feet. Sheik Zadam, who was with us, soon kindled a fire on the waste, and quick as thought, plucked, split up, and broiled a freshly-shot partridge.

Then, going to the brow, we fired occasional signal-guns, and one by one the mules appeared. First came our cook with a lamb, which he had bought in the morning, across his saddle-bow. He threw it down; the active young boy, Sahan, seizing it, killed it, skinned it, and, in a few minutes, offered us, with his fingers, delicious broiled liver and heart. In two hours more the last donkey arrived, and not a canteen was missing.

February 16.— At 6.30 A.M., cold and tired, we turned out to see our excellent friend and counselor off on his sorrowful journey. The sheik sent, as guide and guard with Mr. Klein and his companion, only a single slave, with his spear, as their route lay through his own country; and gave them, under his seal, a letter commendatory to the tribes of the Jordan.

We turned in again for a short nap, for there was no further occasion for forced marches; and afterward, before striking camp, I went a little to the eastward, to examine the ruins of Ara'ar (Aroer), just overhanging the brow, and to take a good survey of the country. The ruins of Ara'ar are featureless, and I could find no traces of Roman temples, though several arches are still standing, and there are the usual number of wells and cisterns.*

While we stood on the edge, looking down into that noble rift, the great birds of prey were sallying

---

* The Wady Mojib, or Arnon, takes its name only a mile or two above this, being formed by the junction of three wadys with running streams. All these ravines seemed of nearly equal depth: the northern one, Sheik Zadam, called Wady Seideh, the name given in all the maps to the central one, which he named Mkharrhas; and the southern small one Bal'hua.

forth to forage. The griffons circled and soared from their eyries, lower down, till lost to sight in the sky; the buzzards lazily flapped their heavy wings as they crossed and recrossed; but, grandest ornithological sight of all, a pair of lammergeyers (*Gypaëtus barbatus*), the largest on the wing of our raptorial birds, kept sailing up and down, backward and forward, quartering the valley, and keeping always close to the brow, the sinuosities of which they followed without a perceptible movement of their wings; only their long tails gently steering them in and out, as each time they passed us, easily within gunshot, on a level with our eyes. They were perfectly fearless, as though they knew the sportsmen had only No. 7 in their barrels; and in the morning sunlight their brown tails and wings gleamed with a rich copper hue, and their ruddy breasts shone brightly golden.

Reluctantly we turned from the brow of the Arnon, resolved to follow down its course at some future day; an intention which want of time prevented our carrying out. Turning due north from our camp, across a bleak and dreary plain, we reached Dhiban, the ancient Dibon, in exactly half an hour. We had abundant leisure, as the baggage had been sent on with a guide directly across the plain to Um Rasas, our next camp; and our road was across a hard plain, without a gully or a wady the whole way.

Dhiban is quite as dreary and featureless a ruin as any other of the Moabite desolate heaps. With its waterless plain, the prophecy is fulfilled—" Thou daughter that dost inhabit Dibon, come down from thy glory, and sit in thirst; for the spoiler of Moab shall come upon thee, and he shall destroy thy strong holds" (Jer. xlviii., 18). Singularly appropriate, too, is the denunciation on Aroer, in the next verse, when we stand on its site just by the edge of the arterial highway of Moab, and look down on the pass of which this place commands so complete a view—"O inhabitant of Aroer, stand by the way, and espy; ask him that fleeth, and her that escapeth, and say, What is done?"

Like Kiriathaim, and so many other Moabite towns, Dibon is a twin city, upon two adjacent knolls, the ruins covering not only the tops, but the sides, to their base, and surrounded by one common wall. Close under both knolls, on the west, runs a little wady, in which, after the late rains, we found a puddle of water here and there; and beyond the wady the even plain ceases, and the country becomes rocky and undulating. All the hills are limestone, and there is no trace of any basalt but what has been carried here by man. Still there are many basaltic blocks, dressed, and often with marks of lime on them, evidently used in masonry; and we found a few traces of carvings on other stones. The place is full of caverns, cisterns, vaulted under-ground store-houses, and rude semicircular arches, like the rest.

The basalt would seem to have been the favorite material of the earlier Cyclopean builders, as in Bashan, and then to have been used up by the constructors of the later town, which can not be much earlier than Roman, at least in the portions above ground.

We went to see the spot where the famous Moabite Stone, or monolith of King Mesha, was found. It is quite within the old city walls, and near what, we presume, was the gate-way, close to where the road has

No. 9. RUINS OF DHIBAN, WHERE THE MOABITE STONE WAS FOUND.

crossed it. Very near this spot it was afterward buried, when the dispute about its proprietorship arose among the Hamideh; and it was then, as is too well known, broken by one party of the rival claimants. From all we heard from Mr. Klein, its first discoverer, and, alas, the only European who has ever seen it

CONJECTURES RESPECTING THE STONE. 149

entire; and from what Zadam pointed out to us of its position, it seems to me highly improbable that the stone has been for 2500 years exposed to the light of day, still less that it could have been originally set up in the spot where Mr. Klein saw it lying, with the inscription uppermost.

I do not presume to guess where "Korcha" was, nor where the stone was erected by King Mesha; but, seeing that all the basalt blocks must have been brought here from some distance, and that there are many others at Dhiban many times the size and weight of this tablet (for though it has been called "this huge block of basalt," it only measured three and a half feet by two feet), it seems most reasonable to conjecture that it had been removed from its original position, and used up as building material by the Romans, or some of their predecessors, who were ignorant of, or indifferent to, its import; and that, after lying embedded and secure for ages, it has, through the progress of dilapidation, or by earthquake, been thrown down, or fallen from its place, and the carefully-preserved inscriptions been again exposed to day.*

---

* From the appearance of the ruins near, and from the replies of the Arabs to my inquiries, I can not but believe that the exposure of the celebrated monolith dates only from the earthquake of 1st January, 1837. This earthquake was the most destructive of any on record in Syria, and caused a fearful sacrifice of human life at Safed, in Galilee, where several thousand persons were buried under the ruins. As far as we can trace it, the axis of the disturbance must have passed very near Dibon. Many of the Arabs remember a terrific earthquake

We must bear in mind that the original Moabites disappear from history after the sweep of Nebuchadnezzar's conquests. With them probably disappeared the knowledge of the Phœnician character, for we find abundance of Nabathæan inscriptions of a date apparently older than the Roman conquests, but scarce any unquestioned Phœnician. It would be strangely out of keeping with Oriental habits and ways, if the new-comers had had any reverence for the lapidary records of their predecessors; still more so if, unable to decipher these records, they had respected them.

On the top of one of the knolls there is still a block of masonry, apparently the keep, or castle. Here we photographed, and took careful observations with sextant and compass, to fix our position. Two known points from Dhiban were Jebel Attarus and Jebel Shihan.

Trotter meantime, in hunting about the ruins, distinguished himself by discovering a new Moabite stone. It was a block of basalt two feet five inches high, hollowed and perforated inside to the shape of an hour-glass, and with a massive boss protruding on either side. Its use was not at first divined; but, not far off, he afterward found, in the bed of the wady, the stone which had fitted into the upper cup,

---

which occurred when they were children, and which overthrew many columns and arches in the old cities. Considering the comparative freshness of the inscription on the Moabite Stone, it may probably have been exposed for not more than the last thirty-five years.

IDENTITY OF DIBON AND DHIBAN. 151

and which proved it to have been an oil-crushing press. The upper stone was also of basalt. Happily there was no inscription on it about which to be inconveniently dogmatic; so it was satisfactorily agreed that it might have been the altar on which Mesha offered up his son on the walls of his capital.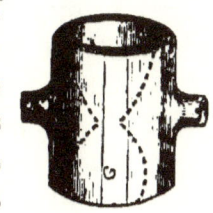

NO. 10. OIL-PRESS.

The smaller fragment was laboriously carried half a mile up the hill, to be preserved as a trophy, when it was found that the camera-bearing donkey had gone on; and the stone is left for more enterprising explorers.

The identification of Dibon and Dhiban can not be questioned. The place was known to Eusebius and Jerome under the name Dabon, or Dibon, and is spoken of by them as κώμη παμμεγέθης παρὰ τὸν Ἀρνωνάν. That Jerome meant on the north side of the Arnon is clear, for he adds that it was in that country originally Moabite, then taken by Sihon, and wrested from him by Israel. The fact of its being three miles retired from the brow of the valley, when we note that there are no intervening features, is not sufficient to raise a difficulty from the expression, "by the side of the Arnon." The name was first recorded in modern times by Seetzen, the pioneer of Moabite exploration. From some passages in Scripture, where Dibon is mentioned (Isa. xv., 2; Jer. xlviii., 18)—"Come down," etc.—it would seem to have been a "high place;" yet Burckhardt observes that "it is situated in a low ground of the Koura." But, looked upon *from the east*, it is on high ground, though low from the *western* ridge; and being placed on two hills, the first that rise from the east, the cry "Come down" would be exceedingly applicable. A similar discrepancy occurs in the description of Medeba, said, by a very careful and accurate observer, who did not visit it, but saw it from the west, to be in a hollow, whereas it is really on a hill.

CHAPTER VIII.

From Dibon eastward.—Beni Sakk'r Flocks and Herds.—The Plain of the Vineyards.—Rhibuyeh.—The Ruins of Um Rasas.—Its Walls.—Abundance of Game.—Wild-cats.—Beni Sakk'r Camp.—Considerate Neighbors.—Deep Tank.—The Raven's Home.—Um Rasas, within the Walls and without.—Three ruined Churches.—Apses still remaining.—Arches and Streets.—Amphitheatre.—Isolated mortuary Tower.—Church in the Plain.—Quaint Tradition and Legend.—Freedom of the Desert.—Intense Cold.—Animal Life of the Plains.— M'Seitbeh.—Ancient Block-houses.—Wady Butm. —Letters from the Brigade.—A long Sunday's Ride.—Crossing the Themed.— Visit to Zadam's Tent.—Westward ho!—Rumors of the Troops.—Ajermeh Camp.—Ride in the Dark.—A Turcoman Guide.—The Camp.—Reception by the Pasha.—Depositions taken down.—A bitter Night.—Beiram.—Grand Salute.—Speculations on Kerak.

FROM Dibon we set our face toward the wilderness, looking eastward on the "Mishor," or "plain country" of Moab (Jer. xlviii., 21). Without mules to look after; without fear of molestation or demands for black-mail; with a bright sun and a fresh breeze, a cool day with floating clouds; with the party in high spirits and perfect harmony; with the sense of entering upon a piece of new country—nothing could be more enjoyable than the ride across the grass country parallel with one of the feeders of the Arnon, the Seil Lejum.

The country differs from that south of the river in

the absence of occasional cultivation. East of Dibon no plow disturbs the soil, and consequently the ground is firmer, and there is a nearer approach to turf in the character of the herbage. The whole of it, far as the eye could reach or glass sweep, was dotted with flocks and herds of sheep and goats, each small flock with their attendant shepherd, often a child, but the tents ("Beit char"—*i. e.*, homestead) invisible, until, in some little depression of a very few feet, we would suddenly ride close upon a group of low black specks of camels' hair, the homes of the Beni Sakk'r. The tribe was now all distributed over this district, while the early spring grass was shooting, which in the summer is here completely burned up. Here one can well understand the reproach of Deborah, "Why abodest thou among the sheep-folds, to hear the bleatings of the flocks?" No wonder, with such a country, that the sheep-masters elected to remain on this side of Jordan.

In twenty minutes after leaving Dhiban, we found ourselves riding up a shallow depression, scarcely to be called a valley, with traces of terraces and walls, now grass-grown ridges, running across it every few hundred yards up the hill-sides. Upon inquiring what these meant, we could get no explanation, but were told the valley was called "Kurm Dhiban"—*i. e.*, the Vineyards of Dibon. The depression was about three miles long. The name has been preserved by men who probably never saw a vine in their lives, and who had no idea of the meaning of the old "dikes," as they might be called—an instance of the persistency of Semitic nomenclature. But more, it was an interesting illustration of a trivial expression in the book of Judges. When Jephthah, in his war against the Ammonites, defeated them on this plain, we read (Judg. xi., 33), " He smote them from Aroer, even till thou come to Minnith, even twenty cities, and unto the *plain of the vineyards,* with a very great slaughter." Here, then, exactly in the route which it was most likely a defeated army of Ammonites from the east would take, the struggle having been at Aroer, the name remains, though in another language, identical in signification. Where Minnith was we know not. It has been suggested that it may be *Menjah,* a site said to be seven miles east of Heshban, but of which name or place we could find no trace on the spot assigned to it, or elsewhere. But at least there are traces here which attest the appropriateness of the name, " Plain of the Vineyards."

An hour east of Dibon is Rujum Selim, a shapeless mass of ruins, on a small knoll. To the north of us, one mile and a quarter distant, were the ruins of Rhibuych; and two very distant ruins were also pointed out to us, Kasr el Alâkhi and Kasr Azizi. We made a detour to Rhibuych, which seems to have been little more than a large block-house, round which a few huts may have clustered.

Far ahead we could see our bourne, marked by a tall, square tower on the plain, with a long mass of ruin crowning a ridge a little to the south of it. This was Um Rasas, a large, solidly-built, square city, far more perfect than any thing we have before seen. The walls of the old city are still entire and intact for a part of their height, and had an imposing appearance as we neared them from the west.

In order to reach our camp, we had to wind round the walls; and as we sharply turned a corner, Zadam cleverly shot a very large wild-cat (*Felis caligata*), an animal I had once seen, but never procured, in Palestine. We afterward obtained another specimen.

Snugly sheltered on a slope, under the eastern wall of the city, we found our camp, tents already pitched, and the union-jack flying. A few yards behind us, close to the walls, were a row of half a dozen tents of Beni Sakk'r shepherds, and very convenient neighbors, ready to supply guards by night and guides by day; while their flocks supplied us with milk and lamb, whenever needed, for the moderate price of about a dollar a lamb. Unlike our guardians at Kerak, these people were too well bred ever to intrude, or even sit about our tents. Never during our sojourn with them had we once to complain of the slightest breach of good manners. Strange as must have been our ways and doings to them, our privacy was strictly respected. They were always ready to do any little friendly office; and if rewarded by a cup of coffee, sat as long as politeness required, and then rose and withdrew; and yet many of them had never before spoken with a European.

A few yards below us was a large open reservoir,

about thirty yards by eighteen inside, and very deep. A flight of steps in one corner enabled the water-carriers to descend about thirty feet, to the surface of the water, which still remains to some little depth inside. Happily, the staircase was too steep to allow the animals to go down and wallow in our only supply of drinking-water, as they did elsewhere. The masonry of this tank was Roman, or earlier, and it has, apparently, been originally domed, the voussoirs of the arches lying now at the bottom of the cistern.

We found two other great cisterns, outside the town, of at least equal size. One of them still contains water, and has the vaulted roof yet entire. There is the opening in the centre, now used not so much by man as by pigeons (the common blue rock-dove), kestrels, ravens, jackdaws, and owls, who resort thither to quench their thirst, and the pigeons and owls, also, to roost. Our arrival was an annoyance to the ravens, for they evidently preferred the open tank in front of our tents; but finding some of the party continually about, and the muleteers on the steps with their skins, the old ravens would put in a vigorous protest, croak indignantly and ominously for a few moments at the farther end of the tank, and then shuffle off to the other reservoir.

As we made Um Rasas our head-quarters for a week, and divided ourselves into two or three parties each day, the place and neighborhood were pretty well ransacked. Um Rasas itself can be better understood by a sketch than by description. The walls have evidently been repaired at some later date by ruder hands than the original builders, and after the same method which has been employed in constructing a Saracenic khan in the neighborhood (Zebib). Probably, in the earlier days of the Caliphate, soon after its destruction, it has been hastily repaired as a Saracen fort for the protection of the pilgrim road from Damascus to Mecca. Now all within these walls is utterly desolate. It is difficult to clamber among the mass of ruins, not grass-grown, but as if the mason's stones had, as soon as dressed, been turned promiscuously out of a wheelbarrow over acres of land. The plan is square. There has been no vacant or open place, square or court, anywhere within the walls, as far as we could judge. But the number of small semicircular arches which are standing everywhere, and which have formed both the roofs of houses and the arcades of streets, is really countless. They remain intact both above and below the rubbish. It was often easy to see the old street among the débris below, as we stepped from arch to arch of these long parallel arcades. To any one who remembers, for instance, the street architecture of Jerusalem from the Church of the Holy Sepulchre toward the Damascus Gate, the solution of these arches is easy.

To traverse and quarter these ruins is a good day's work—one uninterrupted mass, yet with no great or special features, except three churches; one near the north-east angle, another at the south-east angle, and the third near the centre of the east part of the town.

No. 11.   SKETCH OF UM KASAS.

Two other churches, or what seem to have been churches, are to be found in the south-west quarter; but they are now completely ruined. In all of the three first named the apse remains, except the roof. Two have, also, the apses of the side aisles still standing. In the central apse of one the Greek crosses on the bosses of the bead-line along the architrave still remain very distinct, alternating with sculptured knots or figures. Close to the central church we found a large slab with a Greek cross of some size deeply engraved on its face. On several of the lintels still standing were carved crosses and other sculptures, which we photographed.

Standing over the ruins, it was easy to trace the shape of the churches, and even the marks of the elevations at the east end. In one of them there are the old pillars of the side aisles still lying, and the enceinte of the walls and of a porch; so that little more than the roof is needed in the way of restoration. It was strange, indeed, to come across these silent witnesses of a great population, and that a Christian one, in this lonely wilderness, where only wild Ishmaelites pasture, and where we were but the second party of European visitors since the Crusades.

Man has given place to partridge, of which the numbers had not perceptibly diminished by the end of a week, though they had supplied our large party with two plentiful meals daily. This fine bird (*Caccabis saxatilis*) would never be found on these plains but for the ruins. Strictly a rock bird, and found all over the steep hill-sides and cliffs of Syria everywhere —on the plains, wet or dry, it is never found. We never put it up on these rolling downs, though food abounds; but there is not a ruined heap in the country where they are not plentiful, and almost packed. In the ruins also, besides the wild-cat, Trotter trapped the root-eating mole, or *Spalax*, and a pair of a beautifully-marked Gerbille, with a fine, squirrel-like tail (? *Melio melanurus*), which we had not previously met with. The jackal and the fox were, both of them, at home here, in labyrinths which must be to them a perfect paradise.

Outside the walls all is grass-grown; but the suburbs have been extensive, and may be traced for some distance. We could not identify any temples, but soon found that our own camp was evidently under the lee of an old amphitheatre, now entirely covered with turf, and probably only an earthen erection at first. Close by were the mounds of the circus, within which was our camp.

By far the most interesting ruin of Um Rasas, and, indeed, second to few in the country, was "the Tower of the Christian Lady," the landmark we had seen from afar. It stands about one mile and a quarter north of Um Rasas, beyond a number of old cisterns. Its purpose seems marked, not only by the Christian symbols sculptured in many places upon its face and the niches, but by the ruins of a church close by, of which the apse remains. The traditions that cling to it would point to its being a mortuary tower. Though

NO. 12. CHRISTIAN TOWER, UM RASAS.

square, its position reminded me very much of that of the round towers of Ireland, close to the churches. The inside of the tower is completely choked up with fallen masonry, as though there had been a staircase and other work inside, which has been shattered down by an earthquake, of which there are also traces in the crack outside. There is some very neat sculpture and ornament about the eaves of the tower, and on a plinth lower down.

There are various legends connected with this tower, one of which has been related by Mr. Palmer; but as it was told us pretty much to the same effect by Zadam, I may venture to repeat it. It is, that the Christian sheik of the neighborhood had been warned that his son would be devoured by a wild beast on the night of his marriage. Accordingly, when he was betrothed to the fairest maiden of the country, the father built this tower for his son's security, and to it he and his bride retired for the wedding-night. In the morning the son had been devoured, and the bride, who, being in reality a ghoul, had assumed the form of a wild beast, flew away from the top of the tower.

Another legend is to the effect that, before the Christians were driven out by the faithful, they deposited enormous treasures in the top of this tower, and left it in the care of a Jinn. This Jinn has prevented its being overthrown by earthquakes, while all around has fallen, and has filled up the staircase, so that none can ascend. Our party, however, were openly accused of having dealings with the Evil One; and many of the Arabs declared that when Buxton and Johnson went to photograph the tower they were seen looking over the battlement, and had been lifted up there by the sprite. The tale spread, and Zadam himself, intelligent though he be, firmly believed it, remarking that the Jinn might guard and prevent the Bedouin from touching the treasure, yet that Westerners, having greater minds, might overcome the guardian spirit of the place, and get it out.

News travels fast in the desert. Late in the evening a spearman reined up at our door, to tell his sheik that he had heard that the Turkish troops had started from Es Salt for Kerak, and were only about three hours off; that they had orders to take out the Europeans; that they were to find Zadam, and hand them over to his keeping. So official action had been prompt on this occasion.

The calm security and delicious sensation of freedom was very grateful to the new-found brothers of Beni Sakk'r. *They* were evidently much exercised in mind by the ways and manners of their new relatives, who began the day by improvising a bath, spreading a mackintosh sheet in a hole in front of the tents, and sponging *al fresco*, while the hoar-frost yet covered the ground. It *was* cold; the thermometer was down to 27° in the night. All the morning the Arabs sat on the grassy slope of the old amphitheatre, but at a respectful distance from our camp. The photographers had enough to do at home all day. Arrears of journal and cat-skinning occupied us till the afternoon, when Hayne and I had a splendid gallop across the downs for five or six miles due east, to a ruined castle we had sighted, named by the Arabs M'Scitbeh.

The characteristics of these great rolling plains impress themselves upon one as we ride over them day after day—grass in the hollows, and a low gray-green scrub on the slopes, chiefly a wormwood (*Artemisium*), strongly scented when crushed. Stones and ruined foundations of walls are scattered in the lower valleys —sometimes the terraces, too, remaining; but no more of the vineyards that once abounded. Cisterns are hewn in the rocks. Channels, dams, and sluices once were there, but are not more than faintly outlined now. Innumerable white snails with the thickest of shells, and red caterpillars like those of the Emperor-moth, with myriads of larks—the skylark, crested lark, short-toed, calandra, and others—in combined flocks fattening themselves upon them. Here and there a flock of rock-doves fluttering from a cistern; a covey of partridge from a ruin; a pair of Egyptian vultures battening on the offal from a recent camp: flocks, herds, and camels, a few horses and asses, with attendant shepherds and shepherdesses; and a little cluster of black tents in some dell, with a dog or two prowling and hoarsely barking at passers-by, while a few children squat about the doors—these are the only *living* features. "Behold, the days come, saith the Lord, that I will send unto him wanderers, that shall cause him to wander, and shall empty his vessels, and break their bottles." "Joy and gladness is taken from the plentiful field, and from the land of Moab; and I have caused wine to fail from the winepresses: none shall tread with shouting" (Jer. xlviii., 12, 33). As for the ruins themselves, *their* only inhabitants are the wild-cat, the jackal, the fox, the mole, and such like, to be trapped, but not seen.

The kirbet, or castle, of M'Seitbeh itself is a keep raised on a solid platform of masonry, about twenty-two yards square, on the top of a low hillock; it formed a block-house in the centre of an open square, surrounded by a wall, and reached by steps which yet remain. Of the outer walls only the old foundations are left. Below there is a large open cistern, measuring thirty yards by fourteen outside, and similar to that at our camp at Um Rasas, with plenty of water in the bottom, thirty feet below the surface. There have been many inclosures in the neighborhood, and the old vineyards have extended far even beyond this. Not a bit of desert or barren land was visible in this grand panorama; and the camels, sheep, and goats marked the whole sweep of the glass with black patches.

Evening was coming on as we galloped back over the grassy plain, enjoying intensely the sense of security and peace; countless herds of goats, sheep, and camels betokened the wealth of the Beni Sakk'r; and little curls of blue smoke rising here and there revealed where, unsuspected, behind many a knoll, and in many a dell or gentle slope, the women of the tents of Kedar were preparing the coffee, or the evening meal.*

February 18.—We had calculated on a quiet Sunday, undisturbed by either business, alarms, or intrigues; and when we turned out at sunrise, had no idea of the ride before us. Before 7 A.M. a tall negro appeared with a letter, and orders to wait for an answer. The letter was addressed to me at Kerak, or elsewhere, by Mr. Selami, of the English consulate, dated from Salt two days previously, and with the startling news that he was there with the Pasha of Nablous, who had been sent by order of the Pasha of Damascus, and that the troops, horse and foot, with

---

* Among other expeditions made from Um Rasas was one to the Wady Butm, or "Terebinth Valley," in a direction W.N.W., first going two miles south to visit the conspicuous castle of Kirbet Jemail, from which bearings were taken. Its remains are a few arches of the same date as those of Um Rasas, and one well-marked cave, or "matamoros," still used for storing grain, supported by a pillar in the centre. The old roads leading up to it are more clearly marked than at Um Rasas. The neighboring slopes have been covered with vineyards, and water rested in an open rock-pool. Hence north-west to Sfayet Khazal—*i. e.*, the Rock of the Gazelle (the Ghazaleh of Palmer)—where the Wady Butm was first struck. There was water in pools, but not running, in the wady. The ruined fort stands on a mound nearly isolated by the winding of the valley. Next, about a mile and a half west of Sfayet Khazal, is Kirbet el Butm, on a steep hill-side, almost a cliff, in the same wady. Kasr Zafaran, which we afterward visited, was well seen from hence. Next was Kirbet Rujum, on a tributary valley bearing the same name. All were on the left, or southern, side of the water-courses, which, running westward, finally drain into the Arnon.

two brass guns, were to march next morning for Kerak, to set us free. Mr. Sclami added that he had brought £600 in cash for ransom, and was determined no force should be used till he had got us safely out, when the Turks might do what they pleased. I shortly replied, telling him of our peaceable departure, and our camp in the wide Belka, under the spear of Zadam. Strange how news travels in the wilderness, but the messenger had heard of our whereabouts on his road, and had struck twenty miles east at once. As soon as he had had food we dispatched him with our reply.

The messenger had scarcely gone when we felt that the efforts made for us required an immediate and prompt acknowledgment; and that though it was Sunday, and the ride might be very long, yet courtesy demanded that we should at once in person wait on the pasha and apprise him of our position, lest the troops should have a needless and costly march on our account. After breakfast the maps were studied, and we calculated that, having left Salt on Saturday, the soldiers ought not to be very far from Heshban on Sunday night. We now felt the want of our counselor Zadam, who had gone to keep Beiram. It was decided that Trotter and I should go, with Daoud as interpreter, to find the troops, our horses being the best and freshest.

We took also with us a Beni Sakk'r horseman, Sherouan, a ragged dervish, and, with strange inconsistency, a great warrior also, who boasts of having slain thirty men in fight with his own hands—an ecclesiastical warrior worthy of the Crusades. He is, withal, a meek, quiet-looking man, who never talks, and never pushes into the tents. But, more to the purpose, he is the best local topographer, and sure of his own knowledge of all the plain country.

We had to prepare for being out three days, and for sleeping in the open. All being nearly ready, we let down the tent door, had a short morning service, and at 10.30 were in the saddle. Young Sahan insisted on joining us, as we should pass close by his brother's camp. We took a course N.N.E., and crossed the Wady Themed and the Wady Shobek exactly at their junction. A little way down the Wady Themed was a ruined castle called M'Deineh. One rolling down after another, and we descended into the Wady el Jiddreh, the banks of which were fringed with the most luxuriant soft herbage, water in all the pools of its bed, and old gnarled terebinths in thick succession, fringing it everywhere, sheltered under the upper banks. We now found ourselves among bolder scenery than we had expected on the plateau of Moab —cliffs of some height, with many open caves in them, and several nests both of the griffon vulture and the lanner falcon—and soon reached Zadam's tents, in the Griffon, or N'ssour, valley.

The camp was a modest one, as the bulk of the tribe are now far east; but a party of elders were gathered with their young seigneur. Nothing could exceed the dignity and stateliness of the young sheik in his own tent—"an awful don" T. pronounced him. He came to meet us, even held the stirrup as I dismounted, and conducted us to his open tent, where already carpets and cushions had been spread for us; and such carpets! — the richest Persian, quite new, into which we sunk as we sat down. We explained shortly our errand, and that we could not stay for dinner. He assented reluctantly; but young Sahan rushing out, soon returned with a large bowl of cold sheep's-head and rice, which we ate while coffee was preparing.

Coffee over, we started again. On and on we rode, with the range of Nebbeh and Heshban in front of us, up and down the gentle acclivities, and always on rich, though neglected, soil. Everywhere the traces of past cultivation, sometimes patches of present. The ground is just beginning to be carpeted with its spring dress. In the slightest depression there is the richest velvet green; and the most stony slopes have bulbs, cyclamen, and iris bursting forth, and young grass, which promises to be meadow in a fortnight, giving them a delicate hue. On ascending a brow anywhere, countless flocks and herds dotted the landscape; and camels in scattered order, browsing, and lifting their tall necks, fringed the horizon. Yet not a tent could be seen, save when, on a sudden, we happened to descend on a camp hidden in some sloping wady, where herbage and water were near. The shepherds are just now more scattered than at any other time of the year, water is plentiful, and the ewes and she-goats, dropping their lambs and kids, require close attention. Numbers of young camels, many only a few days old, were stalking with their dams; and we actually saw a young camel, about three days old, so far forget the dignity of its kind as to skip about and lead its growling and chiding mother a race as she vainly attempted to keep it solemnly by her side. It was the first time I ever detected a symptom of playfulness in a camel. Clouds of dotterel got up every now and then; and once a large solitary wolf rose within shot, and walked quietly away, seeing, no doubt, that we had no guns. We put up vast packs of sand-grouse, which rose wild and fast as pigeons. Wherever we rode, we could see shepherds hurriedly stalking forth ahead, so as to intersect our path, and, if possible, stop us and ask the news.

Guided by reports gathered here and there, we turned north to find the camp of the Ajermeh Arabs. Old Sherouan, our guide, got into spirits now, and several short gallops took us across a grassy plain, toward the shoulder of a hill, where we could see flocks and herds rapidly converging as the sun was setting. Night had fallen on us ere we reached the camp, a very large one; and by the sheik's tent, marked by the spear with its tuft of ostrich feathers, we drew up, and inquired for the soldiers. Several irregular horsemen came out, and we found our day was not yet at an end; their camp was in the Wady Na'ur, three hours north of us, and these had only been sent in advance to collect provisions and camels for transport. Our Beni Sakk'r declared he could go no farther, for his horse was done up; and the Turkish officer obligingly lent us a wild mounted spearman, a Kurd, who could speak a very little Arabic, to guide us to head-quarters. The moon was kindly in the zenith, and without dismounting we passed on.

The compass showed N.N.W., and the pole-star kept steadily just to the right of the horses' heads; so we felt we could not be far out. From the plain we soon rose among bare, rocky, Judean-looking hills, and wearily plodded our way, three miles an hour, till our guide exclaimed, "Ah! there are the cypress-trees; we are not far!" We soon wound down a rather steep descent, and on a sward sloping down to a little stream there gleamed in the moonlight the long-sought camp. We felt ourselves really the heroes of an Abyssinian expedition on a small scale, as we heard the cavalry bugles, and responded to the sentry's challenge. There were thirty-three large white tents, and a number of black Arab ones, stretched in regular order below us; while many a watch-fire cast a gleam of lurid light on the lines of picketed horses.

We asked for the pasha, and were conducted past a couple of brass howitzers to one of two tents overlooking the camp. A very stout, elderly Turkish gentleman sat on a pile of cushions at the farther end of the tent, with his tray of dinner on the ground before him. He politely handed a cigarette from a silver case, and, through Daoud, who stood deferentially at the tent door, while we sat on the cushion by his side, congratulated us on being out of our difficulties. We insisted upon retiring till his excellency had supped, and were ushered into the other tent, which belonged to his staff — two colonels and two other officers.

In a few minutes an orderly brought in a dinner-tray; and we, who had been fasting since the forenoon, and had been ten hours in the saddle, were not sorry to see it. The service was exactly the same as the pasha's—a large dish of rice, some hot poached eggs, sardines, a well-oiled salad, cheese, and native bread. Coffee followed when we had done justice to the tray; and we were waiting our summons to the pasha, when Mr. Selami, of the consulate, arrived. He had heard that we were at Um Rasas, had gone that morning to find us, and after four hours' ride was turned back by some Arab shepherds, who told him they had seen us riding in search of the soldiers. Our explanations were brief: Mr. Selami's saddle-bags, heavy with ransom-money, had just been deposited in the tent, when we were summoned to the presence to make our official statement.

The secretaries sat on the ground with their ink-horns. Between them and the pasha, on another carpet, sat Mr. Selami; and on the other side the pasha, opposite him, Trotter, and myself, utterly tired out. An orderly in the door-way, and the two colonels smoking their nargiles on the pasha's left, completed the group. A tedious process was the taking of depositions. Name, country, route to Jerusalem, dates, objects of journey, and various other preliminaries, had to be asked by the pasha in Turkish, translated by Selami into French, replied to by me in the same, then retranslated into Turkish, and in that language written down by the scribes. Then came the historic version of the Kerak difficulties, from the Sáfieh to the robbery of Mr. Klein's letter. The tedious process lasted till long past midnight, when the nodding pair were dismissed with a courteous bow, and were told the depositions would be ready to sign in the morning.

To the other tent we retired, with Mr. Selami and the secretaries, to share it with the colonels. The tent sides were open for six inches up, the wind blew keen, the thermometer was below the freezing-point, and we had no coverlets. We turned our saddles up for pillows, wrapped our heads in our water-proofs; but before day-break the cold was past endurance.

At dawn we turned out, not for washing or toilet, with a thick rime on the grass, thankful that we had taken the precaution of bringing camphor and laudanum in our pockets, which we mixed with the welcome hot coffee. To-day was Beiram, the New-year's-day of the Moslems; and we had just been summoned to the pasha's tent, when the order was given to fire a salute from the howitzers, which was at once done, to the amazement of the crowd of Arabs. The artillery-men seemed well drilled, and went creditably through their exercise. Our depositions were now produced in fair copy, read over, translated to us, and then signed and sealed by me in duplicate. The pasha offered us two cavalry soldiers for the rest of our sojourn in the country; but we modestly declined, feeling it far better to show all confidence in the Beni Sakk'r than to seem to distrust either Zadam's power or his good faith. Of course, after our declining this offer, the government had no further responsibility; but we felt we were on safe ground through all the Beni Sakk'r and Hamideh country; and the result proved that we were right.

The pasha then dictated letters to Zadam, thanking him for his good management; to Ibn Tarif, of the Hamideh, commending us to his good offices; and also an open firman to all, to be used when occasion might require. Nothing could exceed his courtesy and consideration. He told us he should have to wait at Na'ur for several days, as he had sent at midnight to Nablous, to telegraph thence to Damascus for instructions, and must await the reply. However, he had countermanded, provisionally, the 500 men who were to follow him from Nablous. The whole of this advance-guard consisted of 170 infantry, 120 cavalry, two field-pieces, and 150 mounted irregulars.

We were asked many questions about Kerak, where the staff, at least, evidently wished to go; but they told us they possessed no plans of the place, and knew nothing of it. We explained the approaches as best we could. Whether the troops should be sent on to Kerak, was no affair of ours; but certainly it was an excellent opportunity of teaching a lesson to a quasi-independent chief who has been the oppressor of the country for years, under the pretext of holding it for the sultan, and who wrings out of the hapless people a sum tenfold that which he pays into the imperial treasury.

Es Salt shows what may be done by securing a settled government, even though it be a Turkish one. When I visited Es Salt eight years ago, it was much in the same state as Kerak is now, and life and property were insecure in the whole of Gilead. The difficulties to travelers were as great as in Southern Moab, and extravagant black-mail was levied by all the petty sheiks. Now that the Pasha of Damascus has placed a garrison there, the fellahin are better off, trade has quadrupled, and the country is as safe for Europeans as Western Palestine. With a garrison at Kerak,[*] and the Beni Sakk'r conciliated, as at present, the imperial government could hold the coast of the Dead Sea as easily as it holds the Lebanon.

---

[*] While these sheets are in the press (March, 1873), we learn tha' the Turks have thrown a garrison into Kerak.

CHAPTER IX.

Return from the Wady Na'ur to Um Rasas.—Royal Entertainment by the Ajermeh.—Our Horses keep Beiram.—Coffee-drinking.—Sherouan's many Calls.—Wandering Tramps.—A Beggar's Hospitality.—Return to our Tents.—Reports of a buried Stone.—Zadam's Account of the black, or basalt, Country eastward.—El Hhurreh.— Stone Cities.—Eastward ho!—Mirage on the Plains.—Gazelle Hunt.—The Hadj Road.—Khan Zebib.—Description of the ruined Khan.—Traces of earlier Buildings.—Remains of a Doric Temple. —Labyrinth of Cisterns.—Prehistoric Remains.—Cairns.—A vain Pursuit after the Stone of Rasas.

WE left the Turkish camp without a guide, and in two hours passed some extensive ruins on a low hill called by the shepherds *Samuk*. From it an old Roman road was distinctly marked, leading down the hill and across the next wide upland.

In three hours and five minutes we reached the Ajermeh camp. The soldiers were all gone. We had met some men driving lambs across the plain for the troops, and had the satisfaction of learning from them, what Daoud was loath to believe, but what the Ajermeh afterward confirmed, that the soldiers paid for all they took, or at least gave receipts, to be allowed from the next payment of tribute. We dismounted at the camp, the largest we had yet seen, and where two tents were marked, by the spear and tuft of ostrich feathers, as the homes of the sheiks.

We at once asked to buy barley for our horses, but were told they had none, and must send miles for it. Barley, we replied, we must have, if we waited three hours for it; and suiting the action to the word, we dismounted. They then invited us into the great tents, for they too were keeping Beiram, the New-year's festival of the Moslems. The tent was full, but a clean carpet was spread for us at the upper end. Daoud now produced the three nose-bags from under his 'abb'eyeh, and, with a knowing look, handed them to a by-stander, as much as to say, "No humbug; the horses must keep Beiram too." The man took them, and soon returned with barley enough for two days.

Meantime guests came crowding in, for the day is spent in visiting neighboring camps and eating the substitute for yule cake. Every one who came in, except ourselves, was kissed from four to seven times on the cheeks by each of the circle, who rose to greet him. A huge wooden bowl was brought, with hot boiled mutton, swimming in the Belka substitute for Algerian couscousou — a sort of coarsely-ground wheat-meal, boiled with milk and butter. We were quite ready for breakfast, and plied our fingers very well, the Arabs being actually civilized enough to apologize for having no spoons or forks for the Franghi. We caused great interest, and no alarm, to a number of toddling youngsters of two years old and upward, who examined our clothes with much curiosity, and were won by a supply of raisins, with which Mr. Selami had filled our pockets at starting.

As soon as we had finished, the bowl was passed on to other guests, and quickly cleared, when another and another made its appearance.

Meantime Daoud, the hero of the hour, recounted the Kerak affair to the eager listeners, who thought we had got cheaply off from such a set for sixty goldpieces. My revolver was handed round, and, by their careful handling, they showed that they were no strangers to the weapon. As an instance of the way news travels, we were informed that our muleteers, who had started for Salt two days ago to buy barley, had long since gone back to our camp, as they had bought a supply at such and such a price, from the S'khoor Arabs, on the way.

The coffee was an elaborate affair, and it was the best coffee I ever tasted. The beans were produced in the husk, beaten out, then winnowed with the hand, roasted and pounded before the fire at which we were warming our toes, and, for the first time for eighteen hours, were enjoying sensation. This coffee is brought overland from Mocha, and is perfumed and fragrant. No less than three cups were supplied to each; and we needed no pressing.

As our horses had now fed, we left, grateful for the hospitality so cordially afforded by those who would certainly have robbed us, had we not been under the Beni Sakk'r shield. These Ajermeh are a wealthy tribe, and more given to agriculture than most of the nomads. The long tracts of corn we had passed through, and also the wide extent of arable land stretching from hence to Heshban, is chiefly cultivated by them and their slaves; and they sell much to the Southern 'Anizeh, with whom they have friendly relations.

We pursued a south-east direction for the first hour, across plains all under tillage for wheat and barley, and at 2.30 P.M., after an hour and thirty-five minutes, passed not far south of the extensive ruins of Ziza. How our guide, old Sherouan, whom we had picked up again at the Ajermeh camp, led us across a featureless country for twenty-six miles, up and down sloping dells, we could scarcely make out. Still, by compass, he was always true, though the day was cloudy, with a bitterly cold wind. To every black tent espied from afar our guide made a detour; and he and Daoud, while we jogged on, levied toll everywhere—kid, camel's flesh, or a bowl of milk—for every caller must be fed to-day. From all quarters the shepherds came striding in advance, to intercept us and ask the news.

On one piece of bleak plain, we came upon the most tattered fragment of a tent I ever saw. It concealed nothing, and revealed the most abject poverty, even for Bedouin. Yet even here was a large heap of brush-wood collected, and the skin of a freshly-killed camel stretched on the ground, while the flesh was being boiled on the embers. Our dervish rode up, and had his chat and lump of boiled meat. The people were not Beni Sakk'r, but a small family of wandering beggars—man, wife, and three children—and had no sheep nor goats—only half a dozen camels. Yet one of these six had they killed for Beiram, and every shepherd within hail must partake of their hospitality for two days. I learned for the first time that even among the Bedouin there is, besides the gypsies, whom we several times met pursuing the same arts of tinkering, fortune-telling, and conjuring, as in England, a class of begging tramps, belonging to no tribe, but wandering where they will, too poor to be robbed, and living on the alms of the shepherd tribes.

At length, just at sunset, we reached the Wady Themed, and knew we were not far from camp. For the first time to-day we had a gallop, and soon espied by moonlight the tall tower of Um Rasas, a mile and a quarter from our tents, which we reached at 6.30 P.M. Beiram was being kept in due style at Um Rasas, to the expenditure of our powder; and one of our muleteers had a narrow escape, from the bursting of his great horse-pistol, the blame of which was, of course, laid on the English powder.

Zadam had just returned, bringing with him the skin of a very fine cheetah, or hunting-leopard, which one of his brothers had shot, as a present for me. Supposing I would use it as a saddle-cloth, he had, unfortunately, cut off the head and part of the tail. It was the only beast of the kind we heard of being killed while in the country; but we several times came across traces of the leopard in the ravines lower down. The cheetah, on the contrary, seems to be confined to the open country, where it preys on the gazelle.

In the morning a mounted Arab, with a long spear, a very fine-looking fellow, rode hotly down to camp, and, dismounting, strode to our tent door, just within which Zadam was seated. With fierce gesticulations, he asked what business we had here, told us that his tribe were the rightful owners, and that his gunners would come down at night and shoot us all. Zadam never moved a muscle, but quietly eyed him; and when he had spent his breath, told him to go to his tent. He then explained to us that the man was the sheik of a small subject tribe, whose domicile was in this district, and probably wanted a little backsheesh, which we were by no means to give, as it was not our business. They had a long conference in the little tent, and the man rode off.

It seemed that our visitor had heard of our searching the ruins, though nothing had been said by us, and Zadam had kept our counsels; and that his object was to get a backsheesh for a "black written stone" which one of his men had found here and buried in the ground. I saw afterward, in Jerusalem, a squeeze said to have been taken from this stone, and which is in the possession of the Rev. D. Stuart Dodge, of Beirut, who has kindly forwarded to me a copy. Whether it be genuine or not I have no means of judging. I can only aver that the evidence is in favor of there having been a black written stone at Um Rasas. The link that can indisputably prove that the squeeze is a copy of the Um Rasas stone is the difficulty. Dr. Birch, of the British Museum, than whom there can not be a better authority, assured me that he has utterly failed to make any sense of the inscription, and that some of the characters are not such as he should have expected to find in a monument of so early a character.

No inscription has yet been found which reveals to us the ancient name of Um Rasas. The modern Arabic name gives no clue, meaning simply "the mother of lead," and is explained by the local tradition that lead (probably leaden pipes) had been found in digging here. But its remains prove that it must have been an important town in the Roman province of Arabia. The Peutinger Tables throw no light on this subject, as they give nothing between Philadelphia—*i. e.*, Rabbath Ammon—and Rabba, or Areopolis—sixty-two miles. Nor can I trace any clue in the Itinerary of Antonine. But in the lists of the stations of the Roman army given in the "Notitia," we find, among many other names belonging to this immediate district, such as Ziza, Areopolis, Bostra, Castra Arnonensia, the sentence, "Ala prima Valentiana *Thamathæ*." We have no other record or trace of the name. But may it not linger still in the Wady Themed close by? Themed and Thamatha would certainly be Latin and Arabic equivalents; and though not *on* the Wady Themed, Um Rasas is certainly nearer to it than any other ruins of importance which we visited. Professor Palmer has suggested to me that possibly the Μέρων of Eusebius, an archiepiscopal see, may be identical with Rasas. See "Desert of the Exodus," p. 413.

Zadam gave us some interesting accounts of the country due east of this, which he has often traversed. We are here about twelve miles west of the hadj road. Beyond the ruins of Khan Zebib, which we are about to visit, and which is close to the road, he assures us there are no ruins whatever in the "white country;" that there are hills of no great height beyond it, and then ground like this plain for three days; very little water, no rivers, but good pasture in the rainy season, becoming scantier as we proceed eastward.

After the three days' journey across the "white," or limestone, country, is a region of black basalt, a "land of black stones." This he describes as being two very long days' journey across; and he thinks, but is not sure, it is about three days' journey from north to south. This volcanic region he calls El Hhurreh. It is, he says, debatable land between the Southern 'Anizeh and the Beni Sakk'r; and the latter never cross it while the former are there. Besides these two tribes, there are sundry small bands of "very bad men," who live there always, and steal camels whenever they can. They are outlawed by both. The country itself he describes as being exactly like the Hauran, which he knows very well, and as full of ruined cities, built of black stone. He described with good pantomime how he had often swung the stone doors, which are still hanging in their sockets. Water can be found in various places, in deep, narrow nullahs.

Beyond this black-stone country, eastward, are two days more of white ground, hilly, but with good camel pasture; and then begins a desert with nothing in it but antelopes and wild cows (Bekk'r el wash)—*i. e.*, from his description of their horns, the oryx antelope and the bubale.

Mr. Drake afterward informed me that he had heard a similar description of this black country, under the same name of El Hhurreh, when traveling with Captain Burton, north-east of Damascus; and there seems no reason to doubt the account. If it be so, here is certainly a rich field for adventurous exploration by any one in search of new ground. We asked Zadam if he could himself conduct travelers over it. He said he could easily do so at the proper time of year, but it would require preparation, and he would be sorry, on account of the outlaws, to go with a less force than seventy spearmen. These, he said, would be enough to overawe any robbers in the country.

February 21.—At sunrise the cry was "Eastward ho!" to visit the hadj road, and explore the ruins of Zebib, which we had seen from M'Seitbeh. For two hours we rode up and down the rolling grass plains. Save a fox-hunt, after a reynard who started under our horses' feet, and showed himself as great an adept at doubling as his English cousins, the ride so far had been without incident. The clouds now lifted, and we saw the watery mist rolling on before us, to make a vain effort to moisten the sandy wastes of Arabia.

Two prominent landmarks were here conspicuous —Jebel Jiahl, about two miles from Khan Zebib, east half south, and Jebel Suaga, bearing south-east, perhaps ten miles distant. For nearly an hour we rode up the course of the Wady Shobek, very shallow and wide. It is the channel for the reception of the drainage of a level plain many miles in extent, surrounded on three sides by ranges of inconsiderable elevation.

The scenery now changed. The sun shone on a dead-level plain without a stone, with only here and there a small tuft of artemisia, about four inches high, and a little plant now and then appearing, roused to life by the recent rains, for the plain had evidently been but lately a wide lagoon. It runs some four miles farther to the low rocky hills. A strange mirage was before us, which lifted the distant objects, and elevated every little tuft into a tree, and the sparse blades of grass into a jungle; while the horses, inspirited by the unwonted smoothness of the expanse, galloped gayly on, and trees sunk to tufts, and jungle melted into grass an inch or two high, as we neared it. We might look in vain for the expected temples and pillars—poorer and poorer did the ruins appear as we approached them.

A herd of gazelle were sighted, some forty or fifty in number, trotting quietly along. We spread ourselves out. Trotter and Daoud, the only ones armed, dashed like wild Indians to the front, while we spurred on, on either side, to turn the herd, if need be. We nearly headed them as they trotted to the left, and then the huntsmen galloped to the head of the herd and fired, but too far and hurried. The gazelles became alarmed now, and the speed of the horses was no match for them.

But the incident had brought us far on our way, and we were near the ruins. We had to rein in. We might have been galloping across a deeply-ridged fallow. For about a quarter of a mile in width, every three or four yards was a deep wide rut, all in parallel lines. We were crossing the hadj road. Files of hundreds of camels, slowly following each other in the weary tramp to Mecca, had, in course of ages, worn the hard surface of the desert into these deep furrows.

Just beyond this strange, weird-like road, strewn with the bleached bones of camels all along its course, where the hills begin to rise, we were at Khan Zebib. The mirage had indeed been deceptive. A large ruined khan, with arches and gate-ways, and a few Greek remains beyond, on a series of mounds, were all that struck us at first sight.

It may be observed that all the maps place the hadj road at this point about eleven miles too far west, each writer following his predecessor. This is easily accounted for, as the Arabs speak of the road as on the other side of Um Rasas. We were soon able to take our sextant and compass observations for Khan Zebib, so as to fix its exact position, having many known points—Shihan, Um Rasas, etc.—in view.

The khan itself is an interesting specimen of the Saracenic architecture of earlier and better days,

NO. 13.   KHAN ZEBIB.

though now allowed, by the slovenly carelessness of the Moslems, who never repair any thing, however convenient or useful to them, to become a hopeless, roofless ruin. Certainly, as Zadam observed, it is not the business of the Bedouin to repair these places, as it is not they who would use them; and the central government, he shrewdly added, would have to send more soldiers than workmen for the task. Such is the progress of disintegration, material and political, in these lands.

Zebib has evidently been built with the materials of an earlier city, and Christian churches have supplied their stones, to shelter the pilgrims to Mohammed's shrine. It is a massive square inclosure, there having been semicircular towers or buttresses on each of the four sides, for strength and defense. The gateways in the centre of the east and west walls open into a large square, round which were arched chambers, six on the north, five on the south, and four on each of the other sides. The outside walls of the khan have once been carefully cemented, but, excepting a few fragments, it is only on the north face that the plaster remains. All the inner door-ways are entire, some of the lintels being sculptured stones from Christian edifices, of which we secured several good photographs. Many of the other stones used up in the building were scratched with curious ornamentation, such as I have not elsewhere seen, but which may probably be late Byzantine work.

Beyond the khan eastward were several hillocks, with the remains of Greek buildings of much earlier date and much more careful masonry. Of one temple a massive angle is left, still partly standing. One building puzzled us, though its plan was very evident, and it must have been a small temple. It was a square of eleven yards. There had been a door to the east, and apparently another to the south (though this may have been a niche), completely broken away. The east and west walls had had finely dressed double Doric pilasters; and many columns and Doric capitals were lying about, though where the pillars had stood we could not make out.

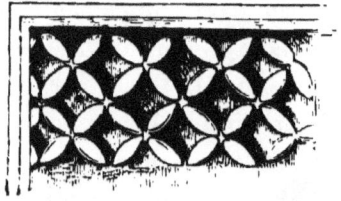

NO. 14.   SCULPTURED ENTABLATURES, ZEBIB.

There had been many finely-sculptured lintels; and numbers of stones with very pretty lace-work of various patterns, apparently friezes or entablatures, strewed the ground around. Wells were in abundance, half-choked and now dry, and a number of natural caves, or perhaps old subterranean quarries utilized, into which we crept, and found some with arches and carefully vaulted roofs, pillars, and walls, all alike cemented, and making an irregular set of chambers of considerable extent. From the plastering, they must have been intended for great water-cisterns; but now they are silted up to within a few feet of the roof, and are used as folds and sleeping-places by the wandering Bedouin. In such a cave David might easily have escaped Saul's notice, as he entered to take rest.

Walking up the hill, a little farther east than what I may call the Greek city, we came upon a number of artificial mounds and circles of stones. Though afterward, in the western mountain range of Moab, we often noticed such remains, yet this was the first time I had observed unquestionable evidence of the cairns of the primeval inhabitants. We longed for tools and time, to dig and open a cist, where, perhaps, we might find ornaments and flint implements. But we could only note these faint traces of aborigines before the basalt-building inhabitants came in.

As we were returning, Trotter noticed a peculiar stone construction in a wall; and we found that the stones on the top of the wall had been formed into a sort of rude sarcophagus for a body, but the jackals had contrived to drag out all of it, except the skull, between the interstices.

CHAPTER X.

Departure from Um Rasas.—Dhra'a.—The Themed.—R'mail.—A riverside Camp.—Zafaran.—A military Keep.—Supplies running short.—Start for the North-east.—Kasr el Herri.—Surveying.—Roman Road.—Um Weleed.—Extent of Um Weleed.—Saracenic Khan.—Roman City.—Streets.—Large Court, or Pretorium Gateway.—Doric Temple.—Date of these Cities.—No Clues to the ancient Name.—Um el Kuseir.—Large Caverns.—Ziza.—Interesting Remains.—Roman military Station. — Magnificent Tank.—Elaborate System of Irrigation in olden Time.—Large vaulted Fort.—Burial-place aloft.—Ibrahim Pasha's Garrison.—Other Forts destroyed.—Remains of Cuphic Inscriptions.—Fine Christian Church.—Variety of wild Animals and Birds.—Return of Convoy from Jerusalem.—Evening Bells.—A Fugitive.—Stripped by the Anizeh.—The Ibex-hunter.—Honesty of our Men and of the Turkish Soldiers.—Sunday's Rest.—Mohammedan Criticism on Christian Inconsistency.

WE had now pretty well explored the district of Um Rasas, and moved our quarters on February 22d. without any definite route fixed. Going north-west by north, after an hour, we rode through the ruins called Dhra'a, a Moabite city of the very oldest type, merely ruined heaps and foundations, with no trace of arches. It occupies the southern slope of a hill. Can this be the Zoar spoken of by Eusebius? The occurrence of the name here, so far inland, may cast some light on the confusion in the references to the situation of Zoar. But the discovery of Zi'ara (chap.

xvii.) seems to dispose of the claims of these Dhra'as to be Biblical sites.

After a short day's ride, we came upon the ruins of an old fortress on the Themed. R'mail stands three hundred feet above the river. The plain below was now covered with herbage dense and rank. Here we descended; and on the velvet turf, close to some large pools in the bed of the stream, our tents were pitched, and the animals turned loose, to graze at will within the natural amphitheatre. Here we spent two days, surveying and exploring the ruins within reach, Zafaran and others.

Our supplies were now getting low, and our convoy three days overdue from Jerusalem. In the larder things looked serious. No more rice; cheese had given out some days; the brandy was getting low; the cakes of chocolate could be counted; only two more boxes of sardines, and one plate of figs. Worst of all, the flour was at an end, and there was nothing to cook with but a little green brush-wood, collected with great pains from a distance. Plenty of lamb and buttermilk, partridge and pigeon *ad libitum*, and tea, coffee, and Liebig to stand a siege. But meat and Liebig, without bread or vegetables, was trying diet already; and without fuel to boil the kettle, the prospect was worse for the future. To add to the dark look-out, we were at the last packet of candles.

Preparations were accordingly made, and at daybreak next morning a convoy of muleteers and five mules, under the guard of a Beni Sakk'r spearman.

were dispatched two days' journey, to Es Salt, to purchase whatever the markets of Gilead might afford, and to return to a camp vaguely defined, somewhere to the north-east of our present one, but of which some wandering shepherd on the way would doubtless be able to give them information. The thermometer in the night fell to 28°—max., 35°.

Next day Zadam advised us to move to Ziza, where he promised we should find very fine ruins, never yet visited by any European. It was only a six hours' journey across the plains.

Leaving the tents still standing and the muleteers dawdling, we set out due north with our sheik and Daoud, who bore the camera and photographic stand packed on his saddle. We were now traversing a water-shed, the whole district being the fruitful mother of infant wadys, up and down which we rode transversely, all of them running due east and west.

We passed Zafaran again, but did not stop, and in half an hour reached Kasr el Herri, on the summit of a high knoll, commanding almost a panorama. On a lower tell, connected with this hill by a sloping shoulder, are extensive shapeless ruins, much grass-grown, called Kirbet el Herri, the old town, of which this Kasr was the citadel. Kasr el Herri is simply a keep, or strong square fortress, with a large space inclosed round it, like the others already described; the inside of the keep, like Zafaran, filled in with stones. Among these was a hole, into which we scrambled, and found it to be a hyena's lair, with a collection of bones, chiefly camels', but also five or six human skulls, and many thigh-bones, rifled from Arab graves.

The old Roman road can be easily traced here, marked by the evenness and regularity of the partially turf-covered lines of stones. The pavement has long since disappeared, and its stones have become upturned, angular, and shapeless, like the rest. Following the line of this road, after a smart ride of thirty-five minutes across a plain, we reached Um Weleed, "Mother of Children."

Um Weleed is a most interesting as well as extensive ruin; and though marked in the maps, I can not find that it has been visited by any previous traveler. It is on an old Roman road, and its remains appear to belong to three distinct epochs. Like all the towns of the "Mishor," or plain of Moab, it stands on a "tell," or mamelon. Within the walls it is more than half a mile from west to east; considerably less from north to south. There are many caves, and traces of scattered houses, outside the city wall, which can everywhere be very clearly traced.

Beginning from the south-west, on which side we approached it, there stands, isolated, below the commencement of the ancient city, a Saracenic khan. It is similar to that of Zebib, but much more perfect, though smaller, and, like it, is built from the materials of more ancient edifices. It seems probable that, along the course of the old Roman road, there passed here a branch line to the hadj road from Damascus to Mecca, for the accommodation of pilgrims west of the Jordan, for whom this would be the easiest route.

Above the khan are large grass-grown mounds, covering old ruins, and now used as favorite Arab burying-places, with the sheep-skin coat of the deceased stretched over his grave. Among these mounds an amphitheatre can be very distinctly traced.

Passing eastward, within the walls, the ruins become distinct, and less covered with turf. The streets are plain, some of them still arcaded with a succession of semicircular arches, perhaps of a late Roman date, which are still standing; with the large flat slabs of stones laid for a roof from arch to arch, and now used as houses and folds by the tribes that occasionally camp here. Many portions of massive wall are of Roman rustic-dressed stone. I found in one place the inverted scallop shell of a niche built into a later wall, and many cornice stones so employed. It would seem from this as though the place had been inhabited since the Roman times; and yet these walls, with the architectural fragments, looked of an earlier and better date than the khan.

Near the east end of the city we found a large open space, well paved with large square slabs, still perfect and clear, and surrounded by ruins and broken pillars, with a few fragments of capitals; as if it had once been encircled by a colonnade. It was forty-one paces by thirty-eight in extent inside, and may have been the old ἀγορά, or *forum*. Immediately beyond was the line of the east wall of the city, built of Roman rustic-dressed stone, and the central gate-way and street, still plainly to be traced.

Just beyond the gate is a Doric temple, twelve yards north to south by ten yards east to west. The door of the temple faced east, and in the centre of the

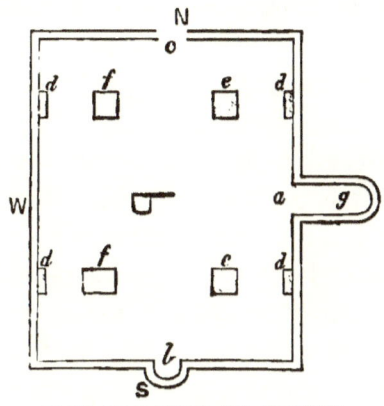

NO. 15.   PLAN OF TEMPLE, UM WELEED.

  a. Door.
  b. Niche.
  c. Door or niche; remains too broken to decide.
  d, d. Four pilasters, formed of one column, and not twin ones, as at Zebib.
  e. Bases of columns *in situ*.
  f. No bases left, but Doric capitals of four pillars lying on the ground, besides those of pilasters, of which three are there.
  g. Sloping débris, evidently the ascent to the door.

south wall is a small semicircular niche, or apse, for the image. Inside the door-way the bases of two columns remain *in situ;* and four plain Doric capitals, and portions of shafts, are lying about. This temple is exactly similar in all its arrangements to the old Doric temple near Khan Zebib. Are these the remains of an ancient Chemosh, or Baal-worship? We found afterward several similar temples in various stages of ruin, all of them outside a city, always at its east end, and with the door to the east, and always Doric, whenever the architecture could be determined.

What is the date of these cities, all so like each other? They are unquestionably far older than the early Saracenic, as we may see by the ruined khans; centuries less weathered, and less hoary in hue. Must they not be at least Maccabæan, as the Roman would be far nearer the Saracenic? It is worthy of note that we searched here in vain for any traces of a Christian church, or Christian traces of any kind.

The most uniform and remarkable feature about all these towns is the vast number of wells, all now dry; and of huge cisterns, or under-ground storehouses, some for water, and others with a bell-shaped neck and small mouth, for storing corn. Nowhere are they more noticeable than here. Not only the place, but its environs, are honey-combed with them. Some are still used by the Bedouin occasionally for secreting corn; and to others, which must have been old quarries, utilized and cemented for reservoirs, they have broken side entrances, to give access to their flocks for shelter.

The name of Um Weleed, like Um Rasas, is another of the vernacular Arabic appellations, which gives no clue to its history or old designation; yet, to judge from its remains, it must have been among the largest and most important, perhaps sixth or seventh, of the towns of the Belka. Not a trace of an inscription did we see; nor, carefully as written stones are looked after by the Arabs, did we hear a whisper of one, either black or white. All we could do further here was to take the bearings for our map.

From Um Weleed, along the Roman road, to Um el Kuseir, was only twenty-five minutes' quiet riding over an easy plain. There is no ruined bridge, as marked in all the maps, between these two places, nor is there any wady for a bridge to span; but there is in one place a piece of old wall, which has been constructed to collect and direct the water coming down the sloping valley in flood times; and this the Arabs called, to us, the "jisr," or bridge.

Um el Kuseir is one of the most conspicuous landmarks of the district, situated on a high tell. A strong massive tower, of which much more remains than of its neighbor, stands boldly out. Below, as usual, is the town, not so large as Um Weleed, and much more ruined.

Our new camp was at Ziza. Here at last we have lighted upon a spot about which there can be no controversy as to its ancient name, unchanged in a single letter. It must, in the later empire, have been one of the most important places of Roman Arabia. Its name occurs in the "Notitia," immediately before that of Areopolis, as one of the chief military stations of the province. "Equites Dalmatici Illyriciani *Ziza*."

We found our camp charmingly situated on a low flat plain, below a ruin-covered ridge, by the side of an immense tank of solid masonry, measuring 140 yards by 110 yards. The bottom was still filled with water, and from the surface of the water to the edge of the tank was seventeen feet six inches. Just behind our tents were the steps leading down to the water, wide and easy, so that horses could easily go

NO. 16.   ZIZA, FROM THE DISTANCE.

up and down. The masonry was simply magnificent. The courses were about two feet each, and many of the single stones six feet in length. The construction is still quite perfect, excepting a stone here and there in the rim, which is recessed back, so as to leave an inside pathway all round. But the

ANCIENT TANK. 199

most interesting portion of all is the very ingenious contrivance by which the tank has been supplied with water. It is sunk at the angle of a shallow, wide valley, just below the rising ground on which the town stood. At its north-east angle, above the top of the tank, are very perfect sluice-gates of mass-

NO. 17.   TANK AT ZIZA.

ive masonry. In a line with the sluice-gates, and also at right angles with them, are great walls, with a solid earthen embankment behind them. The wall at right angles extends some way, and then the embankment is carried on in the same line, continuously, across the plain, so as to dam back the water, which, during the occasional floods, would come down the valley, if the very shallow and wide depression may, by courtesy, be so termed. Higher up, in the middle of the embankment, are another set of sluice-gates, for letting off the waste water after the tank was full.

The whole system, and the artificial sluices, Buxton remarked, were precisely similar in plan to what he had observed in the ancient works for irrigation both in India and Ceylon. But this tank has suffered the fate of the stupendous works of Ceylon, of which it is the pigmy representative. In the course of ages of neglect, the rich loamy soil has been carried down with the rains, and has filled up the wide valley for several feet, choking up the access to the lower sluices, and the water has burst its way through into its old channel by the side of the upper sluice. In the higher parts of the valley there are massive stone breast-works, backed by earthen embankments, to turn the water from other depressions into this central one.

Such works as this easily explain to us the enormous population of which the ruined cities give evidence. Everywhere is some artificial means of retaining the occasional supplies of rain-water. So long as these precious structures remained in order, cultivation was continuous, and famines unknown. But their efficient maintenance was dependent on the supremacy of a domestic government sufficiently strong to enforce systematic industry for the common good, on the part of these scattered populations, and to secure to all of them the peaceable fruit of their labors. This authority was annihilated by the Islamite invasion.

The Moslems did not wantonly destroy the means for artificial irrigation; but if they did not, as seems too probable, at once exterminate the indigenous population, they at least paralyzed all organizations for the common good; robbed the people of every security for the peaceable enjoyment of their industry, until a succession of wars had reduced them all to the position of nomads; and left the miserable remnant of a dense and thriving nation entirely dependent on the neighboring countries for their supply of corn —a dependence which must continue till these border lands, under a settled central government, are secure from the inroads of the predatory bands of the East.

But to return to the ruins of Ziza. The tank does not appear to have been ever directly protected by defensive works. It was the offspring of an era of general security, when the safety implied by imperial rule seemed a sufficient return for works of public utility—when the plain was swept only by the defensive troops of the Dalmatian cavalry, who could water at all times at the reservoir.

The line of circumvallation is half a mile distant; but in the intervening space are two conspicuous buildings, the only ones which catch the eye at a distance, and which stand in bold relief against the horizon, being on the crest of a ridge, elevated considerably above the depression in which the tank has been excavated.

The first and largest of these buildings, apparently of Saracenic origin, consists of a solidly built fort, twenty-three yards by nineteen, with a parallelogram attached, sixteen yards by seven. Both were built, as it would appear, about the same period, and with materials taken from older edifices, many of the stones being sculptured; some of them, by the Greek crosses chiseled on them, being apparently taken from Byzantine churches. One stone in the front wall bears in relief a sculpture of two chariots with horses. The roof of the lower story in each building is still perfect, a fine arched vault, but with no aperture for light, except from the door. Here, during the period of our stay, our muleteers, with our forty beasts, were all comfortably housed.

The attached parallelogram contains another perfect vaulted chamber, opening only from the great chamber, and the staircase leading to the upper story, which is entire, with the exception of the roof. Semicircular arches still span it in two places, and it has many loop-holes and narrow arched windows. There are also several side chambers entire, and the whole has been fitted for engines of war. This upper floor is now utilized as an Arab cemetery, perhaps as a place of security from the hyenas. In one corner there had been a recent burial, with a sprinkling of earth, and great stones heaped over the body. The clothes of the deceased were laid by his grave.

Another staircase led to the roof, and we could walk all round the building on the broad massive wall. This castle, we are told, was occupied, during the war of Mehemet Ali, by a garrison of Egyptians, left here by Ibrahim Pasha, who did much damage to the ruins of Ziza, and wantonly destroyed a very perfect build-

NO. 18. ZIZA. PIGEON-HOLE STONES.

ing in the town, and several perfect Christian churches. Zadam assured us that, before the Egyptian invasion, the large buildings inside the town had their roofs entire, and were often used as places of shelter.

The other castle, to the east of this, is apparently of the Roman age, and has been reduced to a ruinous state by the troops of Ibrahim Pasha. The external walls alone remain, with a conspicuous inner niche, alcoved in the south face. It looks like an old temple utilized, first as a fort, and then as a mosque. In it is a beautifully carved lintel, of very rich late Byzantine, or perhaps Persian work; and other sculp-

NO. 19.   ZIZA. CUPHIC INSCRIPTIONS.

tured stones are built in, as well as some fragments of Cuphic inscriptions.

Eastward from the two castles, on a higher ridge, extend the ruins of Roman Ziza. They are in character a repetition of those of Um Weleed, but more extensive. Near the western end is a fine Saracenic building, quite perfect up to Ibrahim Pasha's time. The gate-way still remains, with its richly carved façade. There are several semicircular niches in the walls, and fragments of Cuphic inscriptions appear in many places on the courses. Several carved crosses, capitals, pieces of frieze; an olive-mill, made of hard basalt, with the solid cone of lava, which fitted into the cup for crushing the berries; and pieces of sarcophagi strew the ground. The oil-press was, in every respect, like the one we found at Dhiban.

But by far the most interesting ruin is one of the Christian churches, placed, like all the others we have noticed, in the east quarter of the city. There is a large apse left entire, and on the south side another shorter aisle, the apse being about three yards short of the other. There are indications of another aisle to the north, but, from the way in which the ruins are heaped, this could not be certainly ascertained. A colonnade has separated the centre from the aisle, and stones, sculptured with crosses, and a column, are lying among the loose stones of the old arches in the interior. We were able to get a good photograph of the south wall of this church.*

Next day a fugitive arrived to claim the protection of his sheik. He had been stripped by the Anizeh, who had left him with no other garment than a cam-

---

* For the description of a curious atmospheric phenomenon noticed at Ziza, see Appendix B.

el's sack, with a hole for his head and slits for his arms. The Anizeh had carried off sixty camels, and other stock besides, in this raid. These are to be distinguished from the well-known Northern Anizeh, who roam between Damascus and Palmyra. Though of the same clan, they have distinct sheiks, and seldom combine, for war or foray, with their Northern cousins. Their territory extends far to the east and south-east of the Belka, and is very poor and waterless, though of immense extent. The Beni Sakk'r seem to have a chronic feud with them.

Zadam was not much perturbed by the news. At least, he had still the advantage over his foes, for in their last raid the Beni Sakk'r had carried off two hundred Anizeh camels. So the question of reprisals would probably be deferred till the great tribal conference at the end of the lambing season, next month. Zadam, however, went off for two or three days, to consult his father and brothers how best to maintain the dignity of the tribe, leaving Sahan and the victim of the Anizeh foray to be our guides in excursions. The latter we found to be quite a character. He was a celebrated ibex-hunter, and on that account was retained for the rest of our time in the country. His pantomimic description of the incidents of hunting the "Bedoon" (ibex) was marvelous. With his wild, rolling eyes, and a sword-blade to represent his gun, he went through the whole scene of detecting, following, stalking the ibex, till at length, sprawling on his stomach, his eyes flashed fire as he aimed the fatal shot. The acting was perfect, and not least his silencing an imaginary loquacious brother-hunter.

We had a satisfactory test of the honesty of our people, and especially of our Christian servant, Habeeb, in the state of our supplies from Jerusalem. They arrived, after a four days' journey, without a package opened. The only levy on our stores had been four bottles of raki by the Turkish officers, whom our convoy had met still encamped in the Wady Na'ur, waiting for orders from Damascus. They had merely asked for some spirits, in return for the hospitality they had shown us. As Habeeb apologetically remarked, "They asked till my face was ashamed, and I gave." It speaks, indeed, well for the discipline and good behavior of Turkish troops (including, be it remembered, two squadrons of Bashi-Bazouks) that a party of unarmed muleteers, without a European with them, should have passed the night alone by their camp, not only without the slightest attempt at pilfering, but without being even asked to surrender any portion of their stores to those who, in their distant march, suddenly undertaken, must, indeed, have been ill supplied with the little comforts so temptingly brought within their reach. We were only grieved that our honest men had not more generously ventured to offer a share of their masters' provisions to those who were in the field solely on our account.

Nothing in the convoy was so welcome as the sack of brown bread. The craving for light wheaten bread can only be understood by those who, like us, have had a daily diet of Arab flat barley dampers for three weeks.

We were struck by the sagacity which all the wild animals showed in the matter of fire-arms, little familiar as they can be with them here. As it was Sunday, we strolled or sat down among the ruins, without our fowling-pieces, and were, consequently, objects of indifference. A fine fox sat and looked at us a dozen times among the stone-heaps, and just walked away as we approached, keeping almost within gun-shot all the afternoon. He is smaller than the English fox, with a grayish back, black breast, and very large bushy tail. This is probably the *Canis variegatus* of Rüppell, though it seemed to resemble in its coloration *Canis melanogaster* of the Italian peninsula. We frequently saw the same species in many different ruins. The Sakk'r falcon sat calmly on his favorite perch, and allowed us carefully to reconnoitre him on Sunday, while the eagle-owls, sand-grouse, and partridge showed a similar contempt for unarmed Europeans.

Much as our refusal to supply powder and shot on Sunday disconcerted our young sheik, Sahan, we found the greatest advantage in enforcing Sunday observance on all our cavalcade; not merely in the value of the regular physical rest for the horses, but in the moral influence over the Mohammedans, who always understand and respect the consistent observance of Christian ordinances. Rigid in their veneration for their own religious institutions, they despise those who neglect theirs; and little do many Englishmen know the contemptuous criticisms to which they are subjected by their attendants for their thoughtless requirement of unnecessary service on the day the Moslems know very well we hold to be " hallowed."

CHAPTER XI.

The Palace of Mashitâ.—Ride from Ziza.—Limestone Knolls rising above the Plain.—Their geological Origin.—Gradual Formation of the Table-land.—Hadj Road.—Palace suddenly in Sight.—First Impressions.—Description of the Palace.—Outer Wall.—Bastions. —Gorgeous Façade.—Octagonal Bastions.—Gate-way.—Delineations of Animals and Birds.—Inner Area.—Inhabited Portion.—Its Plan. — Rich Gate-way.—Corinthian Capitals.—Arch overthrown by Earthquake.—Long Inscriptions.—Nabathæan or Pelvic?—Peculiar Bricks.—Large open Hall.—Vaulted Roof.—Inner Doorway.—Peculiar Capitals.— Large inner domed Hall with alcoved Recesses.—Inner Chambers.—Construction of the outer Wall.— Hollow Bastion.—The Palace never finished.—The Builders interrupted.—No local Tradition of its Origin.—Probably Chosroes II., of Persia, its Builder, A.D. 614.— Campaign of Chosroes.— Conquest of Syria.—Capture of Jerusalem.—Sudden reverse.—Advance of Heraclius, A.D. 624.—The whole East reconquered by Rome. A.D. 632.—Irruption of the Saracens.—Final Devastation of the Country.—Its Disappearance from History.—Sassanian Origin of the Palace confirmed by its Architecture.—Mr. Fergusson's Opinion.—El Ah'la.

NOT many ruins could be descried from Ziza eastward; for the low limestone range, which bounds the eastern limits of the plains of Moab, rises about twelve miles off. To the north the traces of former population were numerous. One pile, apparently a khan, we could distinctly make out with our glasses. Zadam had told us that it stood beyond the great hadj road, and was, he believed, a ruined khan, built by Saladin (to whom every thing great, and not clearly Christian or Roman, is here referred), but that it contained nothing particular, and was just like Khan Zebib, or any other isolated ruin we had seen. It was known to the Arabs merely by the name of "Um Shita," or rather "Mâshitâ"—the former signifying "mother of rain or winter;" the latter, which is doubtless the true rendering, being simply "winter-quarters" (مشتا).

Though assured that we should not be repaid for our labor, we had no intention of leaving any ruin unvisited; and fortunate were we that we trusted not to Arab notions of archæology. An early start on the morning of February 26 brought us, in an hour and a quarter, after a smart canter and occasional gallop over the grassy plain, to the front of the ruin, just after crossing the hadj road, which, with its countless furrowed tracks, presents exactly the same characteristics as at Khan Zebib, farther south.

The ride was diversified by the starting of two herds of gazelle, and of the desert fox (*Canis niloticus*), and afforded a good opportunity of noticing the mode of deposition of the rich soil of the uplands of Moab. The peculiar phenomenon of the many knolls of limestone rock rising out of the soft, level plain of red earth may be easily explained, when we watch the action of the sudden showers on the furrowed sides of the eastern range, and the sweep of sediment which comes down with the floods, and deposits a fine top-dressing on the plains.

Originally the whole of the highlands must have been simply a wide terrace, about thirty-five miles in breadth, rugged and uneven, between this eastern range and the crest of the western mountains of Moab. Water action has, in course of ages, carried down the débris, and deposited it in the inequalities of the surface, until it has at length left only the innumerable knolls and ridges on which all the old cities stand. Had the country been without these excrescences of rock, affording unlimited facilities for cistern excavation, and for the storing of water supplies, it is utterly impossible that it could ever have sustained, as it has done, a vast resident and agricultural population. With them, there is nothing requisite beyond a settled government and the reparation of the old cisterns and conduits to enable a population as dense as of old to resume the occupation of these alluvial plains.

Suddenly drawing rein in front of Mǎshitâ, after a headlong dash at a herd of gazelle across the hadj road, we were astonished at the unexpected magnificence of the ruins, unknown to history, and unnamed in the maps. It has evidently been a palace of some ancient prince. There is no trace of any town or buildings round it. The only remains outside the walls are those of a deep well near the south-west corner. It must have stood out on the waste in solitary grandeur, a marvelous example of the sumptuousness and selfishness of ancient princes.

We were at first perfectly bewildered by the va-

A PALACE IN THE WASTE. 213

riety and magnificence of the architectural decorations. The richness of the arabesque carvings, and their perfect preservation, is not equaled even by those of the Alhambra, though in somewhat the same style. The whole consists of a large square quadrangle, facing due north and south, 170 yards in extent

NO. 20. INTERIOR OF RUINED PALACE.

on each face, with round bastions at each angle, and five others, semicircular, between them, on the east, north, and west faces, all, like the wall, built of finely-dressed hard stone.

But it is on the south face that the resources of

Eastern art have been most lavishly expended. There are here six bastions, besides the corner ones; for the fretted front, which extends for fifty-two yards in the centre of the face, has a bold octagonal bastion on either side of the gate-way. This gate-way is the only entrance to the palace; and on either side is the most

NO. 21.   GATE-WAY OF PALACE.

splendid façade imaginable, of which our photographs alone can convey a correct idea. The wall is eighteen feet high, and covered with the most elaborate and beautiful carving, nearly intact, and hardly injured either by time or man.

On the flat wall itself runs a large pattern, like a

continued W, with a large rose boss in each angle. These stand out boldly from the plane of the wall. Every inch of their surface, and all the interstices, are carved with fretted work representing animals, fruit, and foliage, in endless variety. The birds and beasts are fully represented, and not, as in Arab sculpture, melting into fruit or flowers, but correctly drawn.

No. 22.   OCTAGON TOWER.

There are upward of fifty animals, in all sorts of attitudes, but generally drinking together on opposite sides of the same vase—lions, winged lions, buffaloes, gazelle, panthers, lynx, men; in one case a man with a basket of fruit, in another a man's head with a dog below; peacocks, partridges, parrots, and other birds.

More than fifty figures stand in line, with vases, on the west side of the gate-way. All are inclosed in cornices and moldings of conventional patterns, and the interstices filled in with very beautiful adaptations of leaves.

The side east of the gate-way is without animal fig-

NO. 23.   FALLEN ARCH.

ures, excepting two on the panel next the gate. The façade is even more delicately sculptured than the other side, but with fruits and flowers only, festoons of vine-leaves and grapes predominating.

On entering the gate-way, the square inside seems

to have been divided into three parallelograms, the side ones forty-six, and the centre sixty-six yards in width. The two side parallelograms extend along the whole length of the inclosure. The centre one has been divided into three sections. The first section is covered with the foundations of numerous chambers, well arranged on either side, seventeen or eighteen in number, but none of the walls rising much above the ground. They have probably been intended as guard-rooms for the soldiers. The next section has contained no buildings, but has had a large fountain on the west side; and there are uncertain traces of another to correspond, on the opposite side.

The northern and innermost block of the central parallelogram is entirely occupied by the residence itself. The entrance presents a façade divided into three equal parts, the centre composed of a wide central gate-way and two side doors. These have consisted of three archways supported by massive columns of white, hard stone, almost marble, surmounted by debased Corinthian capitals. The voussoirs of the arches have all fallen to the ground, but in perfect order, evidently overthrown by an earthquake, which has shivered the columns, as shown in the photograph. These arches have been semicircular, very richly fluted, and not unlike our own late Norman work. The rest of this façade, above the three lower courses, is all of brick, excepting the pillars and pilasters, which, as well as the foundation, are of stone.

These courses are finely squared and dressed, and covered with long lines of inscriptions in a character quite undecipherable by us, but still very distinct and unmutilated, excepting that, in many places, it has been disfigured by innumerable tribe-marks cut over and between the lines of the original inscription. These later carvings, however, are all very easily distinguishable from the original record, and so appear in a photograph, from the much lighter color of the incisions. Unfortunately, all our photographs of the inscriptions, excepting one fragment, have failed, from an accident before they were developed, and the silent story is left for some future explorer to decipher. The characters seemed to me to differ from the ordinary Nabathæan, and, so far as memory can be trusted, appear like several specimens of the Pelvic character, kindly shown me by Mr. Fergusson.

The bricks, of which, above these three courses, the whole of the residential portion of the palace is constructed, differ from any we met with before or since; nor have I ever found bricks of a like shape and pattern elsewhere, though Mr. Tyrwhitt Drake tells me that, when in company with Captain Burton, he found similar tiles employed in a ruined palace north-east of Damascus. These tiles are square and flat, of the shape of Roman tiles, but much thinner and larger, about three inches thick and perhaps eighteen inches square. The three courses of stone continue, covered with inscriptions, all round the building; but within, the whole superstructure is of brick, excepting the

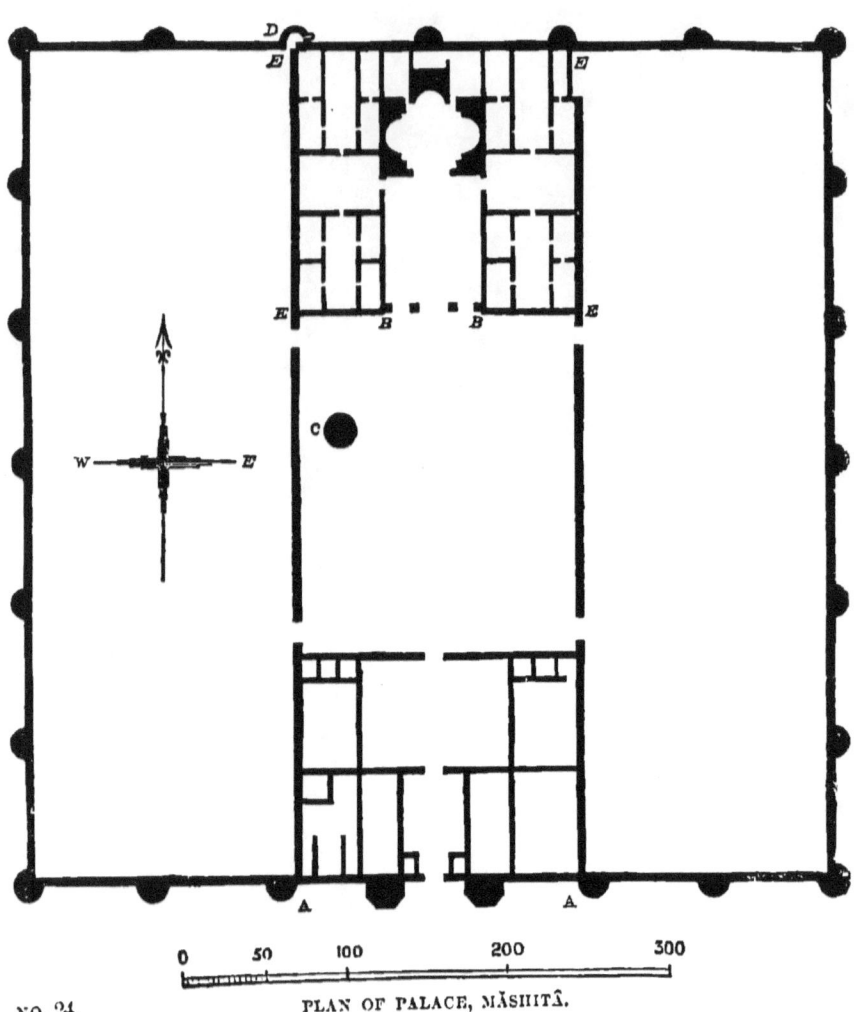

NO. 24.   PLAN OF PALACE, MÁSHITÂ.

pilasters and cornices, with the large stones in the angles, from which the vaulting of the roof springs.

The triple front gate-way leads into a large hall—which, I think, has never been roofed. On either side are chambers, with lofty vaulted brick roofs still remaining, though decayed in places. The access to these chambers is not from the hall itself, but by a circuitous route, through door-ways at the farther extremity of the hall, right and left, which opens by arched door-ways into various other chambers, from which there is access to these.

In front of the hall is a wide door-way, with very massive pilasters of finely-dressed stone. The capitals of these are very elaborately carved, as shown in the photograph, and certainly of no Greek order of architecture, but revealing rather Persian or Egyptian ornamentation. There has been no arch above them, for they simply form the door-way into the grand chamber of the palace, which has had a massive domed roof of brick-work.

The chamber is about fifty feet square in its extreme length and breadth; but its farther end and two sides form three alcoved apsidal recesses, the angles being filled in with solid brick-work, the principal support of the great crypt-like roofs which spring from them. On the right and left of the farther apsidal recess are arched door-ways opening into chambers behind. One of these has no other exit; the others open into a still farther chamber, directly at the back of the great chamber.

The dome being broken through in many places, enabled us to see very clearly the method of construction. The spring of the vaulting of all the rooms is from a row of bricks, slightly projecting, and forming a sort of plinth, the projection being continued in the vaulting. In the arches of the door-ways this projection gives them the appearance of Saracenic or horseshoe arches, though very nearly semicircular. The first row on the face of the arch consists of the square bricks which prevail in other parts; the next, of the thin rectangular tiles before described, set lengthways; then a row of the same thin tiles set endways; after which comes the ordinary walling. The two rows of bricks placed faceways have been cemented; but there are only faint traces of fine plastering elsewhere. The mortar is very strong, and, between the bricks of the arches, forms conspicuous broad white bands.

With the exception of the three chambers behind the central large room, all the other chambers, eleven of them on either side, have but a single access into the farther angle of the great hall. Thus, from any of the inner chambers, it was necessary, as shown on the plan, to pass through three others before reaching the open court-yard.

Turning now to the outer wall of the whole inclosure, we found the circumference perfect all round, varying from five to twenty feet in height. It is very carefully built of beautifully squared stones, each of the same size, and placed alternately lengthways and across, so as to bind the whole in one solid mass. The inside and outside faces are dressed with equal exactness. In the inclosing wall are cut, at irregular intervals, numerous small apertures sloping very sharply downward. They are not defensive loop-holes, for they come out very near the ground, and do not expand as they descend, neither can any view be obtained through them, nor archery used. Though no traces of buildings can be observed in this part of the enceinte, yet where these apertures are made are also large stones projecting from the wall, apparently for the purpose of supporting a flooring which has never been laid down.

One thing struck us much—the very small amount of débris strewn about. Except where the brickwork has become dilapidated, or the walls have been overthrown (evidently, as shown by the cracks, the effects of earthquake), the appearance of the stones is rather that of unused material than of crumbling ruin. The stone is so hard, that it is very little weathered; and from the absence of ruin, it seems impossible that the bastions can have been much higher than twenty feet. They are all of them solid, with one singular exception. This was the bastion at the north-west angle of the brick palace, which is hollow, with an access from the outer square, and has a curious little hollow excrescence attached, as if for a look-out into the country behind.

The state of the external sculptured façade proves that it was never finished. As may be seen in the photographs, several of the stones have their sculptures incomplete. The masonry has been put into its place and then carved *in situ*. In the portion eastward several of the rose bosses are finished, and stand out above the walling, which has never been carried so high. We searched carefully, but in vain, for any sculptured fragments among the débris, and could only come to the conclusion that the builders had been suddenly interrupted, and had left unfinished the decorative part of their plan.

Of tradition the Arabs have absolutely none, though they have on many other ruins—for instance, on the tower of Um Rasas. The name Mäshitâ conveys no idea, except that it is often used as "winter-quarters" for the flocks and herds. Of this there was abundant evidence in traces left by the heaped ordure of sheep and goats in all the vaulted chambers. We may fairly presume that, whoever were the builders, they had left no permanent impression behind them among the tales and traditions which linger so tenaciously among the Arab tribes, and go back to the Jewish and Roman periods.

The palace is no relic of Saladin or the Caliphs, else it would be recognized as such by the Bedouin, who are eager enough to ascribe every thing they can to their early heroes. Besides, the existence of the human and animal figures proves its ante-Moslem origin. But there is no trace of Christian work; and in the Roman times we can not conceive of so sumptuous and truly Oriental a palace being erected in a lonely wilderness, away from cities, and from any military road. The character, also, of the work, and the sculpture, point to a late date. Many of the details are decidedly Byzantine in type; and in the exuberant decoration we have the model of that employed in the Saracenic palaces, as in the Alhambra. We found no other ruin in the whole country which bore the slightest resemblance to Mäshitâ, either in situation, design, or execution.

The whole question continued to be an insoluble mystery to us while we remained in the country; and it was only on our return that Mr. Fergusson promptly and kindly solved the problem for us, and gave the key to it, referring it to the Sassanian dynasty of Persian kings, and to the history of Chosroes II., and fixing the date to be A.D. 614.

The story of the conquests and the defeat of Chosroes, the greatest prince of the Sassanian dynasty, is, perhaps, a nearer parallel to the conquests and overthrow of the great Napoleon than any other event in history.[*]

Under the miserable reign of the Emperor Phocas, of infamous memory, Chosroes, with the Persian armies, overran, A.D. 611, the whole of Northern Syria and Asia Minor. He then advanced to Damascus, and, after reposing his troops in that paradise for a season, invaded and reduced Galilee, and the region beyond Jordan, which offered him a stout resistance,

---

[*] Gibbon, chap. xlvi.

and delayed for a time the siege of Jerusalem, which was finally taken by assault A.D. 614. "The sepulchre of Christ and the stately churches of Helena and Constantine were consumed, or at least damaged, by the flames; the devout offerings of three hundred years were rifled in one sacrilegious day; the patriarch Zachariah and the *true Cross* were transported into Persia; and the massacre of 90,000 Christians is imputed to the Jews and Arabs, who swelled the disorder of the Persian march."

Egypt itself, the only province "which had been exempt since the time of Diocletian from foreign and domestic war, was again subdued by the successors of Cyrus. Pelusium, the key of that impervious country, was surprised by the *cavalry* of the Persians."

His western trophy was erected, not on the walls of "Carthage, but in the neighborhood of Tripoli; the Greek colonies of Cyrene were finally extirpated; and the conqueror, treading in the footsteps of Alexander, returned in triumph through the sand of the Libyan desert." "From the long-disputed banks of the Tigris and Euphrates the reign of the grandson of Nurshivan was suddenly extended to the Hellespont and the Nile, the ancient limits of the Persian monarchy."

We read that, "conscious of this fear and hatred, the Persian conqueror governed his new subjects with an iron sceptre; and, as if he suspected the stability of his dominion, he exhausted their wealth by exorbitant tributes and licentious rapine; despoiled or demolished the temples of the East; and transported to his hereditary realms the gold, the silver, the precious marbles, the arts and the artists, of the Asiatic cities." "He enjoyed with ostentation the fruits of victory, and frequently retired from the hardships of war to the luxury of the palace." The details of his more than Oriental pageantry, carefully collected by Gibbon from contemporary writers, almost pass belief; 960 elephants, 20,000 camels, 6000 horses, as many guards, and 3000 concubines, to say nothing of the gathered piles of precious metals, give some idea of his lavish magnificence.

It was during this transient period of splendor that the then obscure prophet of Arabia wrote a letter to the great king, inviting him to acknowledge *him*, Mohammed, as the prophet of God. Chosroes scornfully tore the letter, little forecasting how soon the Arabian would be master of the East. But this was not to be in his time. Yet he only held together his vast empire for fourteen years.

In A.D. 623 the emperor Heraclius, with incredible daring, commenced the reconquest of the East; and never, in her grandest days of power, did the eagle of Rome swoop more magnificently than in its dying throes, when in the space of three years Heraclius penetrated to the very heart of Persia, compelled Chosroes to return from a distant expedition, to recall his troops from Egypt, Syria, and Asia Minor, captured Ispahan and Salban, and in them the flower of the Persian nobility and youth.

In vain Chosroes attempted to strike a retaliatory blow at Constantinople. Baffled there, he returned to meet the triumphant Heraclius in his third expedition, at Mosul, over the ruins of Nineveh, where on the 1st December, A.D. 627, the Romans were completely victorious, and Chosroes died miserably, a deposed fugitive, in a dungeon, by the hand, or the command, of his own son. Two years afterward Heraclius visited Jerusalem, and celebrated his triumph; and all seemed fair and secure in the Eastern empire, with every rival not only defeated, but utterly crushed, on its frontiers.

It was but a short-lived respite. In A.D. 632 the hordes of Saracen horsemen under the command of Abou Obeidah and Caled poured into the Roman province of Arabia, which embraced Idumea, Moab, and all the country east of Jordan. They speedily overran it, slaughtered its inhabitants, and captured the fortress of Bozrah, the stronghold of the country, five days' march north of the Arnon. Up to the time of their arrival at that stronghold, we are told, they met with no resistance; and, indeed, it is evident that none of the towns of the plains of Moab could, from their position, have sustained for more than a day the onslaught of these warriors.

From that hour the whole of this region disappears altogether from the page of history. Retired from the route of armies, it has been without fortress, town, or inhabitants, to invite a conqueror; inaccessible to ordinary troops from the west, it has remained without the record of one single event on its soil, and its eastern plains untrodden by European foot till yesterday.

Too proud to cultivate—happily, too, careless to destroy—the incurious Bedouin has roamed over its rich pasture-lands, never tempted to loosen a stone, for he needs no building materials, and content if the old cisterns and arches afford a shelter in winter for his flocks.

In every land it has been the builders, rather than the conquerors, who have obliterated the remains of antiquity. The abbeys of England have been the quarries for manor-houses; the Coliseum has supplied the materials for Roman palaces; the stones of many a Syrian temple have found their place, first, in a Christian church, and finally in a Moslem mosque. But the Bedouin needs no mosque; and thus, since the first fury of the victors spent itself, time has been aided by earthquakes alone, and not by man, in the decay of the cities of Roman Arabia. Thus Mâshitâ has remained intact.

The résumé of the history of Chosroes seems to solve every difficulty about the deserted palace, even apart from the architectural features which point to its chronology. Chosroes held this country for only fourteen years at the utmost. Such a mere passing wave of desolating conquest would not be likely to leave any clear or distinct traditions to linger through many generations. The building is certainly neither Jewish, Greek, Roman, nor Saracen, either in its plan or its details. It can only, therefore, be either Persian or Arabian. We know there was a dynasty of Christian kings in Arabia after the time of Constantine; but we have no reason to believe that their power extended into this unquestioned Roman province; and even had it done so, it is difficult to conceive why an indigenous dynasty should ever have selected such a situation for a palace. Mr. Fergusson has pointed out that there are details in the workmanship which can scarcely be older than the time of Justinian; and at that period the Arabian kings certainly held no sway so near the Jordan.

But Chosroes is celebrated for the sumptuous palaces which he caused to be erected wherever he went; and this palace is constructed very much on the same ground-plan as his other edifices, although the details of the workmanship are very different.

He is recorded, after wintering in Damascus, to have invaded Egypt, and that with vast swarms of cavalry. This place would lie in his natural road from Damascus to the Nile, one quite as easy for horsemen as the more westerly route. We are told that he carried away many thousands of Greek and Syrian captives, whom he employed on his works. Some of these he may have employed to erect here a hunting-box, for his sojourn when he passed this way; for we know that he was passionately attached to the chase. As we have seen, the palace has been suddenly abandoned, before it could be completed. This is at once accounted for, if Chosroes be its builder, by the advance of Heraclius, when he was compelled to recall his troops from Egypt and Syria, and, of necessity, to abandon his works. The Romans held the country but ten years longer, and a solitary building in this remote corner had little chance at that time to be mentioned by any contemporary writer. The Saracens had no object to secure in either destroying or utilizing a defenseless, solitary, half-finished pile.

Mr. Fergusson has pointed out several architectural details which convince him that there is internal evidence of the palace being the work of Chosroes. He writes: "The capitals of the outer portals of the brick palace are more like those of the golden gate-way at Jerusalem than others I know, and, if they were alone, might be as old—viz., Constantine's time. But the inner ones could not possibly be carved before Justinian's time: and they are even more certainly integral. It is not quite impossible that the outer ones may have been brought from some of Constantine's buildings at Jerusalem, which Chosroes is said to have destroyed. But this theory is by no means necessary for the date. The Corinthian capital, with very slight change, lasted down to the tenth century."

A Persian architect employing Byzantine workmen might be expected to produce just such a work as this. Many of the details of the sculptured façade much resemble fragments of late Byzantine work at Constantinople; and it was from this that the Saracenic style of decoration was developed.

Mâshitâ, as well as Ziza, seems to have been pointed out from a great distance to Captain Warren ("Expedition East of Jordan, Palestine Exploration Fund," vol. i., p. 293), and we could see several known points from its walls — viz., Ziza, Jebel Shihan, Jebel Sa-mik (whence Captain Warren saw it), Herri, and Jelul. The only ruin to the eastward was a large fort or town about ten miles off, N.N.E. (bearing 220°), in the hills, looking very like Um Rasas, at the foot of an opening in the mountain range, and called by the Arabs Kirbet el Ah'la. We were assured there were no other ruins to be found anywhere to the eastward; and certainly the bare, verdureless hills held out no promise of discovery, though we have ever since regretted that we did not push on to El Ah'la.

CHAPTER XII.

Second Visit to Mâshitâ.—Expedition to Kustul.—Imperial Eagle.—Interesting Character of the Remains of Kustul.—Castellated Temple.—Corinthian Pilasters.—Nabathæan Inscriptions.—Larger Castle.—Vaulted Chambers and massive Bastions.—A Greek Altar exhumed.—Walls for collecting Water.—Kustul-Castellum.—Thenib.—Rujum Hamam.—Views of the Belka.—Southward Migration of the Beni Sakk'r.—Move Camp toward the West.—Azabarah.—Jebel Jelul.—Magnificent Panorama.—Safa.—Trained Falcons.—Women Water-drawers.—Arrival at our camp.—Visit from Fendi y Faiz.—Entertainment of the great Sheik.—Photographing of the Princes.—Escort of the Hadj.—Parting with the Sahan.—Delay at Habis.—Descent of the Wady Habis.—Junction with the Zerka Ma'in.—Contrast between the Highlands of Moab and the Mountains.

February 27.—So unexpected and interesting had been the discovery of Mâshitâ, that a second day was not grudged for its more accurate exploration and photographing, especially as Buxton found that, in the excitement occasioned by its elaborate carvings, he had taken two sets of photographs on the same plates, and, after toiling at developing till midnight, had only one good negative to show.

But time was precious, and accordingly, attended by our old lance-bearing dervish, Sherouan, I set out alone to examine the rest of the ruins to the north of us, where three deserted cities could be made out; and so to finish our map of this part of the Belka as soon as possible, while the rest of the party revisited the Persian palace.

We all began to feel the effects of the climate, and that our camp was not in a spot conducive to health. The thermometer at 24° Fahr. at night, a lump of solid ice in our basins in the morning, and then the scorching heat of the day drawing up the moisture, made the neighborhood of the tank, convenient as it was, rather a fever-trap; and premonitory symptoms warned us to move.

Forty-five minutes' rather quick riding due north, across a grassy plain, with scarcely an undulation, brought us to the first ruins, called Kustul. Game was abundant on the way; and it was curious to see flocks of mallard and pintail feeding among the stunted scrub, in most unlikely ground for duck, who, however, seem able to accommodate themselves to circumstances. A fine imperial eagle sat quietly on the carcass of a kid till I was within ten yards of him, showing his white shoulders in fine contrast with his dark plumage. But I had only small shot; and though successful against the sand-grouse which, plover-like, kept skimming past in flocks large and small, I was tantalized by fox, wolf, and wild-cat—all in turn offering an easy opportunity for a rightly provided collector. This fox of the plains seems to be the same as the Egyptian. In the evening I found that Trotter, riding in another direction, had shot on the plain a duck which proved to be a hybrid between mallard and pintail, the fac-simile of the so-called bimaculated duck of "Yarrell's British Birds."

Arrived at Kustul, I found it a ruin of quite different character from any we had previously visited. There is the ordinary mass of ruins, caves, walls, and arches innumerable, extending over the west side of

NO. 25.   EL KUSTUL.

the hill; but those on the eastern side are evidently later accretions on a much earlier and more carefully built castle; or rather on two castles, of which the northernmost and smaller is far the most perfect. It measures thirty yards by twenty, and has a large semicircular bastion at the north-west corner, surmounted by a balustrade of fluted Corinthian squared pilasters, and an inner staircase leading up to it, still remaining. Inside its south wall is a semicircular niche; and two capitals of pure white marble are lying in the court-yard. This area is partially filled in with crypts of coarser and evidently later masonry.

The building would seem to have been originally a fortified temple, and an outwork of the main castle. This stands on the crest of the hill, immediately to the south of the other, and is eighty-four yards square. All round it have been semicircular bastions of solid masonry, six yards in diameter, and a space of fourteen yards between each. The building has been of two stories at least; but only the lower story now remains, with the foundations, and a few arches of the rooms of the upper one. The chambers have run round the inside wall of this castle, having an open area in the centre, in which two columns are still standing. The crypt roof of the lower chamber remains, and many of the courses have Nabathæan inscriptions, marred, as usual, by tribe marks.

On the ground-floor have been three sets of large principal chambers, on the south-west and north sides, each having a smaller room opening into it on either side, through low door-ways with flat lintel heads. The chambers of the upper story had semicircular arched door-ways of very solid, well-constructed masonry. The size of the lower side-chambers is eight yards by six; and of the nine main crypts, eighteen yards each by six yards, all opening into the central area. The entrance was in the east face; and the old castle seems, at the date of the Christian empire, to have been entirely built in by houses, which abut on it with arches and half-arches, like those of Um Rasas, on every side.

To the north-west of the castle is a large portion of the ancient city, with the usual arches, but also with some singular remains of Greek architecture— one probably a tomb, with elaborately carved lintels of Corinthian character. Below this, again, is a large square tank, in which there was still water.

The Beni Sakk'r shepherds, who surrounded me with much curiosity as I took the angles from the top of the castle, assured me that they knew of a curious inscribed stone which they had buried, but which they would show me. I accordingly accompanied them down a grassy slope to the south, where they exhumed their carved stone, which proved to be a Greek altar, of pure white marble, without inscription, and the greater part of the hollowed surface at the top broken off to make pestles for their coffee-mortars. In its mutilated state it was twenty-six inches high, and fourteen in diameter, with only part of the saucer-shaped depression left in the upper part.

A few minutes' ride down the east side of the hill brought me to a massive wall in the plain, built to dam up the water in the gentle depression, which is the head of a wady running westward. The wall is about six hundred yards in length across the valley, and eighteen feet thick. Of course it has been neglected, and the floods have broken through at the north end of the wall, and worked their way into their old channel, though water runs only after the occasional rains. There is not, however, any grand tank of masonry visible, as at Ziza; but the deposit of soft soil has here been so great that possibly the most important parts of the old works are now buried.

The buildings of Kustul were as great a problem to us as those of Mǎshitâ. From the attachment of the later arches and dwellings of the Byzantine epoch to their walls, we must place them prior to the later empire. Then the many fragments of fine white marble, certainly not indigenous, and which must have been brought, at great cost, from beyond sea, belonged to these earlier castles, which are probably either Herodian or the work of some of the Syrian successors of Alexander. Their shape and architecture are of a character perfectly distinct from any we elsewhere met with. The name, again, of "Kustul"—not an Arabic word—seems to be a corruption of the Latin "castellum," very naturally applied, as *the castle par excellence*, to a castle so markedly different from the square block-houses with which the country is studded. But I can find no clue to the history of the place in either Eusebius, the "Itineraries," or the "Notitia."

After taking observations to fix the site, I rode on due north, and an hour's quick ride brought us to Thenib. The buildings of Thenib cover the whole area of an isolated hill, and are much more dilapidated and ruder than those we had recently been visiting.

Due north from Thenib two miles, I found another ruined heap on a hill, very like the shapeless mass at Remail, merely an old block-house, to which the Arabs give the name of "Rujum Hamam," "the ruins of the pigeons," and well so named. I was now on the edge of the plain, as the hills to the north here begin to rise, forming the conventional boundary between Moab and Ammon, or between the Belka and the Adwân country. No further ruins were reported by Sherouan in this direction, nor could any be seen among the hills north and east; so I turned my horse's head due south to return to our camp at Ziza.

From Thenib and from Kustul I had the finest views of the Belka, as this country is officially called,* which we had yet enjoyed. But not only was the prospect wide and clear; we had also the opportunity of seeing an Arab migration. The law of "cor-

---

* The name Belka is applied, in official Turkish documents, to the whole plain of Moab. But in common parlance the slopes of the Belka mean only the cultivated land running down eastward from a line drawn between Heshban and Medeba, and inhabited by the Belka tribe of Arabs. Yet the Turks are right in giving to the Pasha of Nablous the title of "Pasha of the Belka," for all these plains were for many generations the heritage of the Belka tribe, who about 170 years ago were driven westward by the irruption of the Beni Sakk'r from the east, and compelled to exchange their nomadic for their present semi-agricultural life.

vée," as the French term it, renders all beasts of burden liable to be impressed for the service of an army on the march.

The small brigade which had been sent for our rescue still remained waiting in the Wady Na'ur, and, having already exhausted the camels and the patience of the Adwân and the Belka tribes, had sent on an intimation to the Beni Sakk'r that they should require their aid for the transport of troops and baggage. The news spread instantly through the tribe, and, without concert, each shepherd at once discovered that the pastures were exhausted, and that he must without delay move southward and eastward. The tribe had been distributed over the whole breadth of the northern plain, in little camps of two or three families each, during the season of lambs and kids. At once there was a general migration southward. Very wonderful was the sight. The whole plain, far as the glass could reach, was covered, not dotted, with herds of camels, goats, sheep, asses, in line and file, spreading over the face of the land. The herds of Abraham, or the flocks of Jacob coming from Paran, could not have equaled these innumerable hordes. On one hill-slope eighty-three camels were counted without turning the head.

There was not a cloud on the sky, and to the farthest horizon the moving lines of camels stood out in white dots. We rode past at least seven camps as we returned, each camp containing, on an average, twelve families, and each family averaging twenty camels and four hundred sheep and goats. The women were mounted on camels or asses, the men ahead, and the boys bringing up the rear-guard of lambs and kids. Besides those we passed, there were thousands more, moving on the plain on all sides. At one place we saw over one hundred griffon vultures congregated over the carcass of a camel which had just dropped on its march. We charged them in the gallop, and actually rode among them before they had time to rise; but I had no ammunition. So completely were we upon them, that I struck two with my fowling-piece in the stride. Heavily stretching forward, they commenced by an ungainly run, and at last got their wings, most of them behind us, after we had ridden through them. When they did rise, they actually darkened the air, as they passed in a mass close over our heads.

We had the first sign of spring to-day in the return of the hoopoe, while a swallow took refuge in our tents; yet the thermometer was again down to 24° Fahr. My companions had completed a good day's work at Mäshitâ; Hayne had measurements for an exact plan of the palace; the photographs were successful, excepting those of the inscriptions; and Trotter's gun had done good service, both to ornithology and the kitchen.

We revisited Kustul to photograph, surrounded by a crowd of curious but most inoffensive visitors, for there was still a large camp close by. No worse harm did they do us than emptying our skins and leaving us waterless at luncheon, on a day as hot as the night had been cold.

From Kustul we turned W.S.W., and in a quarter of an hour reached the ruins of Azabarah. The name suggests some connection with *Asabaia*, given in the "Notitia," in this part of the country, as the station of the first cohort of Thracians. Possibly the name yet lingers in the local tongue, and this may have been the older city, while the garrison was stationed in the Castellum, a mile off, round which the new town gradually gathered.

At Jebel Jelul we caught up with the retiring migrants from the north-western pastures. Jelul is a remarkable hill, completely isolated, rising three hundred feet above the plain, and one of the very few places where I have seen a really uninterrupted panorama. It does not seem to have been visited by any traveler, though it is marked in the maps two miles east of Heshban; but it is in reality very far south of it. It was curious to observe on all sides of us, except the east, a double rim of hills, the outer just rising sufficiently above the inner to enable us to distinguish with our glasses the most important points. Er Ram rose above Rasas, Shihan beyond Attarus, and Jebel Jilad (Mount Gilead) beyond Heshban.

After an hour and twenty minutes' farther ride, we reached Sufa, having passed several camps on our way. Almost every depression had beneath its shelter a camp of Beni Sakk'r pitched, halting on their way southward. At one of these we found that the owner was an old sportsman, and had two fine Saker falcons, well trained and docile. They were last year's birds, and had not yet quite completed their hunting education. We had merely halted for a draught of water; but the interest shown in his favorites soon opened the heart of the old man, proud of his pets, the ensign and crest of his tribe. Each sat on its movable perch on either side of the tent door.

The Saker (*Falco sacer*) is much prized here, and is well known as distinct from the peregrine and the lanner, which latter our falconer assured us was a very sluggish falcon, and worthless for gazelle. He was not to be tempted to sell his birds at any price, and treated the offer of £10 apiece with scorn. These birds—obtained, we were told, from the east, and not from the mountains of the Dead Sea—were the only trained falcons we met with.

After taking our bearings, half an hour's easy ride down a gently undulating descent brought us to our tents, already pitched, and the English ensign flying by a dirty pond, but with lovely pasturage, starred with a blaze of scarlet anemone, in the Wady Habis, an affluent of the Callirrhoe.

We had heard in the morning of a great honor being about to be paid us—a visit from Fendi y Faiz, Zadam's father, and the great sheik of the Beni Sakk'r, whose camp was only two hours' ride from the Habis. Daoud had gone on before, to see that proper care was taken for his reception, and with orders to kill two sheep we had bought on the way, and to get the Mocha coffee ready. A visit from a king is not an every-day occurrence, and it required all our stock of dignity, coffee, and tobacco to receive Fendi and his three sons all at once.

On our arrival, we found the old prince there before us, his presence intimated by the number of tall spears stuck in the ground, gleaming by our tents: while a splendid camel, with gorgeous trappings, towered above all the other beasts, and, camel-like, growled his dissatisfaction with all around.

In front of the tents the best carpet and cushions had been spread, and there sat the gray-bearded chieftain, in all the dignity of Oriental sovereignty, with a large retinue of followers respectfully squatted in a circle round him. He rose and greeted us in European mode, by shaking hands; and then we all entered the tent, which had been fitted up in proper divan fashion for our visitors.

He was a man of about sixty-five, with iron-gray beard, strongly marked features, fine and prominent nose, large liquid black eyes, and rather surly expression of countenance; dressed, apparently, in all his wardrobe at once, and perspiring copiously under the oppressive weight of clothing; armed with scimiter and pistol, the sheath, stock, and barrel of which were covered with silver work. Coffee and pipes, which had passed before we came, were repeated, and a heavy conversation of ponderous compliments passed through the dragoman filter. Fendi exhibited great courtesy, and was with difficulty persuaded to stay for dinner, delicately remarking that we could be only guests in his country.

Peacefully as the sun went down on this grand gathering, at the close of one of the finest and most cloudless of days, it was no sooner dark than we heard not only of departures, but of war. Fendi y Faiz was off to conduct the hadj for sixteen days toward Mecca, he having the guardianship of the pilgrims from the Hauran till six days south of Kerak, for which purpose he musters seven hundred camel-men. At the same time Zatum was starting for the east, to revenge the robbery of their camels by a raid on the 'Anizeh, and had summoned all the horsemen of his tribe. Sahan was to go with him, to win his youthful spurs at the age of thirteen.

During the night every one of our Arabs left us to see the departure of the hadj guard and of the raiding party; not even Zadam remained; and our only international representative was the dervish Sherouan. Even our pantomimic friend, the ibex-hunter, was seized with the war-frenzy, and disappeared with the rest. Accordingly, we spent the morning of February 29 in riding over some neighboring ruins, Betan el Bareil, Kirbet el Walch, and Delailat, a little farther to the east. Before 11 A.M. Zadam returned with profuse apologies. Passing the ruins of Habis in half an hour more, we had left the plains of the Belka, and entered the gorge of the Habis, now out of the Beni Sakk'r, and in the Beni Hamideh country.

The ride was a most interesting one down the gradually deepening valley, and afforded a splendid illustration of the contrast between the hill country and the pastoral uplands of Moab, into which Reuben, with his numerous flocks and herds, soon withdrew among the sheep-cots, to hear the bleatings of the flocks; wholly indifferent, from his nomad and pastoral habits, to the retention of the mountain fastnesses and the rough agricultural lands, which the Moabites, builders and husbandmen by taste and position, gradually recovered. An opposite rule to that which obtains elsewhere holds good in this country as to the scenery of the water-courses. The valleys all begin in flat plains, as mere depressions, and increase in wildness and grandeur as they approach the wall of the Moab mountains; and then, instead of rolling sluggishly to the end of their course, the streamlets burst through the range, in a series of rapids and cascades, to the very edge of the sea.

PANORAMA, UPPER ZERKA MA'IN.

NO. 26.

CHAPTER XIII.

Change from the Highlands.—The Hamideh.—Lords of high and low Degree.—Septs and political Divisions of the Hamideh.—Their Habits and Character.—Ornithology of the Glens.—The Callirrhoe. —An Evening's Fishing.—Geology of the Zerka Ma'in.—Basaltic Streams.—Descent to the hot Springs.—The Baths of Herod.— Hamideh Camp.—Nubian Slave.—A Sulphur Hot-bath.—Descriptions of Josephus and Pliny.—Ptolemy's Geography.—Sulphur Terraces.—Rapid Deposits.—Basalt and Limestone.—Palm-groves. —Temperature of the Springs.—Natural Formation of Tunnels.— Primitive Vapor-bath.—Arab Traditions.—Legend of King Solomon.—Sacrificial Rites.—Strange Plants.—The Shrub of Josephus. —The Sulphur Plant.—Orobanches.—Butterflies and rare Birds.— Ibex.—Sunday at Callirrhoe.—Amateur Physician.—Venison and Butter.—Hamideh horned Cattle.

THE transition from the highlands to the mountains is very sudden. Climate and vegetation at once are changed. At first, at the bottoms of the valleys are many patches of flat ground, covered with the richest herbage. In one of these opens we found a camp of Hamideh, into whose district we had now entered. The first sign of our proximity was a large herd of she-asses and their colts, animals not in favor with the more warlike Beni Sakk'r. The camp consisted of fourteen families.

Here Zadam halted, and had a long conversation with their sheik. The manner of both—the nonchalance of the one, the cringing deference of the other—was an amusing illustration of the great man talking with the small one. Zadam, by his contract, was bound to conduct us through the whole of the Beni Hamideh territory, and did not wish to have the expense of their sheik accompanying us. But the poor man, who certainly had few opportunities of backsheesh, urged upon him, "Why should you prevent my going with the Franghi and getting a little present, when you get a large one?" Our sheik consented at last, observing to the inferior magnate that at least there was plenty to eat at our camp, and telling us that the Hamideh came at his own choice, and could not demand a gift.

Our new follower devoted himself henceforward most assiduously to me, as a profitable milch cow, doing the civil most oppressively, and kissing my hand on every possible occasion. Honest and inoffensive we found the Hamideh, one and all, but cringing and mean—in fact, with all the characteristics of those who have been accustomed to be treated as an inferior race.

So far from being independent, as is generally supposed, and has been stated by some writers, there is not a single sept of the Beni Hamideh (or Hamaidi, as some of them prefer to call themselves) which is not the vassal of some greater tribe. All those north of the Arnon are the "teba'a" (feudal subjects) of the Beni Sakk'r, while those south of it have the worse misfortune of having two masters, being for the most part vassals of Kerak, and at the same time compelled to purchase the good-will of their neighbors, the Beni Sakk'r, to whose marauding parties they would otherwise be continually exposed. This position has given them a servile tone and bearing, which is all the more noticeable in contrast with the haughty bearing of the lordly Beni Sakk'r.

Again, there is no unity in the politics of the Hamideh. A number of petty sheiks, each leading a few families, and loath to acknowledge any superior in their own tribe, are enabled, by the configuration of the country, to hold their several valleys in tolerable security. It is no easy matter to lift cattle across from one wady to another when once they have entered the mountain descents. But it is very easy for the lords of the highlands to sally down any ravine they please, and overrun the valleys.

This position of the Hamideh partly explains the difficulties of most explorers of Moab. They have invariably gone to the wrong tribe, and, learning that the Hamideh possess the sites of the principal ruins, have intrusted themselves to the first petty sheik of the tribe to whom they could get access. These chieftains were each powerless beyond their own domains; and endless squabbles over paltry backsheesh, and final disappointment, have been the result. Had our predecessors been as fortunate as ourselves, and got under the protection of the suzerains of the whole country, they would have had free conduct over the lands of the vassal tribes, and we should not have been the first to explore a large part of the country.

We had read that the Hamideh are only semi-nomad, and inhabit huts or houses as well as tents. So far as we could ascertain, they live only under canvas throughout the year, although they do cultivate patches of ground.

In type they show no difference from the other Bedouins; there is no trace of the Syrian fellah, nor does there seem any reason, beyond the bare fact that they inhabit the same region, for supposing them to be the descendants of the ancient Moabites. Their own tradition is that they were driven from the uplands by the Belka Arabs, who in turn have been squeezed out by the Beni Sakk'r.

As we proceeded, the cliffs afforded many attractions to artist and naturalist. A spotted eagle (*Aquila nævia*) was sitting on her nest, beautifully in sight, but ingeniously placed out of reach. For the first time we heard the cuckoo's note resounding in all the glens that run down to the main gorge. The Alpine swift (*Cypselus melba*) delighted us by dashing with lightning speed overhead, up and down the glen, quite safe from the assaults of fowling-piece. The botanical breast was gladdened by many a plant not seen before, as we descended into the warmer regions. The beautiful wild tulip (*Tulipa Gesneriana*) was the most attractive of the spring novelties, gleaming in brightest dress from the crannies of the rocks.

The little river of the Callirrhoe is here, indeed, "fair-flowing," completely buried in oleanders, under which, with difficulty, we pushed our horses, over the recent tracks of wild boar. Emerging on the other side, we rose a few feet into a little plain, knee-deep in herbage, buried in an amphitheatre of hills, a lovely tenting spot. By common consent this was the queen of camps, far beyond any we had yet enjoyed. We had descended 1400 feet to-day. The air was balmy, yet not sultry, for we were still high. A pool was soon found, completely covered by oleanders, where we had a delicious bath, the water being deep enough for a header from the rocks, and a good swim afterward.

A deep basin in the rock yielded seventeen fish to two lines in half an hour. Trotter had quickly extemporized rod and line, and, with a few worms, drew out the unsophisticated fish as fast as he could bait his hook. Equally astonished were he and the fish. The fish were of the same species as those of the Jabbok and the Jordan, one of the *Cyprinidæ* (*Scaphiodon capöeta*, Guld.), a chub-like fish; and a delicious breakfast they afforded us. They were only second to trout, and the best river-fish, next to the *Salmonidæ*, I ever tasted. The Arabs have a prejudice against fish, and, though not holding them unclean, never think of either catching or cooking them. Great was Zadam's amazement at the device of hook and line, by which, as he said, "the fishes catch themselves."

March came in, the next morning, like a cloudless June day, with a fresh breeze, thermometer 65°, and the minimum 46° in the night—a change after 24°. We had nearly six hours to the Baths of Callirrhoe, heavy walking (for we determined to do it on foot), but magnificent scenery. Three hours brought us to the beginning of a basaltic torrent, where we were not sorry that our horses overtook us. At first sight the valley would seem to end here in a broad and rather arid bottom; but really a narrow and rapidly deepen-

NO. 27.   ROCKS AT ENTRANCE OF ZERKA MA'IN.

ing cleft descends from nearly half the height of the mountains on either side. Columns of pentagonal basalt, deep black, and, farther on, a wild gorge with the superincumbent limestone strata laid bare in perpendicular cliffs, render the track steep and circuitous.

BASALTIC STREAMS. 251

In parts of the valley the water disappears, dried up by the sun, or sinking into its shingly bed, the oleanders and the water always keeping company, and preserving each other.

The irruption of basalt is marked and sudden, and seems exclusively confined to the gorge, which it would appear to have filled in, nearly to the sea, in places to the depth of 1000 feet; while the water has afterward worked its way through the softer adjacent limestone to its old depth. Not only has the upper limestone been always cut through, but also the red sandstone, which is continually showing at one side or other of the gully, where the basalt is thin.

The gorge soon became too narrow to be passable, the huge boulders and deep chasms forbidding even wild goats to essay its perpendicular height, and we turned up, not to the higher plateau, but to a lower terrace, about 1300 feet above the stream, which extends a mile or half a mile on each side, and then is walled in by steeply-sloping mountain sides. Again we descended, by the most impossible of horse-paths; again we mounted, after once more crossing the oleander-shaded stream, and followed for a little distance the brow of what is named the lower plateau.

Two piles of stones and a crooked old stick, set in one of them, form the landmark for the descent from the plateau to the historical hot springs of Callirrhoe. Shortly before reaching this point, the waters of the Dead Sea and the whole range of the Judean hills had come well into sight. Before, we had only had an occasional glimpse down the vista of the valley. Wild and broken, the views on this pass increase in beauty and attractiveness on acquaintance. Black basalt on the southern, white and yellow limestone, over red sandstone, on the northern side—each formation broken and furrowed in a different way—scarped rocks, and nullahs, like the cañons of western America, green with waving date-palms and reeds far down the southern exposure, and a winding line of canebreak among rocks 1000 feet below, with one specially magnificent basaltic precipice, barring the valley on its way westward to the Dead Sea—such are the chief features from the top.

As we descended, right upon the famous baths of Herod, we looked down on a scene of strange enchantment. The iron-red rock facing us was gnarled, and contorted into fantastic shapes. The tall palms shaded an exuberant undergrowth of semi-tropical foliage. The stream itself is completely hidden by canebrakes and oleanders, but we could see the bright cascades leaping down the rocks from the hot sulphur springs; and the cloud of vapor rising in long lines told the temperature of the heated waters. The whitish fringe by the edge of each torrent indicated the sulphur with which it is charged. "Last night's camp was perfection; this is Paradise!" exclaimed an enthusiast, as we looked down on a little plateau in the dell, and saw the mules beginning to congregate, where the tents were to be erected for a few days' sojourn.

Before reaching the descent, allured by the birds,

which had drawn me aside in their pursuit, I had left my horse and the party, and afterward, wearied and thirsty, was right glad to espy some Hamideh tents, where I found two or three of our people loitering with the light animals, and enjoying an Arab gossip. A carpet was at once spread and a bowl of soured milk brought me — a most delicious draught on a broiling day. I reclined against a sack, and soon found I had been ushered into the women's compartment, and was an object of great curiosity. All the little ones, from two years old and upward, came to kiss me on both cheeks, in natural expectation of backsheesh.

Among them was a woolly-haired, nearly black boy, of about three years, with good and beautifully regular features. I asked with some surprise if he were an Arab. "Oh yes; his mother is here; she is a Nubian slave, and my husband bought her from Egypt." The mother was at once called from her work and introduced to me; and though black, she was really handsome, and the only good-looking member of the party. The elderly dame, who did the honors of the tent, stroked her affectionately on the face, and appealed to me as to her comeliness.

This was the first time I had had a chance of seeing Bedouin women at leisure, and in their own home; and though the Hamideh have not the best of reputations, we always, during our stay, found them hospitable and unsuspicious. They treated us as simple guests, and never made any difficulties or demands beyond the very legitimate one on the tobacco-pouch, which the ladies appreciated as much as their lords. Though my Nubian acquaintance here was a slave girl, she and her children (for she had a six-months-old babe at her breast) seemed to be on terms of perfect equality with the rest of the family.

When we had reached the bottom of the pass—no easy task, the upper part nearly as steep as the cliff of Ziz, and strewn with basaltic boulders, the lower portion of our descent down the sloping sides of limestone detritus steep as a high-pitched Gothic roof—we next had to force our way through a tangle of trees and canes, and over the rough boulders left by winter torrents. Then we had to scramble over thin sulphur deposits, across hot streams, through sharp and dense canebreaks, or to stumble over rocks, knee-deep in water as hot as could be endured.

At length we descend from a little table of sulphur deposit, by a few rugged crags, to a small grassy flat, strewn with black boulders, on the north bank of the river, which dashes a few feet below us. It is fringed with a dense line of waving reeds and tamarisk plumes; while to the west, only three yards from our first tent, the largest of the hot springs skips down, in one tiny cascade after another, with a cloud of steam overhanging it, and its temperature 130° Fahr., to join the river, ten yards below us. At the junction was a large flat stone, which we constituted our bath-room. On it we could undress, sponge, and take a dip (at least with our feet, if too hot for the body to bear), and

MEDICINAL BATHS. 255

then turn to the other side of the stone, and in a deep pool have a cold, or at least cool, bath. Surely this is the height of luxury — a Turkish and medicinal bath combined *au naturel!*

From our camp we could see down the ravine to its opening, down the far-stretching gorge, where the hills of Judah form a background, the Frank Mountain, the chief feature, framed in a rich moulding, on the one side of basalt columns, and on the other of bright red sandstone.

This marvelous place is historically famous as the resort of Herod the Great, who sought it in his last illness, to find relief from its medicinal baths. It is especially interesting as having been visited by only three or four parties of Europeans in modern times. Irby and Mangles in 1818, the Duc de Luynes in 1864, and Dr. Chaplin, of Jerusalem, with Mr. Klein, were the only travelers who seem to have actually visited the springs. Burckhardt passed to the eastward, De Saulcy did not get so far, and Lynch only ascended a mile from the shore. It is, however, described both by Pliny and Josephus, but very shortly. The latter ("Antiq." xvii., 6) merely says that Herod "went beyond the River Jordan, and bathed himself in the warm baths that were at Callirrhoe, which, besides their other general virtues, were also fit to drink. And this water runs into the lake called Asphalitis."*

* Ποταμόν τε περάσας Ἰορδάνην, θερμοῖς τοῖς κατὰ Καλλιρόην αὑτὸν παρεδίδου, ἅπερ σὺν τῇ ἐς πάντ' ἀρετῇ καὶ πότιμά ἐστιν. Ἔξεισι δὲ τὸ ὕδωρ τοῦτο εἰς λίμνην τὴν ἀσφαλτοφόρον λεγομένην.

On the statement of the potability of the water, it may be observed that, though impregnated with sulphur, we found some of the warm springs not at all nauseous, and drank of them freely, while we were there, without inconvenience. The water only slightly flavored our tea.

Pliny's account is as brief, but not so accurate. Placing Machærus on the south, instead of the east, side of the Dead Sea, he says, "On the same side is the hot spring of Callirrhoe, with medicinal virtues, proclaiming in its very name the fame of its waters." —*Pliny*, v., 17.*

This is almost the only reference of Pliny to the country east of the Dead Sea. In a subsequent paragraph, in his account of the Essenes, he incidentally shows that the contrast in fertility between the east and west sides of the lake was noticeable in his time; for he speaks of the Jewish anchorets on the west side as avoiding the unwholesome shore, but living in society among the palm-trees, which do not approach the shore on the west side, though they grow to the water's edge on the east.

Ptolemy's description of this region is extremely vague; and though he mentions Callirrhoe as on the east of Jordan, he inserts Jazer between it and Machærus, and separates these altogether from the province of Arabia, in which he places the neighboring

---

* Eodem latere est calidus fons medicæ salubritatis, Callirrhoe, aquarum gloriam ipso nomine præferens.

towns of Ziza and Zoar; while Masada is transferred from Judea to Arabia Petræa. Kerak, however, he gives in its proper location, under the form of Characmoab (Χαρακμῶαβ).

To describe Callirrhoe itself is almost as difficult as to photograph it. The latter we found impossible, so far as to obtain a general view of the gorge; for from no place could a complete view of the whole be got into the camera. Buried in a deep cleft of the magnificent ravine, the Callirrhoe gives no signs of its neighborhood to the traveler on the heights, or on the lower plateau, which we called the Terrace. It is only on approaching the northern edge of this that one sees the chasm, with its sides sometimes rugged and sloping, a mass of basaltic boulders; or when we look farther down the course of the stream, built in by a wall of columnar basalt, like Staffa or Iona, but 1200 feet sheer.

Looking to the northern side, the general appearance of the face differs much from the southern. Less steep, but more impracticable, and 200 feet higher, the white limestone is unbroken by basaltic streams, and barely tinted with vegetation till near the bottom of the ravine, where the red sandstone appears. From this point it is thickly scarped by deep and precipitous nullahs running down to the stream, each of them a mass of canebrakes hollowed by the runs of wild boar, and tall palm-trees waving over them. From the foot of each issues a hot spring; or else a little purling rivulet of smoking-hot sulphurous water winds its way down, and then, near the bottom, becomes a series of tiny cascades.

Great black cliffs of sulphurous deposit fringe the north bank, some of them fifty feet high, and some even 150, formed by the incrustation from the mineral springs, which is still rapidly increasing. Even these black and volcanic-looking tables are covered with strange and unwonted plants, some of them mentioned in detail by Josephus, and referred to subsequently in this chapter.

For Roman ruins, or any traces of the residence of Herod during his sojourn here, we searched in vain; nor are any coins left on the surface, as there were in the time of Irby and Mangles. No wonder; for so rapidly formed is the sulphurous deposit, that any thing the Romans built must now be many feet below the surface. The river and the hot torrents simply keep their channels open, burying themselves deeper every year.

It is to be observed that, while all the basalt is on the south, all the springs issue from the north, and that they all emerge just at the junction of the red sandstone and the limestone. The stratification does not appear to have been much disturbed; but higher up in the ravine the line of the basalt, resting perfectly horizontally on the limestone, is finely shown. There the wady seems to have been filled in with a mass of conglomerate, of which a pudding-stone, formed principally of well-rounded basaltic blocks, a yard square, is the chief ingredient. Through this filling in the torrent has gradually again worn its way, leaving the huge boulders, which render passage almost impossible.

The nullahs, studded with palms, are undoubtedly the features of the valley; and every one of them supplies a hot spring, which sometimes emerges at the top, and comes dashing down; and at others, bubbles up with tremendous force at the foot, just where the conglomerate begins.

In a reach of three miles there are ten principal springs. The first, which is not very hot, and only slightly sulphurous, consists of five distinct little springs, which issue from the ground under the rocks, on a little plateau at the base of the cañon. The second, third, and fourth are similar springs, issuing from the foot of palm nullahs, or cañons, above where our camp was placed, each hotter and more strongly impregnated than the last.

The fifth, that already mentioned, which passed close by our tents, is the largest of all, temperature 130° Fahr., and rises at the very top of its ravine, half a mile up, at the foot of a cliff, in a mass of brush-wood overhung by palms. Before it reaches the open below, it receives two considerable tributaries, bubbling out of the earth and rising several inches in the air. Here it has formed one sulphur terrace after another. At the base of one of them is a curious phenomenon — a group of palm-stems completely petrified into a sort of white, powdery chalk, which crumbles at the touch. The steam of this cascade can be seen at the distance of a mile or two.

The sixth spring starts only at the foot of its nullah. The seventh and eighth springs, the most remarkable, and perhaps the most characteristic of all, start very near together, half a mile lower down than our camp, very high up, but still at the base of their little ravine. Hence there has once descended a sloping platform of sandstone, which has now been raised to a large flat terrace of sulphur crust and black deposit, burying, I suspect, the old Roman baths.

The two springs bubble forth at the foot of a cliff with amazing force, each forming at once a basin a few feet in diameter, from which they flow down but a few yards, when they suddenly disappear under the black incrustation, which looks much like a cinder-heap consolidated, and which is by far the largest and most elevated shelf of sulphur deposit in the whole valley. Under a thin crust one can hear the gurgling waters working their way pretty close to the surface, till they reach the edge of the cliff, where they form cascades, or, as the Arabs would say, "water-hills" (*jebel moia*), into the main stream.

The springs evidently have buried themselves in tunnels of their own construction; and elsewhere we could see the process actually going on. The mineral matter is rapidly deposited on each side of the channel; and gradually the spray, which is incessantly leaving its insoluble sediment on the edge of the crust, forms a dome; the key-stone of the arch being, of course, the last step in this natural tunnel-building process.

Over these hidden channels the Arabs had in three places very ingeniously constructed their primitive medicinal baths. A basin had been hollowed out large enough for a man to sit in, and at the bottom a hole perforated down to the stream, about six inches in diameter, through which the sulphurous steam rushed up. The patient strips, squats in the basin, throws his burnoose over the bath, and is steamed as long as he can endure the heat. Our Arabs contrived a still hotter bath, immediately over the first exit of the springs, by an ingenious construction of branches laid across a pile of stones on each side, over which they placed brush-wood crosswise, and then, stripping, placed their cloaks over their heads, and enjoyed a parboiling. Some of our party essayed the experiment with their clothes on, with the uncomfortable result of a hot ducking, which they were not inclined to repeat.

The ninth spring is also very large, but, starting higher up in the ravine, is much cooler before its waters are accessible. The tenth and last spring is the hottest of all, its waters 143° Fahr., and that some way after it has emerged. Though its cascades are not so fine, it adds, perhaps, the largest and most sulphurous volume of water of any of the series. Below these springs the water of the Callirrhoe becomes very gradually cooler, until at its mouth, seven miles down, it registers 70° Fahr.

The Arabs have many strange superstitions and traditions about these springs. We had the greatest difficulty in keeping our men in good humor during our eight days' camp here, in spite of the abundance of forage, food, and water, and, still more, the opportunity it gave them of indulging in that sweetest of Arab luxuries, the "dolce far niente," because of a proverb, "Take thy bath at the Zerka Ma'in, thank Allah, and be gone." They have a firm belief that the evil spirits let out the water from the lower regions because of its healing properties, lest it should assuage the pains of the condemned; but, at the same time, that they are too near for any one to escape injury who exposes himself after night-fall to their influence.

Another tradition is that the springs were opened by a servant of King Solomon, who had discovered these sources of healing to be very near the crust of the earth, and who therefore dispatched this man to tap them, selecting him because of his deafness, lest he should be deterred by the threats of the Evil One.

In connection with this superstition, we saw the only instance of the practice of sacrifice I ever met with among the Bedouin. On Sunday our muleteers begged for a lamb for dinner, which we gave them. This they carried up to the source of the bath springs, and then chanted long invocations to the deaf servant of King Solomon, who had made these fountains, to hear them, and to preserve to the waters their healing virtues. They then performed a number of strange incantations, stretched the lamb on its back, cut its throat over the spring, kindled a fire, and roasted it whole. As soon as it was cooked, they ate the inwards, and then the rest of the flesh on the spot, quoting verses of the Koran, and singing deprecatory verses against the powers of evil, during the whole of their feast. When they had finished, the bones of the sacrifice were carefully collected, and, with the ashes of the fire, were calcined by fresh fuel, and finally were all cast into the spring, to avert, as they told us, the ill consequences of the Evil Eye, which had been upon us for our presumptuous camping in the home of the spirits.

The botanical peculiarities of Callirrhoe must strike even the most unobservant visitor. One plant, an asclepiad (*Dæmia cordata*), which we called "Josephus," from the historian's grotesque description of its appearance and properties, we think we have rediscovered. It grows but sparingly, only on the "moraines" of the chief sulphur spring, and just below its "glacier." A twining shrub, it supports itself upon itself, the young branches clinging to the dead stems of the previous year. The flower is small, of a dull purple, with a perfectly white centre; the fruit large, in pairs, and of a most extraordinary shape, something like the pines of an Indian shawl pattern, and exuding an astringent, milky juice when broken. Its seeds are in a long string, each winged with a fine cottony down, like the "osher."

Another plant of very limited area, which we only

observed on the sulphur and the basalt rocks near it, we named the sulphur plant. It is a crucifer, not unlike a wall-flower in form and growth, with its root orange, its stem and bark sulphur color, its leaves and fruit-pods a brick-dust orange, and its flowers a paler orange. Every portion of it reeked with the odor of sulphur, and altogether it had a most jaundiced look.

Splendid orobanches, of two species in particular, one pinkish purple, the other bright yellow, thrive on the roots of the *Atriplex halimus*, sometimes in large tufts, each flower-stalk more than three feet high, and covered with blossom from the ground upward. An exquisite rose-colored geranium abounds among the stones. Where the soil is a little richer than usual, it is a mass of the night-scented stock; and the interstices of the rock are gay with scarlet ranunculus and masses of sorrel and cyclamen.

Butterflies of gorgeous hue and great size, papiliones, and danaides; charaxes, thaïs, and parnassia, hover over the shrubs. All the birds—which had been the novelties and prizes of my first expedition to the shores of the Dead Sea—the short-tailed whistling raven (*Corvus affinis*), the bulbul, the bush babbler, the Moabite sparrow, and many a rare warbler, inhabit the thickets or scan the cliffs above them; while on the green spots between impassible precipices both above and below us, we can see the ibex feeding, and tossing back their huge horns till they seem to strike their tails as they bound from rock to rock.

In spite of the interruption of the sacrifice to Solomon's servant, against which we vainly remonstrated with our Arabs, by pleading the laws of Mohammed, which forbade it as idolatry, we rarely enjoyed so quiet a rest-day as our Sunday at the Callirrhoe. In the quiet seclusion of that deep glen, after a week of such hard and absorbing work, there was a delicious absence of all that could distract from the holier and higher thoughts of the day; while the incident of the martyrdom of John the Baptist, in the second lesson, could nowhere have been read more appropriately than almost under the shadow of its scene. Not less in exact harmony with the place and events was Keble's hymn for the day.

High as is the reputation of Solomon's Springs among the Bedouin for their healing virtues, the presence of a "hakim," even though an infidel dog, seemed more attractive to the sufferers in the neighborhood; for many were the visitors from Hamideh camps who found their way down in the afternoon to seek medicine for themselves or their friends—some of them not empty-handed. We had, in passing camps on the heights, been invited to prescribe in various cases, comprising blindness, club-foot, congenital lameness, and stiff joint of twenty years' standing. It was difficult to persuade these mountaineers that any thing was beyond the skill of a European. Our excuses were always put down to ill-will, for they look upon medicine as a sort of magic. Some cases we could relieve, and one grateful wife this afternoon brought with her a kid-skin full of fresh butter ("butter of kine"), the first we had seen during our journey, and which she offered for a very modest price.

Another Beni Hamideh brought in an ibex he had shot, and which proved excellent venison. So we did not fare ill for our Sunday dinner. The luxury of fresh butter we owed to our being now in the territory of the Hamideh, the only tribe we met with east of Jordan who keep horned cattle in any numbers. The Beni Sakk'r have none, for they are wholly unfitted to endure the long migrations of that tribe, though the highlands seem as well adapted for cattle as for sheep. The people of Kerak have only a few, and those at a distance from the city.

But the Hamideh, in these rocky defiles possessing fresh pasturage shaded from the summer sun, and also open table-lands among the hills for winter feeding, find their cattle the most profitable stock next to goats. Camels they have none, and horses very few, but have considerable herds of asses. The cattle are very small, rough as a Scotch kylo, horned, and scarcely larger than the little Brittany race. I do not remember that we ever saw any other color than black. Among the Belka Arabs is a different breed of cattle, much larger, and very varied in color.

Unlike the sheep, the cattle do not, as yet, find their way across Jordan to the markets of Jerusalem or Nablous. Beef is a costly luxury, for the bullocks are as valuable for the plow as the heifers are for milch kine.

CHAPTER XIV.

Visit to Machærus.— Delays at Starting.— Superstitions and Obstinacy of Muleteers.— Wady Z'gara.— Deep Gorge.— Fine Landscape.— Ruins of Machærus.— The Town.— Roman Road.— Fortress.— Citadel.— Dungeons.— The Baptist's Prison.— Pliny's Account.— History of Machærus.— Josephus's Description.— The Maccabees.— Herod the Great.— Fabled Plant.— Siege by L. Bassus.— Identity of the Castle with the Baptist's Prison.— Hamideh Hospitality.— Fresh Butter.— Grand Panorama.— Stone Circles.— Expedition to Attarus.— Horses lost and found.— A wooded District.— View.— Jebel Attarus.— Kureiyat.— Identity with Kiriathaim.— Attarus and Ataroth.

Our first care, after settling camp at the hot springs of Callirrhoe, was to ascertain the site of Machærus, and pay a visit to that spot, which has been vaguely mentioned by two or three travelers (who have followed the account of Josephus) as being on the south side of the Callirrhoe, near the hot springs, but which has not been visited by any one.

To explore the castle where John the Baptist was imprisoned and beheaded, and which became so famous by its desperate resistance in the Jewish war against Titus and the Romans, had been a long-cherished day-dream, at length to be accomplished. It is strange that, in spite of its historical interest, we should have been the first Western travelers since the Roman times who have ever explored it; for the place, though lying out of the track from north to south, is well known to all the neighboring tribes; and its name is unchanged—M'khaur, the exact Arabic transliteration of the Greek Μαχαίρους of Josephus.

We were disappointed of an early start, for Daoud, a servant, and a donkey boy who had been with us on an expedition the day before, and had charge of the camera, had lost their way on the top of the pass, and, belated in the darkness, had slept at a Beni Hamideh camp. Daoud had the housekeeping keys with him, and the prospects of breakfast were poor; but the ingenious Trotter soon extemporized some tackle and secured a good dish of fish in the pools above the entrance of the hot water, while we enjoyed our vapor baths *au naturel*.

Meantime the muleteers, seeing indications of a prolonged sojourn, threatened a mutiny, and prognosticated every kind of evil from man and demon. Pestilence, robbery, and nocturnal visits from the servant of Solomon, so rudely disturbed in his haunts, were the least of the evils inevitable on our stay. Muleteers are certainly typical Bourbons. They learn nothing, and they forget nothing. Abundant as is the herbage of the glen, the horses and mules were daily driven a weary climb up to the heights, lest the sprites should bewitch them; and, delicious as is the water in the stream and pools above the hot springs, teeming with fish, no animal was allowed to drink it, because it was warm, and the convoy were daily watered at some dirty rain-pools above the pass.

Our men were only reduced to submission in the matter of staying here by a reference to their contract, and the assurance that, if they threw obstacles in our way, they would but prolong our sojourn.

At length we started, with a Beni Hamideh sheik for our only guide, and a muleteer with the photographic apparatus. We turned upon the south side, and reached the lower plateau, or terrace, in an hour exactly. The chinks and crannies of the rocks abounded in new and interesting plants, among which the crane's-bill was conspicuous. Just before we started, an intelligent Beni Sakk'r brought in a geranium which even he recognized as rare and curious, and which he had not before seen. It was an exquisite plant, with rich crimson petals, and the centre of the calyx a deep purple. The singular sulphur-loving crucifer was plentiful, and our botanist was bewildered and overpowered by the wild profusion of floral novelties.

Arrived at the terrace, we found it a wide, stony ledge, quite flat, and well covered with herbage, extending back about a mile and a half, and 875 feet above the river's bed at the point where we climbed. The northern side of the cleft opposite to us descends without any such break, from the centre of the mountains to the bottom. Riding due south, we scrambled up the outer ridge of the inclosing range; and in an hour more we were on the water-shed of the pass, looking down into the next wady, a stupendous ravine, very short, and beginning most abruptly from a scarped cleft in the Moab range, which suddenly becomes a sheer precipice, slightly overhanging, 800 feet high, and which must in rainy weather be a magnificent water-fall. It is named Wady Z'gara.

The gorge seems to go down to the Dead Sea, which could not be more than four or five miles distant in a straight line, by a series of steps, 3800 feet; and at the mouth of the wady we could see the little green plain and the heap of stones which mark the site of Zareth-shahar, or Zara, the only town of Reuben on the shore.

The western shore of the lake was spread before us from the northern almost to the southern end, and the rugged and barren-looking plateau of Judea seemed to lie far below us. Jerusalem, Bethlehem, and the hills of Hebron, the dark oasis of Engedi, all stood out clearly before us. To the north there stretched the plain of Jordan, shining bare, sulphurous, and desolate, with a silver thread issuing from the desert waste into the sea. One dark-green patch alone relieved its death-like pallor—the green oasis of Jericho. Mount Gilead stood out to the north, but the haze prevented our enjoying a further view, and we watched a thunder-storm bursting over Jerusalem.

Descending to the south, we rode round the head of Wady Z'gara, on the brink of the rocky ledge, where the wady suddenly becomes an abyss; and as our horses walked or ambled on the fringe of rock, not more than three feet wide, at the edge of the crescent-shaped fall, overhanging it instead of retiring, it needed a steady head to look down, with scarce a foot-breadth between the horse's steps and the edge.

Mounting the next ridge, which runs westward from the backbone range of Moab, we soon came on an old Roman road, which had formed a paved way from the Callirrhoe to the Herodian fortress, but which is now merely a rugged line of upturned squared stones.

Following by its side, we passed a bold, prominent cone, with flattened top, and an immense heap of stones, the remains of some old city on the ridge at its shoulder, and soon after reached the ruins of M'khaur—the town, not the fortress. They covered perhaps a larger area than any site we had yet visited; but though we rode through and through, we could not find a single relic worth photographing.

The ruins occupy a group of undulating hillocks, and cover, in solid mass, more than a square mile of ground. The place can never have been strategically defensible, and must have depended for its security on the castle above. Round the ruins, on all sides, are gentle slopes, rising into the surrounding and higher hills.

These slopes are all cultivated for corn (rather a novel sight to us) by the Hamideh, whose neighborhood was also indicated by the equally unusual occurrence of a small herd of horned cattle feeding. Among these rugged mountains we are out of the land of camels, and are in the hill country of cows and asses.

One ruin, M'khaur, possessed, in common with the more eastern Moabite cities, a small temple toward the sunrising, on exactly the same plan, and of the same size, as those already described at Zebib and Um Weleed. It is plain, therefore, that, up to a period not far removed from its final destruction, fanatic as may have been its Jewish population, there must have been a large proportion, either Greek or Syrian, who enjoyed full liberty to practice the rites of the sun-god worship.

Having looked down the wells of M'khaur, in one of which we found water, while perhaps over a hundred into which we peered were dry and choked up with stones, we turned to the north-west, where, separated from us by a narrow and deep valley, not quite a mile across, stood the ancient fortress, on the top of a conical hill. The line of access was clearly marked by an old Roman road, the line of which we followed, which wound, by a somewhat circuitous course, to the southward.

Arrived at the southern shoulder of the cone, we skirted its base, at the same level as the town we had left. Below us, in a deep valley covered with rich herbage, was a Bedouin camp, from which several armed men joined us. Riding round the hill, we climbed a lower ridge on the west side, whence the summit is easily accessible, and dismounted.

The citadel was placed on the summit of the cone, which is the apex of a long flat ridge running for more than a mile from west to east. The whole of this ridge appears to have been one extensive fortress, the key of which was the keep on the top of the cone, an isolated and almost impregnable work, but very small, being circular, and exactly one hundred yards in diameter. The wall of circumvallation can be clearly traced, its foundations all standing out for a yard or two above the surface; but the interior remains are few. One well of great depth, a very large and deep oblong cemented cistern, with the vaulting of the roof still remaining, and—most interesting of all—two dungeons, one of them deep, and its sides scarcely broken in, were the only remains clearly to be defined. That these were dungeons, and not cisterns, is evident from there being no traces of cement, which never perishes from the walls of ancient reservoirs, and from the small holes still visible in the masonry, where staples of wood and iron had once been fixed. One of these must surely have been the prison-house of John the Baptist.

Descending on the western side 150 yards, by a very steep slope, we reach the oblong flat plateau which formed the fortified city, at the east end of which, just under the keep, is the wonderful pile of stones, the carefully-collected material of the once formidable fortress.

There is a weird-like desolation about it, though not the savage nakedness of Sebbeh (Masada); for vegetation is abundant, and the hills are all covered with herbage. Yet that heap stands out most spectrally, 3800 feet above the Dead Sea. Behind us rose several higher, but rounded and featureless, summits; and Jebel Attarus was hid by intervening hills. The view in front, of the west side of the Dead Sea and

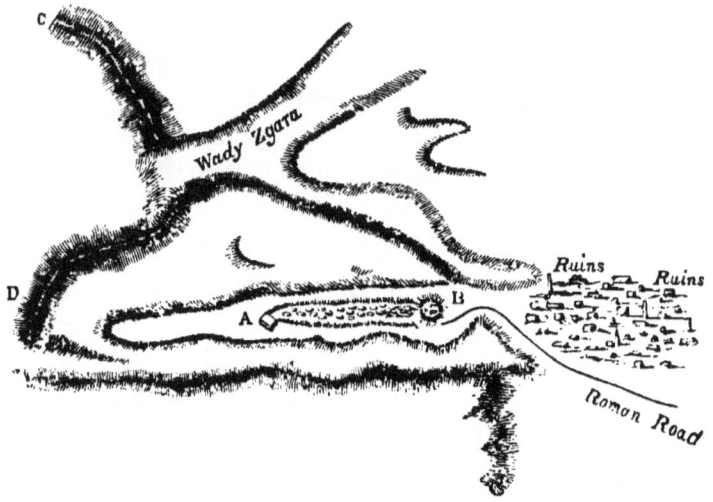

NO. 28. PLAN OF MACHÆRUS, AND THE RAVINES ROUND IT.

A, Square Fort. B, Citadel. C—D, Western Valley of Josephus.

the hill country of Judea, with Jerusalem and Nebi Samwîl, was simply grand, the details similar to those of the view from the ridge we had crossed in the morning.

Walking along the ridges to the west, we found, at the distance of a mile, the foundations of two square towers, which had evidently been the outworks of Herod's citadel. Our examination was interrupted by a heavy thunder-storm, from which, however, we found a convenient refuge in a cave on the east side of the cone, large enough to shelter all our party and our horses.

The history of Machærus is interwoven with that of the last struggle of the Jews against Rome, and its site is accurately described by Josephus. Pliny also mentions it, but with less accuracy, placing it, correctly enough, to the west of the Arabian nomads, but to the south, instead of the east, of the Dead Sea. He also calls it the second fortress of the Jews, next after Jerusalem (Pliny, v., 16). But that his statement of its position, south of the lake, is an inadvertence, is evident from the subsequent paragraph, in which he states that it is on the same side as the springs of Callirrhoe. Machærus is also mentioned by Strabo (lib. xvi.) among the fortresses on the east side, not far from Jericho.

But it is from Josephus that we derive the fullest account of this fortress and its eventful history. It was one of the many places east of Jordan fortified by the Asmonean dynasty, at the period when the Jews, under the Maccabees, had recovered more absolute power over these outlying regions than their nation had ever exercised since the disruption of the kingdom after the death of Solomon—the period to which we may most reasonably assign the building of those crowded cities whose ruins stud the plains and hills of Moab.

Alexander, the son of Hyrcanus I., the builder of the remarkable castle of Arak el Emir, was its founder; and after his death his widow, Alexandra, handed it over to her son Aristobulus. Taken and destroyed by Gabinius, it was restored immediately afterward. But it was Herod the Great, the builder of Masada and Herodium, who rendered it the most formidable fortress of the eastern side. Perceiving at once its importance, as the south-eastern outpost of his kingdom, he lavished all the engineering resources of the age on its fortifications, and laid up within its walls an enormous supply of military material, and provisions for the support of a besieged garrison.

Josephus describes its position at some length, and certainly with some exaggeration. But the details of his description are easily identified on the spot. He states ("Jewish War," vii., 6) that the walled portion of the place was situated on a very rocky hill, elevated to a great height, thus clearly distinguishing between the fortress on the ridge, just described, and the wide open town which we had previously visited.

The historian next describes, but neither distinctly nor accurately, the four valleys which form its defense. That which cuts it to the west he states to be sixty stadia in length, as far as the lake, agreeing pretty accurately with our calculation of its distance from the sea. This he considers the deepest of all the valleys; but he represents three of them as so deep that the eye can not reach their bottom, and that it would be impossible to throw an embankment across them. The latter statement is certainly true, and the former is an ordinary Oriental hyperbole; and if, as I conceive, Josephus speaks not from personal acquaintance with the locality, but from the descriptions of others, it is very possible that he has confused the deep valley to the north with the ravine of the Wady Z'gara just beyond it, which is far more abrupt, and down the dizzy gorge of which it is not easy to gaze steadily from its edge.

Strategically, the valleys north and south may have been impassable; but they are not so precipitous as might be understood from the description. The valley to the eastward, a branch from the southern gorge, is certainly not less than Josephus represents it—one hundred cubits—and is very steep.

The wall of the citadel is stated to have been 160 cubits in height, and to have embraced the royal palace. Of these, of course, there are no traces, excepting the foundations and the enormous pile of stones mentioned above.

Still less can we identify the gigantic species of rue, which Josephus describes as large as a fig-tree, with its marvelous properties. Some light is, however, thrown on the myth by the description in the next paragraph of the root *Baaras*, which is of a flame color, growing in a place of the same name, evidently in the Callirrhoe, which the historian speaks of as "the valley that encompasses the place on the north side." It is needless to repeat the grotesque account of the properties of this plant, or the method of obtaining it. We imagined we had discovered the plant which gave origin to the fable, in the strange crucifer, growing by the baths on sulphur deposits, with root, leaves, bark, and blossom, all of the odor and color of sulphur.

The siege of Machærus was made by L. Bassus on the east, the only side where an intrenchment could be attempted. The garrison at once abandoned the lower city to its fate, and concentrated all their efforts on the defense of the well-provisioned fortress. By incessant sorties they interrupted and baffled the Roman works; and hence we find no remains, as at Masada, of the great mound of the assailants. The place at length capitulated, in order to save the life of a young, noble, and popular leader, Eleazar, who had been captured by the Romans in one of the sallies; and thenceforward Machærus never appears in history.

But its all-absorbing interest to us is, of course, its connection with the imprisonment and death of John the Baptist. It is curious to note that Josephus records it as the fortress to which Herod relegated his wife, the daughter of Aretas, king of the Arabians, when she discovered and resented his guilty passion for his sister-in-law Herodias; and that it was also selected by him as the prison of the Baptist, persecuted on her account.

There has been some difficulty raised as to the correctness of this statement, because Josephus immediately afterward ("Antiq.," xviii., v. 2) adds that Machærus, at the time Herod sent away his wife, was subject to Aretas. He had before stated that it was on the frontier of the kingdoms of Aretas and Herod.

But as the queen immediately fled from it to her father's residence at Petra, the probable explanation would seem to be that Herod, during the time of his connection with Aretas, had allowed him to occupy it, though he soon afterward resumed it. We have seen already that he had fortified it, and laid in great stores of warlike materials; and he visited it in his last illness. It is, therefore, in the highest degree improbable that he ever allowed it to pass completely out of his hands; and the account of John's imprisonment is too precise to admit of the supposition of a mistake on the part of Josephus, respecting an event which must have attracted the deepest interest and attention. We can not, therefore, relinquish the conviction that, standing on Machærus, we are on the scene of one of the most thrilling and tragic events in Gospel history.

As we came down from the citadel, the Hamideh from the camp below, who had attached themselves to us for the whole morning, and had most civilly attended us, insisted on our going to the bottom of the southern valley, to visit their camp. As it lay not far out of our course, it was difficult to refuse their hospitality. They were shepherds, certainly not rich, but knew how to give welcome to strangers. About a dozen tents were stretched in a row along the bottom, where there was only level space enough in front to tether the black cattle. These form the chief wealth of the clan, and are brought down, like the sheep, from the mountains every night. Horses they had none. The men were all, with the exception of our hosts, absent with their herds; and as we passed along, the women and troops of little children at once disappeared.

We were ushered into the farthest and largest tent, which had the women's apartments curtained off at each wing, and was entirely destitute of furniture. Carpets were promptly brought from within, and spread in a circle, and a huge bowl of buttermilk at once passed round. Most grateful was the beverage. We expected nothing more, and motioned to depart; but our hosts solemnly signaled to us to remain. In vain we pointed to the sun, already turning to the westward, and reckoned the hours we had to ride. The old man, who seemed to be the chief, sitting next Hayne, affectionately embraced his neck, and gently stroked his stomach, while his guest despondingly mused over the plants he should miss if we had to hurry back under the shades of evening.

Soon savory fumes were wafted over the black hair partition which shut in the women's apartment. The wife of our host made her appearance, actually sat down in front of us, and talked with our Hamideh sheik, to whose tribe this camp belonged. She was fair, and had remarkably fine and well-cut features, with a refined cast of countenance, and must have been beautiful when young. She was, apparently, about forty years of age. We heard her recount the ailments of an invalid who, as far as I could understand, was suffering from liver complaint. Being told

I was a "hakeem," the sick man came out, and detailed his symptoms. Being without an interpreter, I was obliged to rely on my own Arabic lore, and desired them to send the next day for such medicines as I could supply.

At length the savory dishes appeared—first, a great pile of smoking hot bread, or rather flat cakes, deliciously baked, and the best we had tasted since we left home; next, a great wooden bowl with several pounds of fresh butter, clean, and just churned. Fresh butter we had never found in our travels before the Zerka, and it was indeed a luxury. Taking a flat loaf apiece, with each morsel we pinched up, Arab fashion, a good lump of butter; and I do not think we got through much less than half a pound of the dainty per head. The presence of a herd of black cattle—unwonted sight—on the slopes behind explained the phenomenon of butter. A little tobacco and shot was all the compliment we could offer in return; but we were able to satisfy the hopes of the children, who toddled round the circle for a kiss, with a silver piece for each; and we left in good odor with our wild hosts.

We found an easier route by the head of the Wady Z'gara, on our return, and accomplished the ride back in two hours and a half. On the top of the ridge, between M'khaur and Z'gara, we had a yet finer view than in the morning. Here, for the first and only time, I have looked on the Dead Sea in unbroken length from south to north. Description is out of the question. Beneath was spread the Lisan—the salt mountain and the opening of Wady Zuweirah to the south; to the north, the mouth of the Jordan, with the dreary Ghor, the fertile Jericho, and the cleft of the Kelt up to Jerusalem. Along the farther shore were Sebbeh, Engedi, Feshkhah, and the range of white cliffs, backed by the rugged hills of Judea seamed with fissures. A grand thunder-storm clearing, gave shadows and rain mists, and lent distance and indefiniteness to the view. Far to the right was Kurn Surtabeh, half-way to the lake of Galilee, and Mount Gilead to the north. Still the haze veiled Hermon. The foreground was one of surpassing grandeur; peaks and unfathomable-looking ravines — red, white, and black, as sandstone, limestone, or basalt, predominated—seemed to tumble in wild confusion, one on the top of another, till they plunged into the blue waters of the sea; and still the little green oasis of Zara showed, in the opening of the chasm, in front of us.

We saw many rare and interesting birds to-day, and many fine plants rewarded Hayne's enthusiasm. The scarlet anemone carpeted the higher grounds, the equally gorgeous ranunculus the lower dells. Several pairs of Tristram's grakle, with their ringing, bell-like whistle, showed themselves, but, when shot, fell hopelessly into the abyss; and a large flock of over a hundred of the rare wedge-tailed raven (*Corvus affinis*) wheeled for half an hour over our heads as we descended to the Callirrhoe.

In the course of this excursion we found, especially on the plateau, several curious circles of stones, similar to those which have been described in the wilderness of Sinai, and evidently the work of the prehistoric inhabitants of the country. They are not so large as the stone circle near Bethel, known as the stones of Beitin, and are composed entirely of basaltic boulders. In this district we observed seven or eight such circles, and repeatedly came upon them afterward; but here they were not associated with the dolmens, so abundant to the north of the Callirrhoe. The largest blocks were not above four feet in diameter, and were neatly arranged in a circle of a hundred yards or more in diameter. The small size of the stones seems to show that the men who raised them had no idea of quarrying blocks for this purpose, but contented themselves with the material that came easiest to hand. But the absence of dolmens suggests that they may be the work of a tribe whose mode of sepulture was different from that of their neighbors, as here were many small tumuli, varying in character from those which occur in the dolmen district.

Another expedition from the hot springs was to Attarus, the ancient Ataroth, situated about three or four miles east of Machærus, and to Kurciyat, an ancient Kiriathaim, Kirjathaim, or Kerioth (Numb. xxxii., 37; Josh. xii., 19; Ezek. xxv., 9; Jer. xlviii., 24).

Three of our horses had been missing for three days, supposed to be stolen; and we had some hopes that, if they had only strayed, they might be recovered on the line of country which leads by Attarus to the highlands. Charged urgently by our muleteers to sweep the country for their lost beasts, we felt ourselves like Saul traveling after his father's asses. The owner of one of the horses wept like a child as he implored us to find them. Poor fellow, his whole fortune had been invested in his horse, and he owed half the price in Jerusalem, where, returning horseless, he must go to prison for his debt; and out of the three shillings a day he received from us, he could do little to make up the money.

Our fame as hakims had spread by this time, and no less than three parties did we meet on their way to camp for medical aid. The first part of our road was the same as that to Machærus; but when we had mounted to the crest of the ridge, we left the hill of M'khaur on our right, and wound round the next set of hills by the side of an ancient roadway, of which the engineering, well managed, as it skirted each shoulder, though now worse than useless, could be easily traced. The road was evidently in connection with the one which led down from Machærus and Callirrhoe to Zara and the sea. We passed an old site, El Hamman, and, winding among deep-cut valleys, we crossed a charming little stream in a miniature ravine, Wady 'K'nif, an affluent of the Callirrhoe.

The little wadys, rocky and green, were full of bushes, and on the slopes were patches of cultivation. Wheat, barley, and tobacco were laid down, as we mounted 2500 feet above our camp, and 3500 feet above the sea. Turning sharply to the south, a steep ascent brought us to Kirbet Attarus.

Unwrought stones lying in heaps, ranges of broken walls, lines of foundations scattered over a long ridge, large caverns and circular cisterns—such is all that remains of Ataroth. Out of the caves were, generally, growing fig-trees or gnarled old terebinths. A new feature in the district into which we had entered were the number of isolated and venerable trees with which it was dotted, chiefly terebinths, none of them in woods or groves, but growing on hill-tops, sides, or valleys, alike—everywhere singly, solitary sentinels, hanging out signals of distress to their next neighbor.

The view from the ruined keep is wide and grand. The day was superb, a fresh breeze and warm sun, a delicious air, like one of the first days of summer in England, the horizon perfectly clear; Bethlehem and Jerusalem, Gerizim and Gilboa, visible with the glass, across the sea; Shihan peering over the plain on the south; while eastward many a little dot on the wide plain betokened to us the position of the places among which we had been roaming for the last month, as Um Rasas and Ziza. But the castle hill of Machærus, only three or four miles to the west, was shut out by the intervening range, which left us no view of the gorge of the Dead Sea, excepting the corner by the plain of Jericho.

Though Ataroth has been on the top of a hill, yet the summit is a wide flat platform. From this a gentle slope and rise leads us, by the side of an ancient Roman road, through a park-like country, to Jebel Attarus, the old citadel, distant an hour's walk. The fortress is actually lower than the town, but, being an isolated mamelon, is more easily defensible, and has evidently been strongly fortified. The ride was in-

NO. 29. TEREBINTH-TREE ON ATTARUS.

teresting and refreshing, varied by patches of green corn and trees; and though the terebinths were still bare and leafless, the almond-trees were already in flower, clothed with a sheet of rosy white, to say nothing of red-berried Oriental mistletoe on their limbs, and gorgeous tulips in the crannies of the rocks.

The view from Jebel Attarus is much more circumscribed than that from the town, and the ruins have no special feature of interest. The place is a flat-topped cone, with the foundations of a wall which has once inclosed the whole crest; and an enormous pile of stones in the centre, the débris of some very large fort, forms a cairn some thirty feet high. By the side of the heap grows a fine old terebinth.

Jebel Attarus long did duty for Pisgah. Burckhardt, passing three miles to the eastward, espied the cairn and the tree, and conjectured them to be the remains of the altar and grove of Baal. But no one had mounted the hill to find that the cairn is more than three hundred yards in circumference, and that the prospect is peculiarly circumscribed. It is also far too much to the south and to the east.

No traces of building exist here, other than the fort itself. There is, however, an admirable view of the wadys eastward, which feed the two rivers of Moab. We looked northward into the glen at the junction of the Jiffar, the Habis, and the Ma'in, where the three form the Callirrhoe, or Zerka Ma'in. Southward, we traced the Arnon cleft from Aroer to its mouth; and we could satisfactorily ascertain that the intervening country was featureless, with very few ruins.

We have often found that the Arabs of Moab, like Roderick Dhu's men, start from the hill-sides when least expected. Halt for a few minutes anywhere, though there is no trace of human existence near, very soon some Bedouins will spring up. Here, as we sat down to lunch, up came the brother and mother of Na'ur, the Hamideh sheik, our solitary guide, who were watching their cattle, lest they should stray

NO. 30.   THE ZERKA MA'IN.

among the crops. Then came a stray Beni Sakk'r, an old acquaintance, who had been grievously disappointed to find we had left our previous halt, while he, on hospitable thoughts intent, had hurried off to milk his camels for our benefit. He had followed us three miles, and firmly refused a backsheesh.

But the most satisfactory recognition was that of our horses. The quick eye of the Hamideh soon espied three horses quietly luxuriating in a green patch of wheat on the other side of the hill. They had wandered far, but certainly had good discrimination to find the best pasture. Great was the joy of Daoud, while the Hamideh kissed us all round in an ecstasy of delight. But three days of the sweets of liberty had not yet wearied our steeds, and it was only with much caution, when one of their number had been entrapped, that they were wheedled into following our cavalcade, at a careful distance, back to camp.

Kureiyat was the next place to be visited, about three miles south-east of Attarus, and situated on sister hillocks, half a mile apart, both covered by the ancient city. The ruins are extensive, but utterly featureless; and between them and the Arnon are very few remains of any extent. We can scarcely doubt that this is either Kerioth or Kiriathaim. Whichever it be, the twin hills explain the Hebrew dual and plural terminations, and render superfluous the ingenious conjectures which have been formed on the presumption that the dual termination was merely an attempt to Hebraize a foreign sound. A southern Kureitun, near Kerak, also a twin town, has already been described (p. 114). One of these sets of ruins is, therefore, probably the *Kerioth*, the other the *Kiriathaim* of Jer. xlviii., 23, 24. The Kureiyeh of the Hauran, near Bozrah, seems far too distant to have been grouped with the other Moabite towns named along with Kiriathaim.

Eusebius mentions Kiriathaim as close to the Baris, and ten Roman miles west of Medeba. As this Baris is probably the same as the Baaras of Josephus, it must be either the Zerka Ma'in or one of its affluents; and the account of Eusebius is, therefore, not very incorrect. Burckhardt has suggested the inconsiderable ruins of Et Teim, near Medeba, as Kiriathaim; but he did not visit them. We found them insignificant, and I can see no ground for the conjecture, nor any tenable argument for rejecting the claims of Kureiyat to be the Scriptural site.

Equally clear seems the identification of Kirbet Attarus and Jebel Attarus with the Scriptural Ataroth and Atroth (Numb. xxxii., 34, 35), or Atrothshophan. Here we find the same name repeated. On the spot we find two places of the same name two miles apart. The objection which has been raised against the identification (B. D. *in loco*), that Ataroth is said to have been taken and built by Gad, whose southern frontier was Heshbon, falls to the ground, when we observe (Numb. xxxii., 34) that precisely the same objection would apply to Dibon and Aroer, still farther south than Attarus, and about which there is no question. The true solution seems to be that Gad and Reuben were much intermingled, like Judah and Simeon.

CHAPTER XV.

Visit to Zara, the ancient Zareth-shahar.—Volcanic Soil.—Rich Botany.—Descent to Dead Sea.—Ancient Road.—Scouts ahead.—False Alarm.—Beni Sakk'r and their Camels.—Vegetation and Springs of Zara.—Hebrew City.—Baths, hot and cold.—Birds.—Along the Shore.—Rugged Path.—Mouth of the Callirrhoe.—Romantic Glen.—The Ibex-hunter.—A rough Scramble.—Water-fall.—Home at last.—Sunday in the Gorge.—The Ibex and its Habits.—Unsuccessful Hunt.—The Hakim.—Medical Cases.—Ornithology of the Callirrhoe.—Our Postman robbed.—Topography of the District.

HAVING climbed the hills and traced the feeders of the Callirrhoe to their mountain sources, our next aim was to get down to the shore of the Dead Sea by the unvisited Zara, the "Zareth-shahar in the mount of the valley" of Joshua xiii., 19; and afterward to explore the coast about the mouth of the Callirrhoe.

Warned by our guides that this could not be accomplished in one day, and that the roads were all but impracticable, we started, prepared to sleep out, with a compact supply of good food; water we were sure to find. Vainly did our Arabs protest against the idea of sleeping in the open, and conjured up alarms of Beni Atiyeh and all sorts of "Titchmanns," or murderous enemies, who were in the habit of prowling in this no-man's land. We knew that, accompanied by Zadam, we need not fear any thing worse than an attempt at horse-stealing.

The sun had not risen when we were off; and on making the platform on the top of the pass, we turned toward the south-west. The plain was everywhere covered with broken fragments of basalt, few of them more than ten pounds weight. We had with us Zadam and two muleteers with camera, etc., mounted; while two Beni Sakk'r and three Hamideh on foot, with their long guns, completed the party.

At the end of the plateau we begin to ascend hills covered with a mass of scoria and volcanic cinders, many in large blocks, but with no solid basalt on the top of the limestone. We now cross the head of two gorges, which start from the same point, to join the Callirrhoe, one on either side of the great basaltic cliff which bars the valley to the south-west of our camp. Soon nodules of hard basalt are mixed with the lighter scoriæ. We pass the crest, and are treated with another series of landscapes of bewildering grandeur; while at our feet every black boulder is framed in the loveliest flowers—a setting, springing one can hardly see whence, and living one can hardly think how. ' Geranium, iris, ranunculus, red poppy, and composite plants of endless variety, especially the geraniaceæ, delight us all, and glut Hayne's collecting cases.

We now leave the cinders and crude basalt, which looks just like a mountain of slag left by some Titanic blast-furnaces. The descent to the Dead Sea from hence is just over 2000 feet—easy at first, but when we leave the limestone and come on the red sandstone, rugged and precipitous. The strata, as usual at this distance (six miles) from the sea, begin to dip at an angle of 45°. An old Roman or Jewish road is clearly seen, winding in zigzag along the slopes, and here and there carefully built up and paved, but now, for that very reason, wholly useless and impracticable, being reduced to a rough ridge of stones. Near the top of the ridge are the ruins of some old fortress, composed entirely of basalt, and without a name. Not far from it are several stone circles, yet earlier remains, none of the material having been shaped or dressed, and identical in character with the primeval circles mentioned in the last chapter.

When we have descended about seven hundred feet, our course, for path there is none, becomes very difficult among the red sandstone cliffs, from the masses of basaltic boulders which strew it everywhere, and which are piled in wild confusion in the embayed flat of land at the bottom. Scouts are here detached, as the pasturage of Zara is rich and abundant, and no one knows whether Beni Atiyeh, or other freebooters, may not be making free with it. Every now and then we see one of our ibex-hunters signaling to us from some distant crest, after creeping to the brow, and scanning carefully every nook for a possible foe.

At length the signal is made from far that there are camels on the plain and Arabs on the hills. But soon this disquieting problem is happily solved: they are a camp of the Beni Sakk'r—old acquaintances—with whom we had traded for lambs at Um Rasas. They had come here with a herd of weakly and nursing camels, in order to feed them on the canebrake tops, which, as Daoud explained to us, are "castor-oil to camels' stomachs."

Not only was their presence here welcome as old friends, but it was a guarantee that no other loafers could be in the neighborhood, and that we might safely wander at will. Our guard were happy, and ready to spend even two nights here; for what Beni Atiyeh would venture where a Beni Sakk'r had pitched? On our asking Zadam how his people had come here, so far out of their own territory, he replied, with manifest pride, "True, the land is not ours, but our people are many, and who shall dare to prevent them from going where they please? You will find them everywhere, if the land is good for them." One of the many advantages this, as we had found, of belonging to the strongest, where might is right.

At length, after three hours' ride, we reached the Dead Sea shore at Zara, which is wrongly placed in the maps, being really three miles south of the mouth of the Callirrhoe, and in a wide, open belt of land beyond the opening of Wady Z'gara. The surrounding mountain crescent is beautiful, both in form and color. The sandstone, gilded by the sun, presents the most gorgeous coloring, red predominating; but white, yellow, and brown patches and streaks abound. Groves of tamarisk and acacia, and all the strange tropical shrubs of Engedi and the Sáfieh, the osher alone being absent, gradually give place to huge tufts of a sort of Pampas-grass ten feet high, and then to impenetrable canebrakes, which reach to within a few feet of the pebbly shore. The shore gently slopes, and the chord of the embayed oasis is about two and a half miles across.

The plain is full of springs of hot water, sometimes sweet, but for the most part slightly sulphurous, and which make the whole canebrake a swamp. Most of these springs sink into the gravel as they approach the sea; but three of them continue their course above ground, tumbling over little slabs of limestone and sulphurous incrustation, and forming tiny cascades along the edge of the shore. The belt of verdure closes abruptly to the north, where the sandstone cliffs form a bold promontory, standing out of the water; but southward it continues, slightly narrowed sometimes to a mile or less, as far as the headland which closes in the view, just north of the mouth of the Arnon.

There can be no greater contrast than that between this coast-line and the western shore, or the Lisan. There we have the desolate marl, broken only at Engedi, by a patch of scanty verdure. Here there is not a trace of the marl, and springs and streams of sweet water abound. Clearly, the post-tertiary marl deposit could not hold against these steep cliffs, and has long since been washed away; for where the rocks do not come sheer to the sea, they break away in avalanches of boulders to the firm pebbly beach. Though chiefly of many-colored sandstone, yet there are many masses of basalt, and also great blocks of pudding-stone formed of rounded boulders of basalt, embedded in carbonate of lime.

Of Zara, the old Hebrew town of Zareth-shahar,

No. 31. ZARA.

but little remains. A few broken basaltic columns and pieces of wall, about two hundred yards back from the shore, and a ruined fort rather nearer the sea, about the middle of the coast-line of the plain, are all that are left, beyond the identity of name.

Of Roman, or later work, there is not a vestige. Yet these poor relics have an interest of their own. We are looking here on perhaps the only surviving relic of the buildings of the semi-nomad tribe of Reuben, prior to the Babylonish captivity. Of any subsequent permanent occupation of the site there is no trace.

The oasis lay entirely out of the highway of the Moabite plain: it leads nowhere, and it is very evident, from the scanty remains elsewhere, that the later colonists never affected the sultry nooks down by the sea, though a few shepherds may have pastured and partially cultivated the fertile soil in winter and spring. Enough is left to show the plan of the place, similar to that of the most primitive villages of Western Palestine, as they exist to-day. There has been a sort of central tower or keep, on a little rising hillock, round which the hovels of the village clustered in a circle, surrounded, doubtless, by a wall, of which no traces can be made out. The material must have been chiefly basalt, roughly hammer-dressed, and without any attempt at squaring or smoothing the surface. Neither Lynch nor any other explorer appears to have visited Zara. Just to the south is a very conspicuous peak, called Abou Sheebeh.

The choice of baths at Zara was tempting. First, there was the warm salt sea, in which, or rather on which, to disport and perform aquatic gymnastics. Then one had but to step out and free one's skin from the brine by a mixture of douche and shower-bath under the ledge, over which a fresh stream tumbled to the lake; or, if a warm sulphur bath were preferred, those who had sufficient endurance to bear parboiling had but to go a little higher up, and simmer in a bubbling pool of the temperature of 130° Fahr. For myself, a sponge at that heat was quite enough.

But the air was scarcely cooler than the springs—95° in the shade, and what in the open I do not venture to guess. There was enough, in the amazing richness, novelty, and beauty of the scene to the naturalist, to compensate for any rise in the thermometer. The familiar note of more than one English warbler struck the ear, and the lesser white-throat, chiff-chaff, and blackcap hopped from twig to twig, enjoying perpetual summer; while large Nubian butterflies lazily flapped their wings among quaint shrubs and bushes, covered with flower-spikes, yellow, pink, or white, but almost all of them nearly destitute of foliage.

Thoroughly exhausted at last, we enjoyed our dinner under the shadow of a rock. The freshly-killed lamb had been brought; and though the salt had been forgotten, we found the Dead Sea water an excellent substitute, and its bitter improved the flavor of the insipid viand, while water warm from the cascade was more suited to our heated frames than cold water, which exists not here.

From Zara we went, by the shore, to the mouth of the Callirrhoe. Trotter alone had sufficient confidence in the prowess of his horse, or in the strength of his own bones, to attempt it in the saddle. Our animals followed, led by the muleteers. The distance

NO. 32.   MOUTH OF THE CALLIRRHOE.

was about three and a half miles, the track was a scramble on and over large boulders, and on the ledges and sides of cliffs overhanging the sea—something like the Corniche, only with much richer coloring. We soon crossed a lovely little gully running down to the sea, and full of palm-trees, with a stream at the bottom. One of the most exquisite bits of form and coloring was a bold headland of crumbling and jagged red sandstone, pushing right forward into the water, round which we scrambled. Two other gullies had palm-trees, and rivulets of hot fresh-water running down.

The charm of the coast-line was complete when we reached a triangular spit of land running out into the sea, about half a mile each way, densely clothed with tamarisks and jungle. In a moment, at its southern corner, we were in the bed of the Callirrhoe, at the mouth of its gorge. So narrow is it, you are quite unconscious of it till it is reached. Picture a wild ravine, never more than one hundred yards wide, and in some places only thirty, winding between two rugged lines of brilliant red cliffs, six hundred feet high, which stand perpendicular, but sometimes seem to meet. The water, in a large and rapid lukewarm stream, rushes to the sea, over and among boulders of granite, sandstone, and conglomerate, under the dense shade of tamarisk-trees, choked with canebrakes waving their tall feathery heads. An emerald fringe of maiden-hair fern hanging from the rocks skirts the line of the stream to the very mouth of the gorge. When we had strolled up some six hundred yards, the limestone first appeared far above us, on the top of the red sandstone, but only on the north side; and here we found the first palm-trees now remaining in the valley.

Intent on outdoing our predecessors, if any, and hearing that it was possible to force our way back to camp along the course of the river, we took some views, and dispatched our horses, servants, and guards, to find their way back over the hills southward. This they did by a route they described to us afterward as much worse than the descent to Engedi, and where the animals, led the whole way, had many a fall. We took with us only a Beni Hamideh ibex-hunter as our guide, and started up the glen.

The deep shade of the gorge was delicious, after the broiling we had had at Zara, and in our scramble along the shore, with the sun beating upon us from the south-west. And now began a series of adventures, difficult enough at the time, but most enjoyable in the retrospect.

Every turn presented a new view. Now leaping, with guns slung on our shoulders, from rock to rock; now stumbling among boulders, up to the hips in the warm water of the dashing stream; now struggling through tangled jungle; now climbing slopes of rotten débris that looked impassable a few minutes before; now crawling up a jagged rock on hands and feet; at length we reached a point, on a shelf at a dizzy height above the stream, where we had just room to stand. We halted for breath, and our ibex-hunter proposed to lead us along a ledge skirting the face of a precipice, by a niche a foot wide, with hundreds of feet below us as well as above.

Though Buxton and Trotter were ready for it, the others, being neither ibex-hunters, nor Alpine-club men, rebelled, and we compelled our guide to descend again to the bed of the river. I was in the rear; and here Hayne had a narrow escape, when, in the descent, I dislodged a boulder of some hundred-weight, which dashed down the ravine with the reverberation of thunder. He was just in its course, when he turned round at the shouts of those above him, and, barely in time, moved out of its way. We reached the water, and had now the advantage of our barefooted hunter, who did not relish the sharp points of canebrakes and jagged rocks. On we waded, through the treacherous depths of the warm stream, plunging sometimes headlong, or pushing through dense jungle, till we had rounded the next headland.

But now, what our Hamideh called a "jebel moia" —*i. e.*, "a mountain of water"—a water-fall, some one hundred feet in height—compelled us to take to the cliffs again. Perched, after a fatiguing and perilous ascent, on a narrow ledge half-way up the cliffs, we saw afar our long cavalcade of horsemen on the opposite side, looking on us, as we sat, from the dizzy height, too far to signal, but evidently having spied us, and supposing we had lost our way. A short rest, and another tremendous climb was before us. Alas! the folly of attempting such a feat as heavily weighted as an unfortunate British soldier on a march, with gun, pistol-belt, compass-case, field-glass, powder, two shot-belts, bowie-knife and cartridge-case, flask, and other *impedimenta*, on one's person. Kindly did my companions relieve me of my superfluous weight, which they distributed among them, while B. aided me with arm or coat-tails, as the lie of the land permitted. Contemptuous pity showed itself in the smiles of our ibex-hunter as, at each fresh point gained, I was glad to pause to recover wind and head.

At length there was an end of this dizzy scrambling. We gained a curious, flat-topped ridge of limestone, along which we walked. It was not more than two feet wide at the top; and we looked down, on the one side into the Callirrhoe; on the other, down the slopes of the next gorge, to the north. This ridge stretched for a mile or two. Still there was a long reach, and many a climb up and down cliffs, before camp could be reached. At length, we finally took to the water. Many a stumble and many a tumble were the result. J. indulged himself and his gun in two involuntary hot baths.

Our last difficulty was to weather a smooth, rounded cliff, overhanging a small lake of hot water. Now, to have one's head-gear repeatedly abstracted by some thorny creeper, and to be in danger of plunging headlong into a lake of the temperature of 120° Fahr., as you clutch convulsively at the excrescences of an overhanging rock, which are provokingly rounded and smooth, is somewhat trying at the end of a day of eleven hours under an Eastern sun, especially when that sun has just gone below the horizon, and you remember that you are too near the equator to have much twilight to aid you.

There is no moon, and our camp is divided from us by a hot stream, shut in by walls of crumbling sulphur, and embosomed in the thickest of canebrakes. Are we near? Our ibex-hunter, who himself has begun to show signs of fatigue, breaks out into a rhapsody of Arab melody, deafening and excruciating to a musical ear, but welcome now, for the "Alhamdu l'Illah!"—"Praise be to God!"—would not have come forth in such stentorian tones unless we had been near the tents. In another minute we creep under a bamboo thicket, and emerge in front of our homestead, steaming and sodden with hot water.

A bathe close by, and then gallons of soup, tea, buttermilk, and bitters, cleared off incrustations without and quenched thirst within; and far into the night we sat discussing the haps and the mishaps of the most successful, original, and enjoyable day we had ever had.

After such a week of expeditions, a Sunday's rest in the depths of the Callirrhoe was welcome indeed; and the coincidence of the history of the martyrdom of the Baptist occurring in the services of the day, just after our visit to Machærus, as well as the appropriateness of Keble's hymn, was not unobserved. We enjoyed, too, the privilege of joining with those at home in the Holy Communion office, though perhaps not after a strictly rubrical fashion. In the afternoon many Hamideh visitors severely tested our medical skill, one woman bringing with her the not unacceptable fee of a kid-skin of fresh butter, while one of our Arabs brought into camp an ibex he had shot.

For two days more we rested in this romantic and delicious dell. There was work enough for all in clearing off arrears, though one was rather tempted to sit in the tent door and watch the little herds of ibex through a field-glass, as they gamboled, unconscious of our proximity, from point to point among the basaltic columns opposite, on the heights above us. One fellow I could see, as he leaped from needle to needle, tossing back his enormous curved horns till they seemed to strike behind his tail, and then, in his bound, gathering all his four feet and lighting with them all close together on a little point of rock on the face of what seemed a smooth wall of cliff, followed by the rest of the herd in single file. Once I saw him make a drop, and break the force of the fall by lighting on the front of his horns. The knees of the ibex are singularly adapted for his mountaineering life. Even in the young kid there is a hard callous, without any hair, on the front of the knee; and in the old animal this callous is hard as a camel's foot, with sinews of prodigious strength attached to it.

But though the ibex were numerous enough, they were not easily got within stalking distance, and the tremendous depth of the ravines rendered it hopeless to attempt a second ambuscade when the herd had been once alarmed. Indeed, our sportsmen only had two shots, and those not successful, to reward them for a heavy day's work. One of these, however, was very close; and had it not been for the awkwardness of his position at the moment, Trotter might have rivaled our Hamideh guide, and brought home two horned trophies. The ibex venison we all pronounced to be the best food we had tasted in the country, and infinitely superior to the *chevreuil* of a Swiss table-d'hôte.

Those of us who did not attempt the feat of ibex-hunting had enough to do at home—one with his photography, and another with his botany. Hayne found himself at his wit's end with a glut of plants, new and strange, every press gorged, every sheet of paper occupied, and every nook of the tent crammed with "hasheesh"—*i. e.*, cabbage—as our Arabs contemptuously termed his treasures.

Medical cases still occupied much of my time. A successful guess in treating one case had raised my reputation, most inconveniently for myself; and my declining to operate on the spot for dropsy was ascribed to malice; while only prejudice against the true believers deterred me from setting right a stiff joint where a bullet had been lodging for twenty years. Our pharmacopœia was not extensive: the most popular remedy was croton-oil—two drops a dose; and invariably a perfect cure was reported. Ophthalmy, the plague of the country, of course, we could satisfactorily treat, as we were well supplied with caustic and sulphate of zinc.

Ornithology, had we had more leisure, would have well repaid research in this sequestered glen. The red-winged grakle (*Amydrus tristrami*) sent forth his sonorous whistle, far out of shot, in the cliffs above, but even here proved himself the wildest of birds. The exquisitely-colored Moabite sparrow (*Passer moabiticus*), peculiar to the Dead Sea basin, and discovered by us in our former expedition, concealed itself in the thick reeds, or ran up the stems, with a merry chirrup, to pick the seed-tufts. The little sun-bird (*Cinnyris oseœ*), with his plumage glancing with metallic lustre, puffed out his orange tufts from his shoulders, as he hopped among the tamarisk twigs; and many of our English summer birds were enjoying perpetual summer here. The square-tailed raven (*Corvus affinis*) had a rookery in the basalt cliffs, and a large flock passed over our tents morning and evening. This is a most interesting bird to watch—full of antics, and very jackdaw-like in some of its ways. In their flight these ravens often gamboled like the roller, dipping perpendicularly, and performing somersaults in the air. They have three distinct notes—an alarm-cry—"whew-ho"—a call-note, something like the jackdaw's, and a whistling, musical caw of satisfaction.

We had thoughts of moving camp, when an Arab, whom we had sent a week before to Jerusalem, arrived with our mails, bringing every one news from

England, our latest being twenty-three days old. Our postman had had a narrow escape in coming up from the Jordan Valley. The night before he reached us he had been stopped by a band of robbers, eight in number, belonging to Kerak. On finding he had no money, they threatened to kill him, but contented themselves with opening the packet of letters, and ascertaining that they contained no coin; and after stripping him, and taking from him the store of tobacco he was bringing for our servants, finally let him go. Probably he would have fared worse, had he not told them he was a Beni Sakk'r, and that his sheik was in the neighborhood, when prudence induced them to give back the packet of letters.

The band consists of forty men, employed chiefly in horse and cattle lifting from the Hamideh. They divide themselves into smaller bodies, but have a common rendezvous in the mountains, known only to themselves. The neighborhood of this marauding band warned us that it was time to move camp; for though Zadam threatened summary vengeance on any whom he might catch, it was more than probable that some of our horses and mules, which were allowed to wander at will on the mountain side, might be lifted during the night, in spite of the sharpest lookout our men could maintain.

Before leaving this neighborhood we spent an evening in catechising the local Hamideh who hung about our camp on the topography of the district. It was difficult to elicit the simplest facts, and most of them were utterly ignorant of the country a few miles beyond their own pasture-grounds. By dint of cross-questioning we made out the names of most of the hills and wadys on either side of us, and ascertained that no ruins had escaped us.* Of one thing they were firmly convinced—that our only object in visiting the country was to seek buried treasure, and that we had already been successful. It was in vain to deny or ridicule the notion: they would only quietly smile; but nothing would disabuse them.

---

* The only ruins on the western edge of the plateau, between the Callirrhoe and the Arnon, unvisited by us, seem to be Sug'hat and Ed Deir, both of which we had made out through our glasses. The wady to the south, between Machærus and the Arnon, is known as Wady Beni Hamideh. To the north we had Jebel Azzenah, then Wady 'Anazeh, Jebel 'Anazeh, and Wady and Jebel Hajilah, apparently the same word as the Hebrew "Hill Hachilah," on the western side. (1 Sam. xxiii., 19.)

CHAPTER XVI.

Departure from Callirrhoe.—Night Alarm.—Horses stolen.—Pursuit.
—Camp Fires.—Wild Seclusion.—Ascent to the Highlands.—Primeval Remains.—Dolmens.—Corn-fields.—Gazelle.—Ma'in, *Baal-Meon*.—Balaam's Progress with Balak.—His Stations.—Medeba.
—Pigeons.—Alarm of Shepherds.—Farewell to the Hamideh.—A Beni Sakk'r Farmer.—Tenure of Land.—History of Medeba.—Its Citadel.—Isolated Columns.—Inscriptions.—Colonnaded Square.
—Churches.—Immense Reservoir.—Richness of the Soil.—Part with old Friends.—Letter from the Adwân.—A Jericho Naturalist.
—Endless Villages.

At length we must leave the most charming of camps, and bid farewell to the rightly-named Callirhoe. Our people, full of Arab superstitions, by no means shared our reluctance. Our first night was to be spent in the upper Zerka Ma'in, where we had pitched on our way down. But, after sending up our convoy by the most direct route, we employed the day in further investigations southward. After a long and interesting detour of ten hours, we reached our old camping-ground, just after sunset, without recognizing it, and found our white tents already mounted on a lovely slope overhung by fig-trees and oleanders, which shade the stream, at the foot of Jebel Humeh.

Dinner over, we had a little excitement. We were discussing the plans of the morrow with Zadam, when the alarm of thieves was raised, and we were called on to seize our guns. The robber band, of whom we had heard from our postman, had found us out, and had carried off a horse and a mule. They were quietly sneaking up the hill with them, and a muleteer in full pursuit, when one of them turned and aimed a large stone at him. The companions of the thief called on him not to fire, lest an alarm should be raised. But Zadam and Daoud were already climbing the hill, and a whole volley of small arms was instantly fired off, to warn the robbers of our strength. They at once left their booty, and concealed themselves among the rocks, while a young Beni Sakk'r brought the animals back in triumph, and performed a sort of war-dance round the camp fire. Certainly, after hearing the report of some twenty barrels in succession, they must have been bolder than ordinary Arabs to make a second attempt. Yet soon after, a horse's pickets were loosened, and another alarm given, when a party of men could be seen in the starlight, as they fled up the hills.

The camp scene was picturesque. The night was now pitch dark; several great camp fires were blazing, for fuel was plentiful, and the men in circles sat or stood round them, the glare reflecting the gleam of the guns, while the situation was discussed. The jackals howled on one side; the signal-calls of the robbers were detected, very near us, on the other. Sheik Na'ur stood up, Arab fashion, by the fire, and made sonorous proclamation, in terms which re-echoed round the inclosing hills (for our camp was completely shut in on all sides), that we were men of peace, and at peace with all; but that if any one disturbed us, or touched a beast of ours, the sheik of the Beni Sakk'r would shed his blood on the spot, and, after this warning, it would be on his own head. Vigorous and partially successful efforts were now made to light up the hills, by kindling the brush-wood and dead trees on the banks of the stream. While the glare was rising, we retired to rest at midnight, lulled to sleep by the calls of our guards echoing round the hills, to keep themselves and their friends awake; nor had we, after this alarm, any fear of finding ourselves minus a horse before morning.

Our camp in the valley of the Upper Zerka, though not the most picturesque we had lighted on, was yet a most perfect ideal of wild seclusion. A saucer-shaped dell, into the depths of which the sun can not peer till he has mounted high on the meridian—an oleander-shaded stream running through its centre—a perfect circle of rugged mountains all round, without affording a glimpse of any possible entrance or exit (for the stream enters at right angles at one end, and escapes at right angles at the other, with overlapping hills to cover the passages)—and a lovely slope of rich herbage, fringed by wild fig-trees—such was our sequestered home for the night. We needed no barometer to tell us we were getting into high ground, for the thermometer fell to 39°; and the cold, with our late vigils, did not conduce to an early start.

To the top of Jebel Zerka, as the northern ridge is named, was only half an hour's ride, when we turned and could look down into the basin, where our laggard muleteers were still loitering over the embers of the watch-fires. We followed without interruption the track of an ancient road, which continues right across the highlands, by Maon and Medeba, to Heshbon. We were now once again on the plateau of Moab, with rocky swellings instead of plains, and with gentle-sloping valleys, the mothers and nurses of the ravines which plow the bowels of the rocks down to the Dead Sea.

Part of our route was by the side of the Wady 'Atabeiyeh, which runs down south to the Zerka, a short and rapidly deepening valley. Here, on a rocky upland bank, we came for the first time upon a dolmen, consisting of four stones, rough and undressed: three set on end, so as to form three sides of a square: and the fourth, laid across them, forming the roof. The stones were each about eight feet square.

From this place northward we continually met with these dolmens, sometimes over twenty in a morning's ride, and all of exactly similar construction. They were invariably placed on the rocky sides, never on the tops, of hills; the three large blocks set on edge, at right angles to each other, and supporting the massive stone laid across them, which was from six to ten feet square. They are favorite stations for the Arab herdmen, whom we frequently saw stretched at full length upon the top of them, watching their flocks. The dolmens appear to be confined to the district between the Callirrhoe and Heshbon: in similar districts to the south of that region, they never occurred. I have, however, in former visits to Palestine, seen many such in the bare parts of Gilead, between Jebel Osha and Gerash.

NO. 33.   SKETCH OF DOLMEN.

It is difficult to understand why they were erected on these hill-sides. I never found one with a fourth upright stone, and in many instances the edifice had fallen: but in such cases the heap always consisted of four blocks, neither more nor less.

From the shallowness of the soil, there could have been no sepulture here under-ground; and there are no traces of any cairns or other sepulchral erections in the neighborhood. It is possible that the primeval inhabitants erected these dolmens in many other situations, but that they have been removed by the subsequent agricultural races, who left them undisturbed only on these bare hill-sides, which can never have been utilized in any degree for cultivation.

Still, it is worthy of notice that the three classes of primeval monuments in Moab—the stone circles, dolmens, and cairns—exist, each in great abundance, in three different parts of the country, but never side by side: the cairns exclusively in the east, on the spurs of the Arabian range; the stone circles south of the Callirrhoe; and the dolmens, north of that valley.* This fact would seem to indicate three neighboring tribes, co-existent in the prehistoric period, each with distinct funeral or religious customs. Of course, the modern Arab attributes all these dolmens to the jinns.

Having reached the crest, we are now on easy riding ground—sometimes flat plain, covered with green corn, or else the gentlest ascents and descents; while, all along, we follow the tracks of the old road, be it Jewish or Roman, marked by its bold edging of stones, and here smooth between the parallel lines,

---

* One cairn only, surrounded by a circle of dolmens, is found in the north-west.

undisturbed by the wooden plow; so that we often ride along the centre of the road itself. On all sides are the long lines of foundations, which indicate the boundary-walls of ancient fields or vineyards, perhaps the patrimony of many a Reubenite. Men are plowing in all directions with oxen, or sowing barley—the wheat being already six inches high—and flocks of pigeons afford us many a passing shot.

The territory of the Beni Sakk'r had begun on the top of Jebel Zerka; but they are no agriculturists, and most of this wide corn plain is tilled for them by slaves, or by their dependent vassals, the Abou Endi.

A herd of gazelle was started among the corn. Trotter and Buxton went after them on foot, while Zadam and I, having no bullets for our guns, rode hard round the base of the hill to the other side, with the hope of turning them. It was a pretty sight to see the graceful little antelopes trotting gently along the edge of the ridge, just on the sky-line. Unfortunately, the wind was against the hunters. On reaching the shoulder, and turning sharply round, we found ourselves within twenty yards of the herd, which looked at us for a moment, and then, tossing up their heads, bade us farewell, and scampered off in the wrong direction.

The chase had brought us on to the hills of Ma'in (Baal-meon), with its ruins of vast extent. These occupy the crests and slopes of four adjacent hills—one having evidently been the central city, and connected with the next by a wide causeway. The remains are of the ordinary type—foundations, fragments of wall, lines of streets, old arches, many carved stone, caves, wells, and cisterns innumerable. Some curious cavernous dwellings, built up with arches and fragments of old columns, are still occasionally used by the Arabs as folds and sleeping-places.

Baal-meon had, in the time of the later prophets, reverted to Moab, and must have been a city of importance, since it is spoken of by Ezekiel (chap. xxv., 9) as "the glory of the country." It continued to the Christian era, and is mentioned by Eusebius, under the same name, as a very large village ($\kappa\omega\mu\eta$ $\mu\varepsilon\gamma\iota\sigma\tau\eta$) near the hot springs, and nine miles from Heshbon. He adds that it was the birthplace of Elisha. It does not appear to have been an episcopal see.

The view from the highest crest is very fine, but too far recessed to show the depression of the Dead Sea. There is a very clear exposure of the southern wall of the Zerka Ma'in ravine; and northward, Jerusalem, Gerizim, Tabor, Hermon, and Mount Gilead can all be descried, through the distant haze, by the glass.*

---

* This was a remarkably good position for ascertaining the topographical details of the immediate neighborhood. West of Wady Habis, a small deep wady, Wady el Bekker, runs down to the Callirrhoe. From Ma'in, a spur of the plateau, forming a sort of ridge, runs due west, called Masloubeiyeh, to the north of which the Wady Anazeh descends. A Roman road runs along the ridge from Ma'in as far as the edge of the plateau, where it divides, one branch turning south to

I have drawn attention to this view, from its bearing on the history given us, in Numb. xxii., of the progress of Balaam with Balak. Balak met the prophet at the banks of the Arnon, the frontier of his kingdom (verse 36).

He then takes him to Kirjath-huzoth, "the City of Streets" (verse 39), probably Kiriathaim (described chap. xiv., p. 290), and its high place, the top of Attarus, with its commanding prospect. This is the first conspicuous eminence north of the Arnon.

Then, proceeding northward, the next day he brings him on to the high places of Baal (verse 41), or Bamoth-baal—probably Baal-meon—evidently, from its name, sacred to Baal, and which was changed by the Reubenites into Beth-meon (Numb. xxvii., 38). This was the second position whence he had a commanding view of the future country of Israel.

Afterward they proceed to Pisgah, or Nebo (chap. xxiii., 14); and finally to the top of Peor, facing Jeshimon—*i.e.*, the ridge north of Nebo and due west of Heshbon—where there is a group of ruins, which,

---

the hot baths, and the other descending direct to the shore. We found that Et Teim (the conjectural Kiriathaim of Burckhardt), instead of being, as marked on the maps, between Heshbon and Ma'in, in the open plain, is really just south of Medeba. Several ruins unmarked on the maps are visible from Ma'in northward, but west of Medeba. Two miles north of Ma'in is Kirbet el K'feir, and about a mile west of the latter is M'Shuggar. In a hollow between these, but to the north, is a small ruined heap, Rujum Abdallah; while three miles N.N.W. of Ma'in is Rujum Seyieh. None of these names suggests connection with any historical ancient site.

as well as Nebo, will be afterward described. Thus, with every reasonable probability, we have the identification of the four sacrificial stations of Balak and Balaam.

A ride of an hour and a half, all the way by the line of the Roman road, brings us from Ma'in to Medeba. Medeba, though it does not cover the square miles of Ma'in, has been a city of great importance. It is in much better preservation than the former city; and its vast reservoir, some standing walls, and a few columns still erect, form conspicuous features in the landscape from a distance.

To be again on the open plain, with its long stretches of grass, gave a pleasurable sensation of freedom, after our most enjoyable time in the rocky valleys. Much of the country was under cultivation — the Abou Endi on one side of us, the Beni Sakk'r on the other; tents in every hollow, countless flocks and camels. All bespoke security, and mutton and milk in abundance.

We found our camp already pitched under the shelter of the rising ground of the city, and looking forth to the east, with an uninterrupted view of the plain and its spring tenants. We at once strolled forth, with the best archæological intentions; but, finding birds in abundance, were seduced by less scientific propensities, and returned at night with heavy bags, and three days' dinners secured. Hearing a somewhat rapid fusillade, really a most innocent slaughter of pigeons, the shepherds in the neighborhood fled in fright, concentrated, reconnoitred our party riding up the hills, and sent a herald to inquire what the warlike demonstration might mean.

Being now out of the Hamideh territory, we here finally parted with Sheik Na'ur and all his men. Zadam, too, left us for a few days—a very practical proof that we needed no guards here. The little great man, the humble footman chief of a small mountain tribe, was an amusing contrast to the proud chieftain of the lordly Beni Sakk'r; but he was especially careful to impress upon us that he, too, was a real sheik. There are lords of high degree and of low degree here, as elsewhere. Zadam bows, Na'ur kisses our hands, and is somewhat cringing. The very moderate parting gift of five gold pieces, well earned, was enough to evoke a torrent of gratitude, and affectionate kisses to all the party round.

Our ibex-hunting friend, whom we nicknamed Abou Bedoun (father of ibex), was at home here, and one of the very few Beni Sakk'r of high degree who turned his attention to agriculture, cultivating the rich soil of the ancient bank and the neighborhood of the old city by his slaves, and claiming, though a nomad, distinct personal, and not tribal, possession of the land. This exception to the ordinary Arab system seems to be admitted without difficulty, where the ground is unsuitable for pasturage, and prevails still more generally among the Abou Endi, the Belka, and other more stationary tribes. It is certainly a tacit recognition of the fact that, however suitable tribal or common enjoyment of the soil may be to a pastoral people, it can not practically co-exist with the simplest or rudest agriculture, but at once gives place to individual proprietorship.

Abou Bedoun and his friends were very constant evening visitors, as he had pitched his tent hard by, to watch the getting in of his seed, and had an eye to tobacco and other luxuries when the labors of the day were over. But we had the advantage of his local knowledge, and it would have been impossible to find a better guide.

The remains of Medeba itself indicate a high state of prosperity in the Roman period; but its history extends centuries further back. It must have been among the most ancient of the cities of Moab, for it is mentioned with Heshbon and Dibon in the antique poem quoted in Numb. xxi., 30, before the conquest.

Allotted then to Reuben, we find it held for a short time by the Ammonites during the reign of David; for it was before the gates of Medeba, on the fine plain to the east of it, that Joab gained his great victory over them and the combined hordes they had brought to support them, with their 32,000 chariots from Mesopotamia, Syria-maachah, and Zobah — in fact, from the whole region between the Jordan and the Euphrates (1 Chron. xix). In the time of Isaiah it had again reverted to Moab, along with the other towns in this district.

After the return from captivity, it was alternately in the possession of the Jews and of the Gentile tribes, and was the scene of several important events. Here John Maccabæus was captured and slain, for which his brothers Jonathan and Simon took a bloody revenge (Joseph., "Antiq." xiii., 1). It afterward surrendered to Hyrcanus, at the end of a six months' siege. It remained from that time in the hands of the Jews. It retained its importance in early Christian times, and was an episcopal see, as mentioned by Eusebius. Its bishop appears several times in the records of the Eastern councils.

Medeba is not, as it appeared to Palmer, looking at it from the higher ground to the westward, in a hollow, but on the top of a "tell," round which the old city extended a considerable way into the plain eastward, bounded on the south by the wady of the same name. Taking the top of this "tell" as our centre, where there has evidently been a sort of citadel, we command a view of the whole extent of the ruins. In few places are the lines of roads and streets more clearly to be traced. A gentle declivity on the west side is immediately succeeded by a rise, honey-combed by a labyrinth of caves, which have all been once a dépôt for the supply of water, stored up for summer use.

Beyond the base of the hill the city proper does not seem to have extended westward; but the slope has been a wide suburb of scattered buildings, with several roads, still plainly marked by the parallel double lines of stones, and half-way up has stood a large temple. This has still two columns standing close together erect, conspicuous objects from far. They are only eighteen feet high. It is rather perplexing to find that the capitals must have been mounted on the columns at a later period, subsequent to the destruction of the temple. Each of them is far too small for the shaft on which it stands; while one

NO. 34.   COLUMNS AT MEDEBA.

is Ionic, and the other Corinthian. Across them has been laid a large block of stone, which has, at least, performed the useful office of keeping the pillars erect.

Passing round by the north flank of the hill, we see extensive foundations outside of the city wall. We found a Greek inscription of five lines on a tablet;

and although we could not satisfactorily decipher it, yet it would not be impossible, with time and patience, to do so. We also found, on a very large cornice-stone, a Latin inscription of some length; but this is hopelessly weathered and past deciphering. On the southern slope of the hill, built into an ancient wall, was another plain stone, which has borne an inscription, now all but obliterated, and which appears to have been in Phœnician characters.

The chief extension of the Roman city has been on the plain to the east of the hill. The wall of circumvallation can be clearly traced. The access to Medeba, on this side, has been by a paved road leading to a finely-built massive gate-way with two side portals. Several cornices of this gate-way remain *in situ*, and the stones of its arch, and many cornice-stones, are lying strewn around. Within the gateway, on the north side, has been a large square, with a colonnade. Six paces outside the columns has been a wall, probably the line of the principal street. The bases of the columns are for the most part in their places, and there is only a space of four feet between each. The extent of the square is 280 paces from north to south, by 240 paces east to west. Within the inclosing colonnade we could find no traces of building; but outside the eastern wall are many traces of isolated buildings on the plain; several of these have been small square temples of the ordinary Moabite type, others perhaps forts, and others certainly tombs. Just beyond the eastern gate is a large

PUBLIC BUILDINGS. 325

deep cistern, or reservoir, now half filled in; and a paved road stretches across the plain from the north-east angle of the city.

The principal public buildings seem to have been in the northern quarter of the city. One oblong

NO. 85.   TEMPLE AT MEDEBA.

building, the use of which we could not divine, was fifty yards from east to west, by twenty-five from north to south, and had door-ways in the centre of the eastern and western faces. Beneath it were solid vaulted cisterns of great depth, beautifully arched. A round temple in this quarter seems to have been subsequently converted into a Christian church. It has four pillars standing at the west end, and a large pentagonal apse, apparently an addition of later workmanship, at the east end. Near this is another vaulted cistern, fifteen yards by ten, containing still a small supply of water, the drinking-place of the ravens and pigeons.

From these buildings upward is a labyrinth of streets, with the ordinary arched constructions, some of them still temporarily inhabited by the Bedouin shepherds. Among them has been a Christian church, with its apse. Inside its walls many capitals of Corinthian columns, which once supported the roof of its aisle, are strewn, and some slabs with Greek crosses inscribed. Near it is another large square building, and another Christian church. A defaced Greek inscription lies among its ruins. ΒΑΟΙΛΕ and ΘΕΟΤ were the only consecutive letters I could decipher. Upon a lintel over an ancient door-way were the sculptured emblems of the sun and moon.

The eastern extent of the city is over 1000 yards. It is at the south-east angle, where the wady turns to the eastward, that the most remarkable relic of old Medeba is to be seen. A mass of masonry dams the valley, forming the sustaining wall of an immense reservoir, open, like that of Ziza. This structure, of beautiful workmanship, far more carefully finished than that at Ziza, is still perfect, though the space of the reservoir, now used as a tobacco field, is many feet deep in soil, washed into it by the torrents from above. It is 120 yards square, built on the same principle as Solomon's pools; and at each end is a carefully-finished flight of steps. The eastern, or lower, wall is thirty feet thick at its base, diminishing, by the regular contraction of its courses outside, to eighteen feet at the top. Inside it is of smoothly-dressed masonry, and buttressed: each buttress is nine feet nine inches, with the intervening spaces of exactly the same width. The present height of the walls above the soil, inside, is only twenty feet. At the north-east corner has been a massive tower and sort of gate-way. From the south-east corner the wall extends a long way across the valley and up the hill, forming a massive dam, which turned the water back to the reservoir. This wall has now been broken down, close to the pool, by the winter torrents. The other inclosing walls are plain, without pilasters or buttresses, and fifteen feet thick, the top of the western being level with the soil outside, carried down against it by the floods.

A very little energy and labor might easily again utilize this noble work, and fertilize the neighborhood. The soil of all Moab, and pre-eminently of this neighborhood, is wonderfully rich—a fine, red sandy loam, which year after year grows successive crops of wheat without manure, and into which one can with ease thrust a stick for at least two feet. The mole-rats (*Spalax typhlus*) seem to be the only scientific agriculturists here, and they swarm. Were it not for their top-dressing, the soil must soon be exhausted. Yet our friend Ayeed, the ibex-hunter, looked upon these heaps with the same disgust with which an English gamekeeper would eye the traces of what he calls vermin.

Four days, including a quiet Sunday, was but a short time to devote to the remains of Medeba and its neighborhood; but it was all we could spare, and very hard did all the party work. Excavations we were not able to attempt; but I have seen no place in the country where they seem more likely to yield good results.

We were now on the frontier of the Beni Sakk'r land, and our companions of the last month began to leave us one by one. Young Sahan came one morning, before the hoar-frost was off the ground (for the nights here were sharp, and did not conduce to early rising), to bid us farewell. Arab-like, he, though a young prince, evidently expected a "tip" at parting, and had no scruples about accepting one. He set off at once for his father's camp, in good heart, to join in the war with the Anizéh, his first introduction to military life. He was a fine, noble-hearted, generous boy, and open to impressions. Would that he had the opportunity of getting some better light and instruction!

The same day, also, we lost the best of our Beni Sakk'r guards, who went to join the fray—the horseman, Nim'r—*i. e.*, "the leopard"—who had been Trotter's companion in ibex-hunting, and had been a watchful, quick, and keen guard and guide for a fortnight. He had a soul above backsheesh, and knew the country well. No intending explorer of Moab could do better than secure, through Zadam, the services of Nim'r. The same evening Zadam, who had left us alone for three days at Medeba, returned from his family camp, bringing with him a present of four lambs—no slight addition to the larder, for we had begun keenly to feel the force of the French proverb, "*Toujours perdrix.*"

On the Sunday morning we received a letter of welcome from my old friend Sheik Goblan, of the Adwân, informing us that he had heard of our being in the neighborhood, and that he was encamped near Heshbon, where we were by all means to go and see him, and dine with him. He added that he was sure we could not leave the country without paying another visit to Amman and Gerash (both, of course, within his district, and involving backsheesh). We were obliged to disappoint him of his anticipated gains, but wrote, through Daoud, in reply, that we should be at Heshbon in a few days, and that he must come and dine with us on our arrival.

We were also surprised by a visit from some Jericho Arabs, who had known me well eight years before, and had heard of our whereabouts through the Adwân. At once they came off to see me as old friends. Among them was my former henchman, Jemeel, who used to collect natural history specimens for me. Perhaps his affection was somewhat stimulated by the hope of a new commission, as he straightway applied for ammunition. We at once equipped him with powder and shot, arsenical soup, and carbolic acid, and bid him meet us in five days, by Jordan. Jemeel certainly did not fail us, and his supply of specimens, when we reached the Jordan plain, attested his industry and prowess, though—alas for my collections!—not his skill in taxidermy.

Our various rides in the immediate neighborhood of Medeba yielded absolutely nothing worth record. The ruined villages lie thick in every direction, seldom more than half a mile apart, but all utterly featureless, and most of them very small. The largest, Et Teim, is the only one noticed by previous travelers by name. It lies due south of Medeba. The others appear to have been unwalled towns, the dependents either of Meon or Medeba, and possessing neither churches nor temples. The oil-press was usually the most conspicuous relic of the past; but their frequency attests a prodigious past population.

The towns farther to the west are of a somewhat different character, and may be grouped rather with Heshbon than with Medeba.

CHAPTER XVII.

The north-west Corner of Moab.—Its many Ravines.—Wheat Cultivation.—Belka Arabs.—Maslubeiyeh.—Splendid Panorama.—Dolmens.—Jedeid.—Nebbeh.— Its Identity with Nebo.— View of Moses.—Ancient Authorities.—Zi'ara.— Interesting Ruins.—Balaam's Views.—Identity of Zi'ara and Zoar.—Position of the Cities of the Plain.—Arguments for placing them north of the Dead Sea. —Mr. Grove's Inference.—Ayun Moussa.—Springs of Moses.— Picturesque Glen.—Cascades.—M'Shuggar.—Ajermeh and other Tribes.—Heshbon.—Adwân Camp.—Elealeh.—Night Search for Camp.—Goblan's Welcome.—His Character.—Tragic Crime.

THE district lying to the west and north-west of Medeba—*i.e.*, that comprised by a parellogram roughly drawn, with the line from Medeba to Heshbon for its eastern limits, and a line drawn through the edges of the brows overhanging the Dead Sea for its western—has many characteristics to distinguish it from the other portions of Moab. Within the space of these few miles the plateau is riven by five or six deep wadys, which, commencing in very gentle depressions, about the parallel of Heshbon, rapidly deepen; while the plain, culminating, just where the wadys begin to descend, in a ridge elevated some two hundred or three hundred feet above it, thenceforward becomes a series of parallel ranges, descending by graduated steps of about six hundred feet, with a ruined city on each brow. Beneath the westernmost brow there is a precipitous descent to another lower strip of grass-land, from half a mile to a mile in width; after which a rugged incline, covered with boulders, leads to the plain by the sea-shore.

All the remains of former civilization are crowded on the upper ridges, and we spent several days in examining these in detail. The wadys in order are, to the south of Medeba, and commencing near Et Teim, the Wady Hawara; next, north of Medeba, Wady Ed Deib, called, when it approaches the sea, Wady Ghuweir; north of this, Wady Jedeid, named, lower down, Wady Ghedeimeh. Between these two latter is a shorter and very steep gully, Wady Burrhoughat. North of these, after crossing over Nebo and Zi'ara, we come to the Wady Ayun Moussa—"Springs of Moses"—or, as it is called in the lower plain, Wady Jerifeh. Beyond these, again, are wadys Heshban and Na'ur, the latter the largest of all, and opening into the plain north of the Dead Sea, the plain of Shittim or the Scisaban.

The first ruin of importance west of Medeba is Jazel, with a heap of stones marking a central fort, and foundations of buildings grouped round it. Soon afterward, proceeding in a north-west direction, we come on a group of ruined villages, consisting of four distinct places, but all bearing the same name, Kĕfeir. Common as double towns are in Moab, this was the first time we had met with a quadruple one. The ruins are about half a mile apart, situated each on a separate "tell," or gently swelling elevation of the uplands.

We had now altogether left the pastoral country, and, instead of herds of camels, had before us an almost unbroken reach of corn land, the wheat well up, thick and vigorous, and of the deepest green; while many yokes of dwarf oxen were dotted about, plowing, under the guidance of negro slaves, for the barley which they were only now beginning to sow. Our guide, Ayeed, took care to point out to us the extent of his farm, assuring us, at the same time, that no Beni Sakk'r ever drove a plow himself, but left all such menial toil to his slaves. When a man came up to us, and most civilly requested us not to ride over his wheat, this very commonplace incident made us feel as if we had really returned to civilization.*

At Jazel we entered on the territory of the Belka Arabs. This tribe was once the ruling race of the whole country; but, about 140 years ago, the Beni Sakk'r pressed upon them from the south-east, gradually drove them completely out of their fair pastures, and hemmed them up into this little corner. The tradition of their former power still remains, and the whole of the highlands of Northern Moab, as far as M'Shita and Zebib, are known to this day in the Turkish governmental vocabulary as the Belka. The pasha of the east side of Jordan, whose head-quarters are at Es Salt, is known only as the Pasha of the Belka.

---

* From these hillocks we had a good view of many ruined sites to the south and south-west, between the Wady Ed Deib and the Wady Hawara, as M'Kheir, M'Seyik, Gouajiyah, and others.

The slopes of the Belka are by no means unbroken. Out of the fine, light, red soil continually rise little rocky rounded hills, with very gentle slopes, half their surface the bare rocky shelf, all limestone, and the rest covered with fine short herbage, completely burned up in summer. The little knolls are studded with dolmens, exactly like those described above.

Judging from the number both of plows and camps, which were always large, the Belka population must be, for a nomad one, very dense. Population and cultivation have not encouraged animal life. Scarcely a partridge was flushed. Rock-doves here and there; stone-curlews, jackdaws, and vultures, were the only large birds we saw. Now and then a fox was started; and once, as we were coming over a little brow, a grim, solitary wolf leaped to his feet, and walked very quietly away, looking at us over his shoulder. But by the time the guns were unslung and charged with ball, he took care to quicken his pace and desert us.

The whole of the ridge running westward between wadys Ed Deib and Jedeid is named Muslubeiyeh; and this name is given indiscriminately to many ruins on its various knolls, causing hopeless confusion in their identification. Many short and steep wadys run down either north or west. One of them, Burroughat, starts from a heap of ruins of some size, bearing the same name. All the ruins to which we rode in this district, and they were not a few, were similar to each other—utterly overthrown heaps, the barest fragments of walls, no arches left, and generally a large heap of stones in the centre, where once the central fort has stood.

The highest point toward the east has been crowned by a fortification of greater importance than the others, known by the name of the ridge, Muslubeiyeh. The top is flat, with a precipitous descent from its western edge. The ruins are very unlike those of the Roman times. There has been a circular wall round the town; and outside it, at the eastern and accessible end, has stood a square fortress, of which only a few courses remain above ground. This castle is eighty-six yards square, and stands seventy-three paces east of the circular wall. The total diameter of the place is 289 yards.

The view from this place, especially that of the lower part of the Jordan Valley, is very fine, and can only be surpassed by those from Nebo and Mount Gilead. To our left, on the south, we looked down into the Wady Ed Deib, from its very source. Just beyond it, and running parallel with it toward the Dead Sea, was Wady Hamara. Beyond this again, over the rugged southern wall of the Callirrhoe, peered the hills of Southern Moab; and beyond their tops, in the haze, was Mount Hor, or one of the mountains of Petra. Several rounded brows intervened to the north between us and Wady Jedeid, each crowned by a ruin. Corn patches of deepest green crept everywhere, almost to the crests of the hills, up each gentle depression in their sloping sides.

Below us, in front, and stretching some way toward the Dead Sea, was a plateau covered with corn, undulating, but not sloping, high above the sea, and completely shutting out its edge from our view.

In front the hill country of Judah, from far south of Hebron, stretched in unbroken line up to Gerizim and Jezreel; and other hills, perhaps Tabor and Hermon, could be faintly traced up the opening of the Jordan Valley in the dim haze of the sunny mirage. Farther to our right were the dark pine-clad mountains of Gilead and Ajalon, with Es Salt (Ramoth-gilead) on the side of the former, and Heshbon in front of them. Just beyond the immediate foreground at our feet was spread the lower end of the Jordan Valley, bare, and of dazzling whiteness, as the sun shone on the barren but glittering marl, relieved only by the two green patches of Jericho opposite, and the long green strip of the Scisaban, or the plains of Shittim, close below the hills on which we stood. Over these, in the far distance, we could just detect the green plain of Shechem, and the opening to its valley between Ebal and Gerizim. The whole country of Judea opposite looked naked and rugged, plowed with a complete net-work, or labyrinth, of irregular furrows, till, as the eye reached to Bethlehem, or Jerusalem, they were lost in the distance. The pale earthy brown of the western country was unrelieved by the slightest tinge of color. The higher ridges behind us shut out all view of the plains of Moab.

The camps of the present inhabitants dotted every

little valley, and the dolmens of their ancient predecessors every hill-side, as we looked northward up the course of the Jedeid toward Nebbeh, or Nebo. M'Ileiyat, which we visited, nearly an hour due north of Muslubeiyeh, is merely a large pile of shapeless ruins, and a few foundations on the top of a hill. Descending from this, we wound up the side of a gentle rising valley, an affluent of the Jedeid, with picturesque cliffs below us, sheltering occasional pools in the little stream, which was now dry in parts of its course.

Signs of population were on all sides—Arabs bathing in some of the pools, blue-clad women washing linen in others. Many were the dodges of the old ibex-hunter to delude us by side-paths to the constantly-recurring black tents, which promised him the chance of a draught of "leben," or curdled milk; but, with deaf ears and fixed faces, we set our horses' heads toward one hill-top after another, regardless of the assurances of our guide, in his most silvery tones, "Leben tayib menhone" ("The milk is good here").

At the head of the valley stands an ancient fort, Kirbet Jedeid, which would call for no remark, being exactly like all the others, a mere square block-house, were it not that it was the only one we found in which the walls are still tolerably perfect, and show the closely-built buttresses which strengthened the solid masonry.

From this castle, crossing the valley and mounting on the other side, we reach the third parallel ridge north of Medeba—that of Zi'ara, the highest hill of which is Nebbeh. The ruins of Nebo are on a mamelon, slightly depressed and projected from the line of the main ridge, which runs north and south from Heshbon to Ma'in, and are about two miles west of its crest. There is a very perfect ancient roadway from the eastern plain to this place, and thence down to the lower terrace. But the ruins themselves consist of nothing more than foundations.

Anxious to verify exactly the view of Moses, we paid three visits to Nebo; but we were not so fortunate as on my former visit, when, for the first time, Nebo was identified. On each occasion there was a haze from the heat, which dimmed the distant features and outlines, producing a sort of mirage, which rendered it most difficult clearly to trace distant objects.

Still, we had a clear distant view of Western Palestine and the whole Judean range from far south of Hebron up to Galilee. We could see the west side of the Dead Sea from Engedi northward, Bethlehem, Jerusalem, and Nebi-samwil (Mizpeh). Ebal and Gerizim were very easily made out, and the opening of the vale of Shechem. Carmel could be recognized, but we never were able to make out the sea to the north of it; and though it is certainly possible that it might be seen from this elevation, I could not satisfy myself that I saw more than the haze over the plain of Esdraelon. The rest of the view was like that from Muslubeiyah, only that a corner of the Hauran

Mountains (Bashan) could be caught in a depression of the Gilead range. Hermon certainly could be made out in a clear atmosphere, over the Jordan Valley, the whole of which lay open as far as Kurn Surtabeh; but the haze rendered it very indistinct, if, indeed, we saw it at all.

However, after testing repeatedly every view in the neighborhood, I am perfectly satisfied that there is none which equals in extent that from Nebo—*i. e.*, from the flat ridge which rises slightly about half a mile behind the ruined city, and which I take to be the true "field of Zophim, the top of Pisgah." The prospect described above from Muslubeiyeh is, perhaps, richer in the detail of the foreground; but, not being so completely projected forward, does not yield the same distant glimpses northward.

From Nebo we looked down on our right, northward, into the Wady Ayun Moussa—"Springs of Moses"—which rises to the north-east of it, and runs out into the Ghor Seisaban—"Plains of Shittim"— opposite Beth Jeshimoth. In the lower part of its course it is called Wady Jerifeh. It was dotted with trees, bright green spots, and occasional patches of cultivation, wherever it was more open than usual.

By this wady would be the natural ascent to Nebo from the plains below; and by it, doubtless, Moses ascended with Joshua to the crest of the range. We could trace the line of the path the whole way up. Three other ravines, up which there are paths, lead from the same plains to the heights—one by the

Wady Heshban,* to the north of Ayun Moussa; and the Wady Na'ur, north of this again, the largest of all these valleys. The farthest up is the Wady N'meirah.

But these are all too far north to have led to any point which can afford such a panorama as that from Nebo. Indeed, there can scarcely now remain a doubt on the mind of any investigator as to the identity of the site, and the exact harmony of the Scriptural topography with the actual facts. Besides, although Nebo had escaped modern research until 1864, the name and place were well known to early Christian writers; and Eusebius expressly mentions that "it lay on the other side Jordan, in the land of Moab, and is shown to this day, six miles to the west of Heshbon." (Δείκνυται εἰς ἔτι νῦν ἀπὸ ἕξ σημείων Ἑσ-βοῦς εἰς δυσμάς.)

The names of Nebo and Nebor (Ναβώς and Νάβαυ) seem to be confused by Eusebius; but probably this Nebo was the old city mentioned in Isaiah (xv., 2), and which perished at the destruction of Moab, nor was again rebuilt. Unlike the other towns, it shows no trace of Roman or later work. Zareth-shahar was the only other site in this part of the country where those great builders do not appear to have left their mark.

The lateral range, which culminates in Nebo, ter-

* In "The Land of Israel" I erroneously stated that the Wady Heshban runs into the Na'ur. I have since ascertained that it has an independent exit into the Jordan.

minates bluntly in a lower brow some distance to the west of it. While standing on the hallowed site, we detected in front of us a bold spur pushing forward, at a rather low elevation, due west, and apparently overhanging the head of the Dead Sea. Half an hour's hard riding, without drawing rein, up and down the shoulders of many a brow, brought us to the summit of a bold headland, projecting westward, between Wady Jedeid to the south, and Ayun Moussa to the north.

The place is known to the Arabs as Zi'ara, and has been one of considerable importance. The pile of ruins is very large. The brow of the hill is flattened, apparently artificially, and its slopes are steeply scarped, to the depth of about twenty feet, with traces of a wall of circumvallation below.

In the hill itself, on the south side, about thirty feet down, has been excavated a magnificent cistern, with a finely vaulted roof, which is still quite perfect, with the two square traps in the roof through which the water was drawn up. We entered by the side, where an entrance has been laboriously broken open for the purpose of sheltering flocks; for water has long since ceased to accumulate in the cavern. We could trace the method by which it was fed, through cemented conduits, entering it near the top, and which brought down the drainage of the higher slopes to the cistern.

The citadel of the place has stood at the east, or projecting, end of the platform. Next adjoining it is an old temple, with the bases of four columns *in situ*, and about a dozen columns lying prostrate, but unbroken, in a row in close order—overthrown more probably by an earthquake than by man. There have been side aisles, running north and south, by the side of the columns; and from some indications at the east end, which is heaped with rubbish, I think the temple may have been utilized as a Christian Basilican church. To the south of this temple are the ruins of a Christian church, with its apse remaining; and eastward, another fine deep tank, which has once been vaulted, like that below, but the roof of which is now broken in.

The near foreground was more interesting than from Nebo, and the undulations, on all sides, abound in stone circles and dolmens. The view was indeed superb, though the distant prospect was inferior to that from Nebo. Still, it must be much the same as that which greeted the eyes of Balaam from Baal-peor; and again it vividly brought back the realization of the glimpse granted to Moses: "This is the land which I sware unto Abraham, unto Isaac, and unto Jacob, saying, I will give it unto thy seed: I have caused thee to see it with thine eyes" (Deut. xxxiv., 4).

The ground fell in terraces, for 3000 feet, to the Jordan Valley; so that the plain of Shittim seemed to be spread in its whole extent at our feet, like a map—the lower course of the Jordan and its mouth, together with its plain as far up as opposite Shechem. The hill country of Judea and Samaria as

THE CITIES OF THE PLAIN. 343

far as Carmel was visible, but we lost Tabor; and the more distant peaks of Hermon and Bashan were shut out by Mount Gilead.

We had, however, a rare opportunity of cross-questioning our guide, and mapping all the nearer wadys, which have been already named. The long Ayun Moussa, to the north of us, was an interesting feature. Dry now in its upper part, we could see where the waters burst forth, with a life-giving gush, from under the cliffs, and the series of tiny cascades by which it bounds down the valley.

I have pointed out minutely the features of the view from Zi'ara, because they have a very important bearing on the identification of this ancient site, and corroborate in the minutest particular what, I am convinced, is one of the most important results of our expedition—the identification of Zi'ara with the *Zoar* of the book of Genesis. There is an identity, more exact than often occurs in ancient and modern nomenclature, between the Hebrew צוֹעַר (Zo'ar), and the Arabic زَعرة (Zi'ara); and it is to be noted that the Jerusalem Targum writes the name צֹעִיר, still more closely identified with the Arabic.

It seems evident, on a careful examination of the Scriptural account of "the cities of the plain," that they must have been situated in the "ciccar," or "ghor," of Jordan, at the north end of the Dead Sea. It is unnecessary to recapitulate at length the arguments for assigning this site. That they were submerged we have no historical record whatever; and the whole tenor both of the history and of geological evidence is directly opposed to such a hypothesis.

There are thus only two possible localities—the lower end of the lake and the upper. Formerly the southern site was assumed (as by Dr. Robinson) without question, from the general tradition, which can not be traced further back than the time of Josephus and Jerome, who speak of a Zoar in that region. This view was further supported by the name of Jebel Usdum (? Sodom) at the south end, and by the name of "Lot's Wife," given to the many pillars of salt detached from time to time from the salt cliffs. But Professor Palmer has found a "Bint Sheik Lot" (Lot's wife) midway up the eastern side, which considerably weakens the force of this coincidence of name.

But for the northern site we have the argument from the simple statement of the inspired writer, who calls them "the cities of the plain," or circle, "ciccar," of Jordan—an expression which can not possibly apply to any other than the *northern* end of the Dead Sea. Abraham and Lot were standing between Bethel and Hai, when "Lot lifted up his eyes, and beheld all the plain of Jordan, that it was well watered everywhere, before the Lord destroyed Sodom and Gomorrah, even as the garden of the Lord, like the land of Egypt, *as thou comest unto Zoar*. Then Lot chose him all the plain of Jordan; and Lot journeyed *east*" (Gen. xiii., 10, 11). Now, from these hills it is impossible to gain a glimpse of the south end of the Dead Sea, shut off by distance and by lofty intervening mountains; while the plain of Jericho, and its far more extensive sister plain of Shittim, or the Seisaban, on the east side of the river, are spread almost at the beholder's feet.

Corroborative arguments may also be found in the incident mentioned (Gen. xix., 28), that "Abraham from Mamre looked toward Sodom and Gomorrah, and toward all the land of the plain," after the destruction of the cities. Though the vale itself is not visible from the hills above Hebron or Mamre, yet the depression between the nearer hills and those of Gilead can be perceived, and Abraham could at once identify the locality whence the smoke arose.

Again, in the account of the raid of Chedorlaomer (Gen. xiv.) we find that the invader, after he smote the Horites in Mount Seir (or Edom), then attacked the Amalekites and the Amorites, in Hazezon-tamar, or Engedi. After this, he met the King of Sodom and his confederates in the vale of Siddim, and returned toward Damascus. The account of Chedorlaomer's route is quite unintelligible if the cities were south of the Dead Sea; but if they were to the north of it, there is perfect topographical sequence in the whole narrative.

The rediscovery of the site of Zoar in Zi'ara also at once explains an expression which has been a most perplexing *crux* to every Biblical geographer. In the view granted to Moses from Mount Nebo (Deut. xxxiv., 3) he beheld "the south, and the plain of the valley of Jericho, the city of palm-trees, *unto Zoar.*" I had always been perplexed by this expression, and was led at one time to suggest that Zoar might have been on the west side, near the headland of Feshkbah (Pisgah), some miles south of Jericho, and visible from Nebo.

But, read by the light of this discovery, the solution is simple enough. The narrative is describing the panorama from north to south, and ends by the feature nearest the spectator—*i. e.*, the city in front of him. Now we detected these ruins while standing on Nebo. They are the nearest feature in the landscape directly in front, perched on a low brow, almost in a line with Jericho, and the object on which the eye would naturally rest in its survey, next after the Jordan plain.

One expression now may be noticed, in confirmation of the identification. Zoar, though on a hill, must have had higher ground behind it; for we read (Gen. xix., 30) that "Lot went up out of Zoar, and dwelt in the mountain . . . in a cave." Here we have higher ground behind Zi'ara, and that, too, pierced by many caves. Heshbon, also, only a few miles distant, was the original seat of the Moabites (Numb. xxi., 26).

It may be added that there is no reason, from the details given us in Scripture, for assigning to the cities of the plain a location on the west, rather than the east, side of the river; and as the plain of Shittim is much more extensive than that of Jericho, and the

Jordan possesses three fords, passable, except during the season of the floods, in its lower reach, it is probable that some, at least, of the four cities were on the farther side.

On referring to Mr. Grove's article in Smith's "Dictionary of the Bible," which I had not previously examined, I find that he has indicated, by *a priori* arguments, this very district as the probable site of Zoar. "It is highly probable," he remarks, "that the Zoar of the Pentateuch was to the north of the Dead Sea, not far from its northern end, in the general parallel of Jericho. That it was on the east side of the valley seems to be implied in the fact that the descendants of Lot, the Moabites and Ammonites, are in possession of that country as their original seat when they first appear in the sacred history. It seems to follow that the "mountain" in which Lot and his daughters dwelt when Moab and Ben-ammi were born, was the mountain to which he was advised to flee by the angel, and between which and Sodom stood Zoar. It is also in favor of its position north of the Dead Sea, that the earliest information as to the Moabites makes their original seat in the plains of Heshbon, north-east of the lake—not, as afterward, in the mountains on the south-east, to which they were driven by the Amorites."—*Bible Dictionary*, "ZOAR."

From Zi'ara we turned northward to descend into the valley of Ayun Moussa—"Springs of Moses"—or, as it is called lower down, Wady Jerifeh. After half an hour's brisk ride, we had to pull up on a terrace and leave our horses, while we scrambled down on foot to the springs below, the proper path down being on the other side of the ravine. Our sudden arrival put to flight, in a panic, a number of Arab women who were filling goat-skins from the precious fountain, and lading a score of asses, but who rushed pell-mell up the opposite path as fast as, with screams and sticks, they could urge their animals.

To describe Ayun Moussa is not easy. One is easily tempted to exaggerate; for in this thirsty land a perennial spring gives an air of fair enchantment to the scene, from its startling contrast with the arid bluffs around. These springs are supposed to derive their name from the tradition of their having been the resting-place of Moses on his way to Pisgah. There are two fountains, or rather two groups of springs, bursting from the foot of a tall line of cliffs. The first group run for a short distance over a shelf of rock, shaded by some fine old fig-trees, under which we sat for our midday meal, which was flavored with water-cress gathered on the spot. A few yards farther on, several smaller springs issue from fissures in the cliff, soon unite their streams on a broad, wide shelf of rock, and then form a pretty cascade, about twenty-five feet high, the effect of which in winter, over the horseshoe-shaped ledge, must be very fine.

The real beauty of the fall is best seen on descending, when the overhanging platform is found to be the roof of a cave with a chord of sixty yards, its front partially built up with stalagmite below and stalactite above, and water dropping in all directions. But who can do justice to the beauty of its adornings? The roof is one mass of pendent fronds of maidenhair fern; the sides are tapestried with them; the floor is carpeted with them. Happy maiden-hair!— here, at least, safe from extermination at the hands of collecting maniacs!

Fig-trees cast their massive shade over the mouth of the cave, and overhang the lower falls very little farther down, and about fifty feet in height. Hence the water hurries rapidly down the wady, dotted with fine terebinths and patches of cultivation. Climbing up again to the springs, we walk along a path under the line of cliffs, till we come to a series of caves in its face, which have been walled up with masonry, leaving only low square-headed door-ways, originally tombs, but now occasionally used as folds by goat-herds.

Near these, the second of the twin "Springs of Moses" bursts from a deep horizontal tunnel in the rock, about fifteen inches in diameter. The volume of water is greater than that of the other spring; and both fountains and stream, clear as crystal, have every stone and pebble of their gravelly bed covered with the glossy black shells of *Neritina* and *Melanopsis*. This stream joins the other, after the cascades, by a series of smaller leaps. We could here look down its course till it enters the Seisaban; and had a peep of a bit of the Jordan Valley, set in a frame of mountain and rock, with green hill-sides in all the lower part.

A good path runs parallel to the water-course up to the last tops of the ridge, before the Wady Heshban and its tributaries divide it from the heights to the north. We soon get into the roots of innumerable wadys, and rise to a series of crescent-shaped knolls, the crest of the ridge, of which Nebo is the southernmost. These all bear in common the name of M'Shuggar, which, however, is more especially applied to the one on which are the ruins of an ancient city of the same name. Each view was new, and we rode unconcernedly at will, with or without our guide, as he stopped to "liquor up" on "leben," at an Arab camp, or took a lazy short cut over the shoulder of a hill, or unwillingly followed our lead.

We were now on the border-land of several tribes, some of them strangers to us, but all peaceably disposed, though they knew nothing of the Franghi. On one hill-side I had dismounted, when alone, to secure a partridge; my horse at the moment espied a camp in the bottom, and galloped off to make some equine acquaintance. Up and down I had to toil, under the scorching sun, for an hour, till at length he was caught among some tent ropes by an old woman, who was in ecstasies over a very trifling backsheesh. Her gratitude would not allow me to depart without a draught of "leben." "She brought forth butter in a lordly dish," and asked if I were a Turkish officer—the only foreigners of whom she seemed to have any notion.

In the valleys were the camps of the Belka tribe. On M'Shuggar were a large party of Ajermeh, housed for the nonce in the tombs and old ruined arches of the city. Between this place and Heshbon was a camp of over sixty great tents of Beni Sakk'r, while lines of their tents fringed the whole way at intervals, during an hour's ride, with their flocks and camels spreading over the eastern plain. Close to Heshbon, on the north, was an encampment of the Adwân, the largest camp I ever saw—comprising, in fact, the whole tribe, with the gaudy Marabout tents of some Damascus merchants conspicuous in their midst.

Heshbon I had visited before, and it has been often described. But there is little, of a place once famed in olden story, for the traveler to see. A large piece of walling at the west end of the bold isolated hill on which the old fortress stood, with a square blockhouse, and a pointed archway adjoining—a temple on the crest of the hill, with the pavement unbroken and the bases of four columns still *in situ*—on the east, in the plain, just at the base of the hill, a great cistern, called by some the "fish-pools of Heshbon," but more probably only the reservoir for the supply of the city—these are all that remain.

On the east was the wide, grassy plain; and here we took our last regretful gaze at the haunts of the past month, with Shihan, Ziza, Kustul, and many other points now so familiar; while the desert hills beyond Zebib and Mâshitâ fringed the far horizon. The cleft of the Callirrhoe faintly shows; and beyond it the table-land south of the Arnon, several feet higher than that to the north of it, forms a background. The Wady Heshban begins just to the west of the ruins and the side of the hill; and the opposite slopes are honey-combed with caves and ancient sepulchres, now the sleeping-places of living goats.

Leaving the photographers at work, Hayne and I rode down to visit the Scriptural site of Elealeh, now El 'Ahl, the road to which is well defined across the plain. Descending the hill, we found ourselves at once in the great Adwân camp. Tall spears, with their tufts of black ostrich feathers, marked the quarters of the chiefs, Diab and Goblan. Men and dogs turned out to salute us—among the former many a companion of my former expedition, especially Goblan's son, who told us his father had ridden down the valley to our camp, to welcome his old comrade. Getting free from them, we spurred at a hard gallop to Elealeh. We were out of Beni Sakk'r land now, and were eyed suspiciously by the strangers we passed. One armed horseman, on the top of the mound, gave us but a cold salute; and as he looked like backsheesh, we sheered off. We glanced at the waif of a column standing solitary among the stone-heaps of desolate Elealeh, peeped over toward Wady Na'ur and the north, and cantered back.

Where was our camp? The sun was getting low, and no time was to be lost. One horseman had remained for us. Our faith in our guide's knowledge was not great; but our halting-place had been arranged to be in the Heshbon Valley, and down the rugged wady we could not well lose our way. It was a romantic little glen, the scenery very Scotch, except for the endless herds of camels, brought here for the foaling season, and each of which had her grunting colt by her side.

We rapidly descended, passing the castle of 'Al on our right. The sun had set, but no water yet in the bed of the wady, and our men would not have pitched till they had found water. At length a frog's croak and a jackass's bray, more welcome than usual, caught our ear. The stream was running freely, with many a little pool swarming with fish—the true "fish-pools of Heshbon;" and soon my old companion of eight years ago, Sheik Goblan, of the Adwân, came forth, with his face enveloped in the folds of a gray "kefiyeh," to welcome me for "auld lang syne."

Goblan had brought two lambs as a present, and Zadam three more; so we had a flock of seven tethered to our tents. Of course, we entertained our visitor and his train at supper. Zadam had gone with his Beni Sakk'rs to enjoy the hospitality of Diab, and the Adwân. It would have implied a distrust of Arab chivalry, had he or his guard remained with us the first night we were in Adwân territory, jealous as the tribes are of each other. Till midnight Goblan sat, recalling old experiences, and lamenting these degenerate, unwarlike days. He is no common character—a tall, spare man of over sixty. As he lifts his kefiyeh to sip his soup, he discloses a long gray mustache, and a ghastly sabre slash on his cheek. His left eye, bloodshot, still shows the mark of his old wound. His eyes are covetous, but his hand is of an almost velvet softness—tiger-like, perhaps, when provoked.

Evil as is his repute, he has some conscience, and is a faithful friend. I once had from him the story of his first crime. When a very young man, riding over the plain, he noticed a horseman before him on a splendid iron-gray mare: the demon seized him— he resolved he would have the mare; and, watching his opportunity, he speared the rider, and carried off the animal. The murdered man was a Beni Sakk'r, though not of Zadam's sept. The man was recognized, and the crime suspected. Years have passed, and Goblan knows not the name nor the family of his victim; but he feels sure that some one has vowed vengeance, and that he shall yet suffer retribution. "I can not sleep," said he, "without seeing the gray mare and her rider before me. But she was a splendid mare! Who would not have killed a stranger for her?" Such is Arab morality—such is man, fallen, but with many a noble trait, yet without the Gospel!

CHAPTER XVIII.

The Wady Heshban.—Goblan's Affection.—Married beneath him.—Botany of North-west Moab.—Ancient Tablets and Tombs.—Changed Features of Scenery.—Circle of Dolmens.—Cairn.—Descent to the Ghor.—Ghawarineh Camp.—Old Acquaintances.—Beth-haran.—Night-watch.—Excursion down the Coast.—Beth-jeshimoth.—Camp of Israel.—Wady Jerifeh.—Ain Suwaineh.—Vegetation of the Shore.—Wady Ghadeimeh.—Clear Atmosphere.—Rich Coloring.—Wady Ghuweir.—Arab Battle-field.—Falcons.—Our Path blocked.—Palm-groves.—A Halt.—Ornithology.—An Arab Collector.—Gale of Wind.—The Tents carried off.—A sound Sleeper.—Ride to the Jordan.—Ferry-boat.—Return to Civilization.—Jericho.—Our old Camping-ground.—Bethany in Spring.—Entry into Jerusalem.—Our Wanderings ended.

The Wady Heshban, in which we camped for our last night in the highlands of Moab, has many interesting and peculiar features. It does not appear to have been followed down its whole course by any previous travelers, as the ordinary road to the Jordan and Jerusalem descends to the north of it. But we selected this route with the view of examining the Seisaban, or plains of Shittim, and especially its southern and unexplored portion.

The wady is full of ruins, old and modern, through its whole course. Just opposite to our tents, on the south side, was the Castle of Sumia, a dilapidated though modern structure, but built by the side of, and with materials from, some evidently more antique remains. It has been a frontier Adwân fortress. Under the cliff, close to the castle, a delicious and copious spring bursts from the rock, and has formerly been used to turn a corn-mill, now in ruins.

Zadam returned to us in the morning; but it required some diplomacy to shake off Goblan and our dozen attendant Adwân visitors. Unlike the Beni Sakk'r, they were perpetually in and out of our tents, assuring us that pure friendship had brought them, and that nothing should separate us till we crossed the Jordan. In vain we demurred to too stately a retinue, till at length, as the old chief was assuring us of his eternal friendship, I gave him a hearty handshake, and during the operation a few gold-pieces passed from my palm to his. The hint was taken that this was a final backsheesh, and, after a little formal hand-kissing, we parted the best of friends, Goblan hoping that ere long I should bring my "sitta" (lady) to see Amman and Gerash; which I promised to accomplish so soon as my purse should be full enough.

Zadam's manners, meantime, were above criticism—unobtrusive to us; toward the petty chieftains and dependents showing a nonchalant and dignified superiority. Among the Arabs, as elsewhere, the husband ennobles the wife—the wife descends to the rank of her husband. Zadam had just concluded a matrimonial engagement (his third) with a daughter of the Adwân, reputed to be the belle of the country; but he scornfully repelled, this very day (as we afterward learned), the proposal of a son of Sheik Diab for his own sister. "No; a Beni Sakk'r may raise an Adwân, but a daughter of the Sakk'r stoops not below her own tribe."

This north-west corner of Moab differs, both in appearance and flora, from the rest. At starting we had to make rather a long ascent on the southern side of the ravine. Marked was the contrast between the rugged red sandstone cliffs, sharp and precipitous, dotted with eagles' and vultures' nests, which formed the north wall of the wady; and the more gentle terraced slopes, covered with luxuriant verdure, unscorched by the sun, which bounded it on the south.

Common home weeds, English dead nettles, black bryony, mingle with maiden-hair and palm-trees. Gray rocks, thrown in massive boulders into the bed of a bubbling stream, and pitched hither and thither among grassy slopes, alternating with crags full of eyries, recall the features of a Cumberland dale. The little sparkling pools, alive with fish, these are surely the "fish-pools of Heshbon," to which the loved one's eyes are likened (Cant. vii., 4), rather than the stagnant tanks of rain-water, which are all that could ever have existed close to the city.

Some of the enormous limestone boulders and blocks, which have fallen from the cliffs and are strewn in the wady, have had chambers, evidently sepulchral, hollowed in them as they lay; and many others have had their faces carefully incised for tablets, of which the inscription or sculpture is now completely effaced.

Several of these tablets are not inferior in size or apparent antiquity to the famed Egyptian and Assyrian tablets of the Dog River, near Beyroot.

The English character of the scene soon changes. The ravine rapidly deepens, and widens to a succession of terraces, on many of which are perched heaps of ruins. We strike away from it to the southward, and, rounding the buttresses of the mountains, again come in sight of Zi'ara and other high points already visited.

The nomenclature of the Arabs for these ruins is limited. All those on the ridge between Wady Jedeid and Ayun Moussa, west of Nebbeh, are either Zi'ara or Muslubiyeh; while all on the range between Ayun Moussa and Wady Heshban are indiscriminately M'Shuggar—the name of the ridge itself. In fact, these minor ruins have no distinctive name, and they can never have been more than most insignificant villages at best. The range running between the Heshban and Wady Na'ur is called Jebel Zabood.

As we descend, we soon find ourselves again in a wide open gorge, dotted here and there by the cairns of stones raised over the death-spot of some Bedouin warrior. A Roman road has once wound down the valley, and we passed two prostrate mile-stones. Sandstone took the place of limestone, and bits of purple, red, and violet hue varied the coloring. We had scarcely been three hours in the saddle when we descended on the edge of the Ghor Seisaban, and entered on an open, undulating plateau.

On the last rocky eminence which pushed forward into it, were the most perfect primeval remains we had found in the country. Round the slightly-elevated crest at the western end of the ridge was a perfect circle of dolmens, each composed of three upright and one covering stone. Several of them had fallen, but the stones were in their places, and it was clear that they had been arranged in a circle round a great cairn, or central pile of stones, which crowned the " tell," and doubtless marked the burial-place of some hero famous in his day, but who lived before Agamemnon.

We debouched on the plain close to where the stream of the Heshban issues. The vegetation had been rapidly changing with the temperature, and now both were truly tropical. Just at the edge of the sultry plain was a large Ghawarineh camp, and troops of stark-naked boys playing at soldiers, with canes for their horses and spears. Black cattle and blue-clad women were roaming in all directions.

By the side of a cane-shaded stream, under a thorny nubk-tree, we sat down to lunch, and soon found ourselves surrounded by a gaping crowd. They were the very same who had stared at us in the Sáfieh, but at a less respectful distance. Meantime they had migrated northward by the shore of the lake, to enjoy the spring pastures of the Scisaban. The same pair of tall, ill-favored sheiks appeared, to pay their respects. How changed their manners now! Instead of hectoring, the caitiffs were cringing. But we did not forget their insults and injuries, and were cold and distant as Zadam himself.

The mules were still far behind; and having agreed to camp at the edge of the wilderness, we dispersed for our various pursuits. The tropical thickets, with their rare birds, were tempting enough to an ornithologist. I strolled on alone toward a conspicuous mound, or "tell," which might be artificial, very like the great mounds of Jericho, and its top crowned with an old Moslem wely, or tomb. Its name, Beit-harran, identifies it unmistakably with the *Beth-haran* of Numbers xxxii., 36, one of the fenced cities built by the children of God, and mentioned immediately after Beth-nimrah, the modern Beit N'meir, also in the Jordan plain, and only a few miles higher up. On the mound, and along-side of it, were a few traces of walls and foundations, all that remains of the "fenced city."

It is to be observed that throughout the whole of the lower Jordan Valley there is a remarkable absence of Roman or other substantial remains. The oppressive heat of the low-lying land probably discouraged permanent occupation, and induced the cultivators to reside on the higher grounds above—as to this day they do, above the fever-stricken marshes of the Huleh, north of the Sea of Galilee.

From Beit-harran I had at least three miles to walk before reaching the open, at the edge of which our tents were pitched. It was night-fall before I reached them; but my ramble gave me some idea of the extent of the Seisaban, by far the most extensive and luxuriant of any of the fertile lands bordering on the Dead Sea.

This abundantly watered and tree-covered district, often now knee-deep with green wheat, extends six miles from east to west, and ten or twelve from north to south. Looking at it from above, we can see how vastly it exceeds the oasis of Jericho; as well it may, with the exuberant gush of water from the springs at the base of the range of the Moab mountains. Its extent and depth are by no means revealed by the glimpses to be obtained from the hills above Jericho. But, like the Sâfieh, its thickets only afford covert for marauders; and it is notoriously the prey of lawless tribes, and the Alsatia of Arab criminals. Our guard, accordingly, were on the alert in our new camp: and our chief went the rounds, inspecting carefully the arms, to see that they were loaded, at least with powder; for noise, as he observed, is the best thing to scare a thief.

To our disquiet, our muleteers acted on the maxim; and every one, if he happened to turn in his sleep, let off a pistol to prove his wakefulness. We now felt grateful indeed to Zadam, who had not insisted on ball in addition to powder. He, however, was out of the way. Having ascertained that the Beni Atiyeh, with whom he had a blood feud, were prowling in the neighborhood, he had taken the precaution of arranging his bed and retiring to his couch with lights in his tent; but so soon as they were extinguished he crept forth in the darkness, and, descending to the banks of the stream, concealed himself in the densest of canebrakes, wrapped in his a'bbe'yeh, where no nocturnal prowlers could disturb his slumbers.

Determined to complete our survey of the coastline, by riding down to the shore as far as the mouth of the Callirrhoe, we made an early start the next morning. The fitful wind, which had gone down toward sunrise, rose again, and blew a suffocating hurricane in our faces, as we rode across the Ghor toward the corner of the sea.

Three miles south-west of Beit-haran, where the vegetation becomes more scant, and the tangle has degenerated into mere scrub, a bare mound rises, utterly destitute of vegetation, but with some canebrakes below it, which project forward, a few green lines, into the belt of waste which fringes the Jordan. These brakes are fed by some brackish springs which issue forth just behind the mound, and to which, if artificial, it probably owes its origin. A few lines of stones are all that remain of what has been once a fortified town. The heap is said to be Beth-jeshimoth. We did not find any name for it among our Arabs; but it must be remembered that they were out of their own territory, and we had no inhabitants of the Ghor with us. To our companions all places beyond their own domain were merely "Rujum"— "a heap."

This knoll is evidently the Beth-jesimuth spoken of by Schwarz, as still known at the north-eastern-

AIN SUWAINEH. 363

most point of the Dead Sea; for it is the only spot answering to his description. The Biblical allusions to the place harmonize with the identification. It was "in the plains of Moab by Jordan, near Jericho," and was the southern limit of the camp of Israel before they crossed the river, Abel-shittim being the northern (Numb. xxxiii., 48, 49), and was allotted to the tribe of Reuben.

From this point the plain as it approaches the Jordan becomes barer and barer, though still the contrast between the east and west sides is most marked—utter desolation on the west, scarcely any marl, and only scantier vegetation, on the east.

Just beyond the mounds, we crossed a little water-course, the Wady Jerifeh, which is simply the continuation of Wady Ayun Moussa. The water here had sunk a few inches below the gravel, but the herbage around could reach it, and was knee-deep. Ten minutes afterward we crossed the bed of the Wady Ghedeid. All these water-courses are, of course, no longer valleys, but mere channels in the plain, with the streams more or less permanent.

In half an hour more we reached Ain Suwaineh, the resting-place of Palmer and Drake, with a heap of shapeless ruins on a knoll just above it. There is a little rock a few feet high hidden among tall canes, and from its foot bursts forth, most unexpectedly, this copious stream, running down almost in a line with the head of the Dead Sea. The water is clear and potable, though slightly brackish. All below it is thick with canes and tamarisks, a few palms springing up among them.

Thence, in twenty minutes, through a marsh covered with rushes and the broad leaves of a sea-lavender (*Statice*), not yet in flower, we reached a lovely running stream, with poplars and willows along its course, and buried in their thickets, sunk among marly cliffs. This is the only spot, except the Lisan, where this formation, so general on the western side, remains on the eastern. About the wady, the soil is cut up into every fantastic shape, worked into mock forts and mamelons, with buildings and bastions that might have trained a Vauban. Very soon after leaving this Wady Ghedeimeh (which is the continuation of the Jedeid, the southern wady of Nebo), we crossed the little Burrhoughat.

We were now out of the Seisaban, and under the headlands along the shore of the Dead Sea; but still the vegetation continued without interruption. Even amidst masses of rocks and boulders there are shrubs. and flowers springing up in every chink. A pretty blue campanula was the characteristic new plant of the first low headland we had to cross. Here alone, during our day's expedition, we met with a number of small basaltic boulders, strewn over the surface—all the rest was red sandstone.

Our track led us over broken ground for several miles, ever and again bringing us to the little pebbly bays between the low headlands. Sheltered from the stifling sirocco gusts by the mountains, which gradually narrow the low-lying "ghor," or plain, of the sea-board, the day was intensely to be enjoyed.

A peerless sky, after the dull and leaden heat-haze of the day before—the sea a brilliant blue, its surface rippled by the breeze—the wilderness of Judea beyond, with light and shade brought out in sharp relief, while the sun was still in its eastern quarter—the foreground carpeted with flowers, sheets of delicate coloring, now pale lilac from a statice, now as softly red, from the sorrel in flower and fruit—such were the chief features of the landscape. Deep green hawthorns among the rocks, and the fresh foliage of the white poplars on the banks of the sea, relieved the eye, after the monotonous coloring of most of the trees and shrubs of the country—a dull olive hue, without the charm of the silvery underleaf twinkling in the breeze.

Scarcely an hour after crossing Burroughat we reached the Ghuweir, the stream which flows from "the ravine of the wolf," Wady Ed Deib, north of Medeba. This would be the very spot in which to camp, for any one bent on a minute exploration of these wild recesses. The stream is sweet and copious, shaded by fine poplars, willows, and the oleander, already in blossom; while its thickets are full of northern blackbirds and thrushes, enjoying here a second summer. The stream, before reaching the sea, crosses a little piece of open plain; but only a few hundred yards farther back it issues from a narrow glen, with cliffs scarcely inferior to those of the Callirrhoe. I explored it for an hour on our way back. Colonies of kestrels were noisily debating far overhead; the fine Alpine swifts had already returned, and dashed, shrieking, from their inaccessible chinks; and a rookery of square-tailed ravens were amusing themselves by the futile pursuit of a lanner falcon.

Close to the mouth of the Ghuweir are a number of small modern cairns, marking some Arab battle-field, called Hawâra, on a long, projecting shoulder; and an insignificant ruined site below, some ancient village, named Anûzeh. Just south of these remains a belt of yellow rock appeared, as if poured down from the mountains above. No doubt it was a sulphurous deposit, for the peculiar plants of the hot springs suddenly re-appeared.* The asclepiad of Josephus abounded, and the sulphur-plant was in profusion.

A little farther on we passed a magnificent cleft, rather than a wady, for it does not reach far into the mountains—Wady Sakk'r. The gully was clad with fine palm-trees from top to bottom, and a pair of Sakk'r falcons were swooping round and round our heads as we approached too near their nest on the cliffs. They had formed, however, too high an estimate of our scaling powers, for the eyrie was absolutely inaccessible. Johnson took the opportunity of photographing the ravine, while we passed on to reconnoitre the nest of a second pair of falcons, equally safe from the most adventurous climber.

* See pp. 268, 269.

Proceeding southward, we were soon face to face with a rugged headland which, at first sight, appeared completely to bar all passage for man or horse. Ayeed, our guide, declared the road to end here, and advised us to sit down and eat, and content ourselves with looking at the mouth of the Callirrhoe through our glasses. As we remained unconvinced, he adroitly led us into a maze of boulders really impracticable for horses, while an overhanging cliff shut out the only view of the real track higher up. His dodge failed, for we announced our intention of leaving the horses and proceeding on foot. A scramble on rocks in his red boots would by no means meet the taste of a Beni Sakk'r, and consequently the path was soon found, and he sulkily led the way.

There are traces of the old and well-engineered road of ancient times. Its terrace remains along the mountain side, broken and interrupted by land-slips and avalanches of stones wherever it rounds a headland or crosses a gorge. As it is, it is a rugged and perilous path. Even the consummate horseman Zadam dismounted. Up and down, along ledges, across boulders, up steep and broken stairs, we led our agile horses, with the thermometer 92° in the shade.

Wherever the spurs of the mountains reach the sea palms begin to clothe the moister nooks, and finally almost fringe the perpendicular cliffs. In one cleft the waving palms covered all the sides of the slope, from the very edge of the shore, where one tree all but laved its fronds in the sea, up to the crest of the overhanging mountains, as far as we could see.

At length, after four hours and a half steady traveling, we are brought up at the entrance to a little palm-tree glen by a face of crumbling conglomerate. We were only two miles in a straight line from the mouth of the Callirrhoe. While our guides and men began deliberately to work a sloping niche up the side of the cliff, and so cut a road for our horses, we clambered up and reconnoitred. There was the spit at the Callirrhoe's mouth, half an hour's easy walk on a plain— an open plain the latter part of the way—but a hopeless mass of boulder and rock for the first half mile. Daylight would not suffice to bring us back to camp, and Zadam would not venture to sleep out in this lawless region, where many a robber band might be watching us, now unseen, from the heights above us.

We reluctantly yielded to *force majeur*, and sat down to our *déjeûner sans fourchette* under the "shadow of a great rock in a weary land," having learned, not for the first time, the difference between theorizing over a map and making progress on an embayed and rocky shore. Our meal over, we turned northward again, but at our leisure: photographer, botanist, naturalist, each had abundance to attract him, and we could not lose our way.

Leaving my horse to follow with the men, I started on foot, ahead of the rest of the party, and scrambled by a course rather higher up than the one we had followed, or made, on our way down. It was well that

NO. 36.

PALM-TREES BY THE DEAD SEA.

water abounded on the route, for the sun had now got to the south, and beat with full force on our backs. The wind had fallen; not so the temperature, 95° in the shade, and, I am sure, 150° in the sun. The rocks refracted the heat. My gun-barrels were so hot I could only just bear to touch them. The Judean hills had now all the shade, which threw the hills and valleys into much bolder relief than when we had looked at them under the full morning glare.

The western hills showed deep purple in the shade. The nearer coloring was gorgeous. The basalt wall south of the Callirrhoe ravine stood out in fine contrast with the brilliant and even dazzling red of the sandstone cliffs above and around me, and with the white glare of the opposite coast. So clear was the atmosphere, that I saw Tabor distinctly, and all the mountains of Samaria northward, and the low ridge of Usdum, forty miles away to the south, and even the very trees at Engedi, twenty miles off, with the naked eye. Oh that we had had such a clear day when on Nebo! The sea below was a strange leaden blue. Such a mass of water so absolutely stagnant I never saw before. In the morning it had been lashed by the gale — now it at once suggested, as its appropriate description, "a sea of molten lead;" while, wherever the spray had struck the rocks a few hours before, the rapid evaporation had left a glittering crust of salt.

The afternoon was far advanced before my friends overtook me, and now no time was to be lost. On we pushed, with many a canter and gallop, through scrub and across the plain. Birds of all kinds, rare and common, tantalized us as we rode, for we had no time to shoot. The summer migrants were traveling northward; flocks of the great spotted cuckoo, scores at a time, rose with their stealthy flight, waving their long tails as though they could scarcely wield them; all our English songsters were mingled with bulbuls, sun-birds, and the rare denizens of Jericho. Now and then a desert hare, and every few steps a quail, started beneath our feet; while partridges, Greek and Hey's, called defiantly from the tops of the boulders as we passed, as though they knew themselves safe.

The sun had retired behind the hills of Jerusalem, and we had barely light enough to descry the white tops of our tents, and to steer our way toward them, when, after eleven hours of an expedition amidst natural scenery the most varied and interesting we had enjoyed in our wanderings, we drew rein—not, however, for rest. On entering the tent, we found it turned into a miscellaneous museum. Jemeel, my old collector, who had visited us at Medeba, true to his word, had come to find us, and had spread, on carpets and couches, the results of his week's hunting. Birds, beasts, eggs, reptiles, beetles, and shells lay strewn in profusion. Among them a large wild-cat, a coney, grakles, hoopoes, spotted cuckoos, hares, hawks, desert partridges by the dozen, a long Naja serpent; and all hinted, by their perfume, that they must be either stowed away or thrown away without delay. Jemeel had, however, profited by his lessons, and had removed the carcasses of the larger beasts. Still a heavy night's work was before me, if any thing was to be safely brought home.

Our last night in Moab was not to be without its ludicrous adventure. The wind, which from sundown had been blowing in sudden gusts of sultry sirocco, at midnight rose to a gale and rocked our tents, though sunk in an apparently snug depression by the side of a stream. Pickets had been driven in, stay-ropes thrown across them, and we flattered ourselves we could defy the storm, which drove suffocating clouds of fine hot sand that penetrated everywhere, and irritated the skin beyond endurance.

Journals were finished, and all had lain down and left me alone, hard at work with carbolic acid and arsenical soap, when, after a violent gust, Buxton appeared in night costume to seek help. The other tent was gone. Presaging the storm, the photographers had, for once, stowed away their plates and bottles, which usually remained on the table till morning. They had not long retired to their mats when the tent was lifted off them.

We turned out to find Johnson lying clothesless and tentless, scarcely yet awakened, on the plain, which was strewn with the débris of the wreck. Straps, clothes, saddles, wraps, and all the lighter paraphernalia of camp furniture, were scattered in all directions. The muleteers were roused, but not the Arabs, who, stolid as ever, slept through it all. At length the wreckage was collected and stored in our tent, into which we all huddled again, but not for rest, for the musquitoes slept not, and the flies would not go to bed.

With the thermometer at 75° at day-break, we were glad to turn out after our sleepless night, refreshed only by a bath among the oleanders, in the little stream. Instead of riding straight across to the lower fords, which would have led us to Hajla (Beth-hogla), and so by Gilgal to Jericho, with our laden mules we preferred to ride a few miles north of our camp, to the ferry-boat, which now takes the place of the pristine fording and swimming. The plain along which we rode was in marked contrast with the western Ghor. There was very little marl, and we never lost a scrubby vegetation till the lower banks of the river were reached. We then wound our way for a mile or two, under tamarisks and poplars, by a charming path, till we arrived at the ferry, some miles south of the spot where I had crossed, on my way to Gilead, eight years before.

This ferry now transports the rapidly-increasing exports from Es Salt and the eastern side to Jerusalem and Nablous. It is a large flat-bottomed boat, passed by a rope from shore to shore—not more than sixty yards across at this spot. Here we bid farewell to Moab and the sultry plains of Shittim. Bathing and filling water-bottles for christenings at home occupied the time till the mules came up.

Landed in Palestine, the first sign of a return to

civilization caught our eyes in the wattled hut of the ferryman and a number of chickens running about— a creature unknown east of Jordan. Invited to coffee by the gentlemanly-looking Charon whose negro slaves work the boat, we crept under a door-way four feet high and sat under a roof. An arsenal of a dozen firelocks intimated that the thickets of the Jordan are still the haunts of outlaws and robbers who have fled from justice.

From the fords we wound for some distance, by the river-side, through a maze of trees with gorgeous yellow orobanches springing up under their shade, and the thickets re-echoing with the notes of the bulbul and of the English nightingale.

From the thickets we ascend to the most desolate and dreary of marl terraces, without a vestige of life, animal or vegetable, till we reach the third terrace, or plateau of the Jordan Valley. At first scrub covers it, which gradually gives place to scattered nubk-trees and a carpet of flowers. Then begin corn-patches and little rills tapped from the springs.

We turn a corner, and soon come on Elisha's Fountain. Signs that we are re-entering on civilization now crowd on our reluctant sight. Small boys rush forward from the corn-patches and the gardens, with open palms, shrieking for backsheesh. Men have mattocks instead of guns on their shoulders. Worst of all, our lovely old camping-ground of eight years ago is no more. The trees have been all stumped up, or pollarded, and the whole is surrounded by an impenetrable line of horrid thorn-branches, and turned into a cucumber-field.

At length, after following the course of the stream for a little way down, though at a respectful distance, we find an opening, and a small space untilled, close to the water, with a good bathing-pool, and a dense shade from trees covered with Indian Loranthus, affording room for tents and pickets. A fellah comes with a bill-hook, and offers to assist in clearing ground for the camp. He informs us that there are a party of Americans camped two miles lower down, and that Cook's tourists, with twenty-one tents, pitched on the open ground above only yesterday.

We have not seen a European since we started from Jerusalem; but the charm of savage life is no more, and Moab has been left behind. We start at once for my old haunts, climb the side of Mount Quarantania, up to the Hermits' Cave, find some Abyssinian Christians keeping Lent there, and return for a bathe in Elisha's Fountain, dinner, and our last night on the ground under canvas.

The next morning was spent in bird-collecting in the thickets, and in examining the sections cut in the mounds of old Jericho by the Palestine Exploration Fund, which still yielded some fragments of pottery. It was near noon when we started for Jerusalem. The rugged path, so familiar in past years, has given place to a well-made road, walled in the most precipitous parts, with series of easy steps in the steepest places. After a halt at the ruined khan, the traditional inn of the parable of the Good Samaritan, and the traditional luncheon-place of all modern travelers, the increase of cultivation in the open spaces in all the shallow valleys since my last visit was most marked.

Bethany is reached, now looking beautiful, buried in fruit-trees—the olive, and especially the almond, now in full blossom. One fig-tree, putting forth its leaves, could even prematurely intimate that summer was nigh. How changed the scenery since we last walked out to Bethany, about two months ago! Here are the first houses we have seen since we left Kerak. The climate, too, has changed since we left the Jordan in the morning, the wind blowing strong and cold, and the sun hidden behind a mist.

Gladly we took shelter under a rock until the mules came up, and the cavalcade formed in procession to enter the city in state. The leading mules were decked out with their trappings and their bells, the foremost carrying the English ensign. This honorable post was not decided before a fight between the rival muleteers as to which had proved itself the best mule. We had, at length, to interfere with threats of force; and great was the indignation of the devout Moslems that the place of honor was won by a Christian mule from Lebanon. The howadji, with Daoud and a pet lamb, Zadam's last gift to him, brought up the rear. Zadam looked in an ecstasy of quiet triumph as he rode over the slippery pavements of Jerusalem, having fulfilled his promise that he would never leave us till he had ridden by our side up Christian Street.

We had scarcely passed through St. Stephen's Gate, when we were recognized by the soldiers who had been sent to our rescue, and whom we had met at the Na'ur. Their congratulations, and those of many strangers, as our horses slid over the pavement, till we reached the Mediterranean Hotel, revealed the interest that had been excited by our detention at Kerak. As we sat at dinner that evening, in Hornstein's comfortable hostel, with Zadam for our guest, his best Arab costume setting off his handsome face and figure, while he complacently quaffed his Champagne, which of us felt not some tinge of regret that our wanderings in the land of Moab were ended?

One morning, a few days afterward, we parted outside the Joppa Gate; Buxton, Johnson, and the writer, to return home—Hayne and Trotter to continue their tour through Syria. Once more the whole party met under Lady Buxton's hospitable roof at Cromer, last autumn. Little did any of them think it was for the last time.

While these last sheets have been passing through the press the sad intelligence has been brought that William Amherst Hayne has been cut off by fever at Catania, in Sicily. How much he contributed to the success of the expedition these pages but scantily testify. But he will not soon be forgotten, either by those who learned to love him then, or by that far larger circle at home, who knew him as the accomplished scholar, the keen naturalist, but, most of all, as the centre of Christian influence among his compeers in the University of Cambridge. With such promise, with such powers, he seemed to be one whom the Church of Christ, to the ministry of which, in heart, his future life was already consecrated, could ill spare. But One wiser than man has told us, "When the fruit is brought forth, *immediately* He putteth in the sickle."

CHAPTER

ON

THE PERSIAN PALACE OF MÄSHITÂ.

BY JAMES FERGUSSON, F.R.S.

DR. TRISTRAM has explained so fully, in the body of the work, the ground on which I ventured to ascribe the building of the palace at Mǎshitâ to Chosroes, the Khosru Purviz of the Persians, that 1 have very little to add, on that branch of the subject, to what he has already said so well. The truth is, the whole argument lies in a very narrow compass. There are in this palace architectural features which, so far as is now known, were first invented in the age of Justinian. The full-bodied convex capitals of the inner palace, as contradistinguished from the hollow, concave, bell-shaped capitals of the Roman-Corinthian order, are just such inventions as mark an epoch in the art which admits of no question, though side by side with them are reminiscences—in the language of the day, "survivals"—of the older and more classical forms. On the other hand, there seems to be an equally certain limit beyond which it can not be brought down. In 632 the Arabs invaded Syria; and they came as conquerors to destroy; and it was not till

INNER PALACE OF MASHITÁ, FROM WITHIN THE OUTER GATE-WAY

long afterward that they attempted to restore or build. Their earliest works, so far as is now known, date from the time of Abd-ul-Malek, A.D. 684–705. He built the Mosque Al-Aksah at Jerusalem, and converted the Church of St. John at Damascus into the principal mosque of that city. Both these works are so essentially rude and clumsy as to prove that even at that age the Arab conquerors were still too inartistic to attempt any thing so beautiful as the palace at Mâshitâ or the Dome of the Rock at Jerusalem. Our researches for a date are thus limited to the century that elapsed between the times of Justinian and Omar; and within this period there seems no one to whom it would be possible to ascribe the building of such a palace as this except to this great hero of the Sassanian race.

The one objection which it appears might be plausibly urged against this view is, that nothing exactly like it is found among the buildings of the Sassanians in their own country. This, however, is not quite correct. The long vaulted halls of the inner palace are found in all their erections from Al Hadhr to the Tak Kesra at Ctesiphon.* And the great sculptured rock-cut arch at Takt-i-Bostan,† which is the most authentic specimen of the architecture of Chosroes known to us, is as classical as this, though differing in detail, as might be expected from its object and its locality.

---

* "History of Architecture," ii., p. 423, *et seqq.*

† Ker Porter's "Travels in Persia," vol. ii., plates 61 to 64. Flandin and Coste, "Voyage en Perse," vol. i., plates 1 to 12.

If any thing remained of his celebrated palace at Dastagerd, we might be able to speak with absolute certainty in this matter; but even its site is a matter of dispute; and though it is probable that the spot may be identified with the ruins at Eski Baghdad—visited and described by Rich*—they are mere unornamented brick walls, without any architectural or sculptured ornament which would afford any means of comparison. The fact is, that all the palaces built on the banks of the Euphrates or Tigris were in brick, and depended for their ornament on carvings in wood or metal, or, in ancient times, on sculptured slabs of alabaster. In Sassanian times these were replaced by plaster; but all these having perished, there is nothing left but the skeletons of the buildings to enable us to judge of the living likeness of the two styles.

Even, however, if the means of comparison were more abundant, we must bear in mind the exceptional circumstances under which this palace was erected. The best years of his youth were spent by Chosroes at Hierapolis, as the guest of the Emperor Maurice, where he no doubt admired and imbued his mind with the glories of the classical buildings of that and other cities of Asia Minor. At the time it is supposed he was erecting this palace, all Asia Minor, as well as all Syria, obeyed his commands, and the best artists of Antioch and Damascus, as well as those of the great cities of Asia Minor, were available for his purposes.

---

* Rich, "Residence in Koordistan," ii., 251, *et seq.*

So far, too, as either history or tradition throws any light on these matters, Chosroes was the most artistic and art-loving of all the kings of his dynasty. As Sir John Malcolm says, "A thousand volumes have been filled by his countrymen with the story of this king and his love for the fair Shireen, and their love for Ferhad the sculptor, or architect."* In so far as Persian history is concerned, the latter was by no means the least important person of the three. He was the friend and adviser of his sovereign, and assisted him in carrying out all the great works that rendered his reign illustrious. It was to his art that the palace at Dastagerd, so eloquently described by Gibbon,† owed its splendor; and we may, perhaps, assume that it was by his advice, and partially under his inspiration, that Mashita attained the prominence which undoubtedly belongs to it.‡

---

* "History of Persia," i., p. 158.
† "Decline and Fall," vol. v., chap. xlvi., p. 527.
‡ Among the MS. drawings bequeathed by the late C. Texier to the Institute of British Architects there is one of a bass-relief at Schiraz, representing the story of Chosroes and the fair Shireen from the time he first saw her bathing, as David saw Bathsheba, the concluding scene of which is curious. It represents the king slaying a lion, as kings of Persia were wont to do from very remote times; and beyond him Shireen sits quietly on horseback, watching Ferhad sculpturing birds and foliage on a rock, or great stone: in fact, just such a subject as we find on the façade of this palace. It might be going too far to assert that this palace was actually executed by or under the direct superintendence of Ferhad, but it certainly looks as if he inspired the design.

RESTORATION.

It is not proposed, on the present occasion at least, to attempt any restoration of the central palace, E E E E, itself (wood-cut No. 24). Its exterior probably always presented the same diapered brick-wall that is now seen, and its only ornamental part was the great triple portal, B B, that led into the hypæthral court. That once was complete, and the whole of the voussoirs of the central arch at least, which was twenty-two feet in width, lie in front, exactly as they fell, and as they appear in wood-cut No. 21. The voussoirs, also, of the side arches, which were apparently eleven feet wide, are, probably, also on the ground, though not shown in the photographs. So that the whole of this façade can easily be restored from the actual remains, whenever any architect has the opportunity of examining them with care.

The case is widely different with the elaborately ornamented façade, A A, that forms the entrance to the whole, on the south side. It certainly never was finished; indeed, there is reason for believing that not one single stone has fallen from its place; what we see now is exactly what the last builder saw when he fled on hearing of the disaster that deprived his master of the dominion of the fairest half of the then known world. The highest block at the left-hand corner had been raised, but not placed in position, and the carvings were left unfinished here and there, and in some places merely outlined, when the great

Pl. 58. ELEVATION OF WEST WING WALL OF EXTERNAL FAÇADE OF PALACE AT MSHITTĀ.

catastrophe arrested the hand of the sculptor. We are thus left entirely to our knowledge of the style derived from other buildings to enable us to say what was originally intended by the architect who designed it.

This façade, which is represented in a restored form on the frontispiece of this work,* extends to 180 feet east and west, between two of the plain semicircular towers of the inclosure. Ample means exist for its restoration to the height of twenty or twenty-two feet from what was the original ground-line. Above that we are dependent on our knowledge of other buildings of the same age and style. These, it must be confessed, are neither so numerous nor so similar as might be desired; but they are sufficient for our present purposes, and admit of the whole being restored with a very fair amount of certainty.

The first thing that strikes any one, on looking at the plan, is the unusual projection of the two octag-

---

* It is hardly necessary to explain that it is quite impossible to make clear to those who are not already familiar with the styles that preceded as well as with those which followed this building, all the motives that guided me in making this restoration without at least an amount of illustrations which is quite incompatible with an appendix to a book of travels. The building, however, is in itself so beautiful, and its position in the history of architecture so interesting, that it well deserves a monograph; and when more detailed measurements are obtained, as well as more extensive illustrations of its sculpture, it may be well worth while to attempt this. At present the reader must be content to take a good deal on trust, unless he will take the trouble of mastering the original authorities quoted hereafter.

onal towers that flank the entrance. All the other towers are only semicircles; but these project more than half their diameter, and they are also quite solid up to the height to which they are built, which would probably not have been the case with towers so purely ornamental without some sufficient motive. It hardly, however, required even these two facts to suggest that they must have been joined by a great arch. So far as is known, no Sassanian building is without this feature. It is as indispensable as a portico to a Greek temple, or a tower or steeple to a mediæval Gothic church. All the Sassanian buildings we know of have this feature, and it is almost equally characteristic of the Christian buildings in Syria in the fifth and sixth centuries.* One of the most remarkable— it may be said, exaggerated—examples of this great arch is found in the Tak Kesra, at Ctesiphon, built by Noushirvan, the grandfather of Chosroes, to which we shall frequently have occasion to refer in the sequel.

In most of the Syrian churches a short pier or pilaster is detached from the flanking towers to carry the great arch; and that is an expedient which would certainly be adopted in modern times; but nothing of the sort exists, or ever could have existed, here: the consequence is, that the arch must have died away against the towers, had it not been stilted, or continued, in some manner. One peculiarity, however, of

---

* See plates of De Vogüé's work, "Syrie Centrale," *passim*.

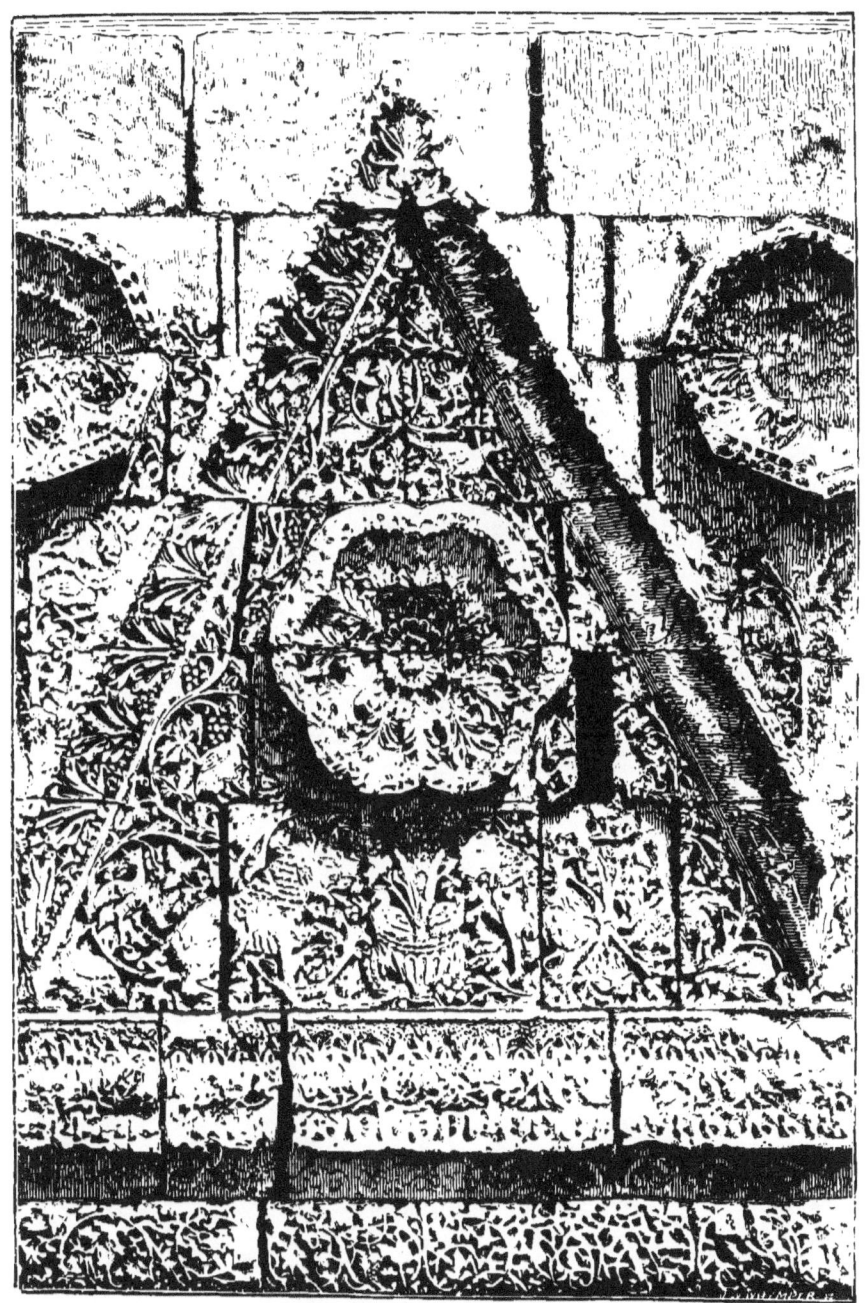

NO. 39. ELEVATION OF ONE COMPARTMENT OF WESTERN OCTAGON TOWER AT MÂSHITÂ.

THE PERSIAN PALACE OF MÂSHITÂ.

all Sassanian arches is that they are all more than semicircles. In the Tak Kesra, as will be observed, the great arch is a semi-ellipse, which is certainly not a pleasing form; but it, or something very like it, occurs in the palaces at Firouzabad and Serbistan.* Luckily, however, there is a very beautiful Sassanian arch, with singularly classical details, at Takt-i-Gero,†

NO. 40. TAK KESRA (FROM FLANDIN AND COSTE).

which is stilted by being horseshoed—if the expression may be used—to the extent of one-tenth of its diameter.‡ As it resembles in style this palace more

---

* For illustrations of these palaces, see my "History of Architecture," vol. ii., wood-cuts 946 to 950. They are taken from Flandin and Coste's "Voyage en Perse," which is the great and best authority on Sassanian art.
† Flandin and Coste, vol. iv., plates 214, 215.
‡ The arch over the great niche in the Pantheon at Rome is stilt-

than any other, I have not hesitated to adopt that form, which seems to meet the case exactly. But I adopt it with more confidence, as, on showing my restoration to Mr. Hayne, he produced from his pocket-book two drawings of an arch in the inner palace at Mashitâ, on which, besides representing it, he noted, on the spot, "Arches distinctly horseshoe."

There can be no great difficulty in restoring the features inside the great arch. The jambs of the door-way exist, and they absolutely demand a horizontal lintel, and a lintel of that extent requires a discharging arch. This feature, it may be added, is nearly universal in the Syrian churches of the preceding centuries: all their door-ways within or behind the great arches are square-headed, but, opening into interiors, their discharging arches become windows, or fan-lights. As this one, however, opens into a court-yard, such a disposition is most improbable; and I have therefore placed in it an equestrian statue of Chosroes, on his favorite black charger, Shub diz, copied from that which adorns his rock-cut arch at Takt-i-Bostan.*

Passing by the principal story for the present, the first suggestion that presented itself to my mind for the third was that it should be a repetition of the

---

ed, or horseshoed, to one-tenth of its diameter, in the same manner. See "Hist. of Architecture," wood-cut 183; Taylor and Creasey's "Rome," plate lv.

* "Flandin and Coste," vol. i., plates 1 to 12. Ker Porter's "Travels in Persia," ii., plates 61 to 64.

lowest, on half its scale. The arrangement of the stories in the Tak Kesra (wood-cut No. 40), and other buildings of that age, seemed to justify this; but when it was so drawn, the probability of this disposition rose to conviction in my mind from a circumstance I must try and explain.

In the island of Murano, near Venice, there is a church, built apparently in the tenth century, but the apse of which, externally, is unlike any thing else I know in Latin Europe. It is surrounded by two rows of triangular recesses in the brick-work, in some of which are slabs of marble beautifully carved, and with devices very easily distinguishable from the clumsy carvings of Venetian builders of that age. There are also slabs with trees, and foliage, and birds, very like those at Mashitâ, and a string-course of that sharp broccoli-like acanthus which distinguishes the age of Justinian. The most interesting fact, however, is, that there is one window on the right hand of the spectator, round the top of which these triangles are carried in the most exquisitely artistic fashion. All these parts, with some of the capitals, had evidently been brought by the Venetians from some ruined Levantine building, as most of the pillars of St. Mark's were brought from Alexandria; but they had not brought away enough to complete the design; so that their own clumsy attempts at imitation betray the forgery to the most unpracticed eye. All this I knew long ago, from personal observation as well as from photographs and Ruskin's exquisite drawings of this apse;* but, till I saw the photographs of Mâshitâ, I never could even guess whence the foreign fragments were obtained. I have now no doubt that it was from some Syrian church near the coast — probably Antioch, or thereabouts—which, being ruined by the Moslem, or an earthquake, was despoiled of its ornaments to adorn this church.

The moment I tried to adapt this Murano arch to that at Mâshitâ, I found that, with a little contrivance, it fitted so exactly that I now feel quite convinced that this is something very like the mode in which it was intended to be finished. This, too, becomes more certain when we refer back to the Tak Kesra (woodcut No. 40), the last great Sassanian building which preceded this palace.

If carefully examined, it becomes evident that, had its architect been clever enough, and been building in stone, he would have carried his third story round his great arch, just as has been done here. Radiating shafts, however, in brick-work were a difficulty he could not face; so we have only the heads of the arches spaced equidistantly with those on the flanks, and starting from the same level, but only carried round as a kind of foliation,† and losing all the

---

* "Stones of Venice," vol. ii., plates 3, 4, and 5.

† The wood-cut No. 40 is on too small a scale, and not sufficiently correctly drawn to make this quite clear, but an examination of Flandin and Coste's plate 218, vol. iv., explains the architect's intention beyond doubt. He evidently was trying, on a scale beyond his means, a mode of decoration which had succeeded somewhere else with more limited dimensions.

strength and depth which the deeper archivolt would have given. The triangular arrangement adopted at Murano, and suggested here, seems to get perfectly over this difficulty, while the want of some such expedient has ruined the effect of the arch at Ctesiphon.

Returning now to the principal story, two suggestions presented themselves. The first was that I have adopted, principally depending for my authority on the Tak Kesra, which seems to justify it, but also because, on the left-hand side, the building is divided in plan into small apartments, which seem to demand light, at least in the upper story.

The other suggestion was that of a great bass-relief. These great sculptured pictures being the favorite style of utterance of the Sassanians from first to last, some forty or fifty of them still remain. A stronger motive, however, than even this analogy was, that in the arch at Takt-i-Bostan, the only really authentic work of Chosroes, there are two great bassi-relievi, probably the masterpieces of Ferhad. One of these represents a great battue hunt after deer, the other after hogs, and either would be singularly appropriate to this hunting-box. Originally, the right-hand side of the restoration was so drawn; but the whole, when covered only with incised ornament in low relief, looked so flat that the idea was abandoned, though, were I drawing the façade again, I would feel inclined to restore it. It may not be what we would consider architecturally the best, but I fancy it is what the founder of the palace intended.

Having got so far, the remaining parts of the elevation presented no great difficulties. The upper part of the left-hand side is taken from the battlements of Lachish, as represented in the Nineveh Marbles in the British Museum, or in Layard's plates,* and from painted details at Khorsabad. Not that I suppose these were standing in the seventh century; but such forms get petrified, and, with slight modifications, reappear again and again, after long periods of time. On the right hand I have adopted a series of arches, such as are found in every Turkish fountain, and in most of their ornamental buildings, just below the cornice. On the whole, I am inclined to think it the one most likely to have been intended, if we adopt the arches for the middle story. This thus becomes a repetition, half scale, of the "piano nobile," in the same manner as the third story was a repetition of the triangular arrangement of the lowest. If, however, we adopt the theory that the middle story was adorned by a bass-relief, then the left-hand design would be most appropriate.

Over the great arch, on the right-hand side, a flying figure is introduced, which is copied literally from the Takt-i-Bostan, and may therefore have been intended here, and in the bass-relief theory would almost certainly have been adopted. In the design as drawn she seems somewhat out of place. The ornaments under the great arch, it may be added, are all copied

---

* Second series of "Monuments of Nineveh," plate 21, *et seq.*

from Takt-i-Bostan, and so are the battlements that crown the wing-walls, though these stepped battlements are common enough elsewhere, both in Persia and India.

It only remains now to say a few words with regard to the two pavilions, with the gallery between them, which rise above the line of the principal cornice. If we look, in the first instance, at the projection and strength of the towers, no one, I fancy, would suggest that they ought to stop with the line of the cornice. But this necessity for artistic harmony rises to nearly a certainty when we come to examine their base moldings. These are Corinthian—corrupt, of course, but of certain well-defined proportions. They are, as nearly as can be ascertained, four feet six inches high; and that is the proportion which a classical architect would assign to a pillar or wall ninety feet in height; and ninety feet, it may also be observed, is exactly half the length of the ornamental façade, which is a very likely proportion in so carefully designed a building.

But, besides these architectural exigencies, the really great argument is, that it is following out what we find took place before the time when they were erected. In the great church, for instance, at Tourmanin, erected in the sixth century, we have exactly this disposition. First, the great arch, with the square-headed door and fan-light inside it; then the gallery between two towers carried up above the arch. In the church all is designed with Doric simplicity and plainness; in the palace, with Corinthian exuberance and richness; but the disposition of both façades is the same, and the tendency in all the façades of these Syrian churches and buildings is to something very like this. Of course, the body of the church itself, as

NO. 41.   CHURCH AT TOURMANIN (FROM DE VOGÜÉ).

shown in wood-cut No. 41, must be disregarded—we are speaking here of the portico, or façade, and of that only.

The little domes that crown the pavilions are borrowed from the palace at Serbistan. I would have liked to add some ornament on the summit, but have no authority for it.

It is almost as much, however, from what followed after as from what went before, that we derive a conviction that this restoration is not far from the truth, for all the Persian and Indian mosques unmistakably took their forms from some such building as this. The Egyptian and African mosques, as well as many of those in Syria, took their forms from the Atria, and other arrangements of Christian churches; but in the East, where Christian architecture hardly existed in these early ages, the path was different. It is, nevertheless, easy to trace back their design to some such building as that at Mâshitâ, which is, unfortunately, however, the only example of its class now remaining—so far, at least, as we at present know.

Almost all Persian mosques, and those especially in Western India—in Gujerat and at Ahmedabad, for instance—have a great central arched door-way, at times merging into a semi-dome, covering a square-headed door-way, but always flanked by two octagonal towers, which in course of time have grown into tall minarets. Between these towers the central part of the façade is always higher than the wings, and is frequently crowned by a gallery, or range, of detached pavilions. The wing-walls, instead of being solid, as here, are generally pierced by one or more openings, but so managed as not to break the continuity of the lines or the solid look of the flanking masses of masonry.

So essentially is this the case, that, taking the Jumna Musjid* at Delhi as a starting-point, it is not difficult to trace the form back to the earliest mosques we have in India. As they only extend backward, however, to the beginning of the thirteenth century, there is a wide gap to be got over before we reach the age of the palace at Mâshitâ. This can only be bridged over by buildings in Persia and the countries between that and India. That such buildings exist, hardly admits of a doubt; but the photographer has not yet reached these regions, and no traveler has had his attention specially directed to the early buildings of the Mohammedan dynasties, which alone can supply the missing link. But from such drawings as exist, and such accounts as have been published, there can be little doubt that the information to complete the series will be forthcoming when looked for. When they are found, they will enable us to explain a great deal that has hitherto been a mystery with regard to the origin of many of the forms of Indian architecture. It is not, however, from its form only that this palace at Mâshitâ enables us to trace the connection between the architectures of the West and East. There is a rich, elaborate style of decoration in India which we can trace back to the tenth century; but there we lose the thread, to refind it, however, in this solitary building. The "rosaces," for instance, between the triangles at Mâshitâ are almost identical with those

---

* Built by Shah Jehan, 1628 to 1658.

that adorn the fair marble temples at Mounts Girnar or Abu; and that peculiar conventional treatment of vegetable forms which is the principal beauty of the façade at Mâshitâ is reproduced — without the animals, of course—in almost all the mosques in Gujerat, especially at Ahmedabad.*

Had it not been that the principal buildings of the Sassanians, or of the Caliphs, were erected on alluvial plains of the Lower Euphrates or Tigris, all this would have been plain to us long ago. As, from their locality, however, these were almost invariably of brick, and depended for their ornamentation on plaster, or carvings in wood or metal, all which have perished, it was not till a building erected and ornamented in stone was discovered that the necessary link in the inquiry was supplied. Many more require to be traced out before the whole story can be said to be complete. But in the mean while this discovery of the palace of Mâshitâ is not only interesting from its own beauty and elegance, but because it is the last, and the only remaining, example known to us of the Byzantino-Sassanian style of architecture, and also because its style was that which eventually blossomed into the exquisitely elaborate forms of the Jaina and Saracenic styles in India.

---

* See "Architecture of Ahmedabad," 100, photographic plates. Murray, 1866.

APPENDIX A.

(See p. 50.)

AURORA AT SEBBEH.

By R. C. JOHNSON.

THE extraordinary display of aurora borealis which was seen on the evening of Sunday, the 4th of February, all over Europe, and in parts of Asia and Africa, was observed by the party while camping at Sebbeh.

It made us, for the moment, wish to be back again in our more northern clime, where we knew that (fine as the display was with us) it must be much more splendid. However, if we missed seeing it in its more brilliant aspect, we were consoled by being able to witness a phenomenon which rarely occurs in latitudes so far south as $30°$.

It was first noticed at 7 P.M. (on going outside the tent for the purpose of observing the Zodiacal light, which presents in these latitudes a much more imposing spectacle than in latitude $53°$ N.); and we watched it at intervals until midnight, when it had become much fainter. It was at its brightest phase about nine o'clock, local time (the longitude E. is $35° 28'$, or two hours and twenty-two minutes), when a well-defined coronal arch was formed, which extended in Azimuth nearly $90°$ from N.W. to N.E., and in altitude about $28°$, almost reaching the pole-star.

The prevailing color was yellowish, with occasionally a purplish tinge. The streamers shot up from the horizon and then faded away; but the display was totally devoid of those large colored sheets of lambent light which were so conspicuous in higher latitudes.

We found the Arabs who were about the camp observing the aurora with but a slight degree of interest. They never looked at it for more than a few minutes at a time, and informed us that it had very seldom been seen by them, and that they did not know any thing about it.

APPENDIX B.

(See p. 205.)

ACCOUNT OF A CURIOUS PHYSICAL PHENOMENON WITNESSED AT ZIZA.

By R. C. JOHNSON.

On the evening of the 24th of February, about eight o'clock, when leaving the tents with Dr. Tristram for duck-shooting, on the banks of the large reservoir at Ziza, we both noticed that our path was encompassed by a semicircular halo of faint light, the origin of which was for a few moments rather puzzling.

At this time the moon was about nine hours past the full, and, shining with that lustre which is so well known to travelers upon a table-land under Eastern skies, like a ball of molten silver, appeared to stand out in strong relief against the intense deep blue of the celestial vault. Upon attentively considering our position with regard to the moon and the halo, we found that it was exactly that required for the formation of a rainbow; and we evidently saw a *lunar rainbow on the ground*, or, to speak more correctly, a *lunar dew-bow*.

Since returning to England, I have made some inquiries, but have not yet found a description of this curious phenomenon; nor have I met with any one who has noticed it. This seems strange; for it was so conspicuous that we did not fail to perceive it immediately on going out, on that and on two other nights.

I had many opportunities of admiring the wonderful clearness of the air upon this table-land, as shown in the increased brilliancy of the stars. They shone with so steady a light that twinkling was reduced to a minimum, and the different colors could be easily distinguished.

Four especially were very striking—Sirius, with its intense white light; and Rigel, with perhaps just a perceptible tinge of blue, shining in splendid contrast with the orange of α Orionis and the ruddiness of Aldebaran. With a first-rate Cooke achromatic of only two inches aperture, the detail visible in the nebula of Orion, and the stellar clusters in Canis Major, made one long to be able to bring to bear upon them, in such a situation, the exquisite defining and space-penetrating powers of my nine-and-a-quarter-inch Browning, with reflector.

APPENDIX C.

ON THE FLORA OF MOAB.

BY THE LATE W. AMHERST HAYNE, B.A., TRINITY COLLEGE, CAMBRIDGE.

THE specimens on which the following sketch is founded were collected in February and March, and have been allocated to their proper orders and genera in the Herbarium at Oxford, kindly put at the disposal of myself and the Rev. H. E. Fox, by Professor Lawson.

The district referred to as Moab must be understood to consist of a parallelogram, in rough measurement, some fifty miles from north to south, by thirty from east to west, bounded on the west by the Dead Sea and the Jordan, on the east by the pilgrim road from Damascus to Mecca, and extending from the oasis of the Sáfieh, on the south, to the gorge which runs down from Elealeh and Heshbon to the Jordan Valley, on the north, and including that portion of the plain of Shittim which lies between the water-course and the Dead Sea, now known as the Seisaban. Out of this parallelogram eliminate a block at the south-east angle, and you have a good idea of the country worked, which might be aptly delineated by a capital P.

Within this area three climates, if not three floras, are included: we experienced winter, spring, and summer in three successive days: one night, clad in every available vestment, we shivered between our blankets, while the water froze into block-ice in the basins at our feet, and the thermometer registered 24° Fahr. The next, we sat out round a camp-fire and enjoyed the open air and the warmth at the same time; and the third, I wrote my journal with my coat off, with the thermometer at 76° at midnight. For the sake of convenience, therefore, I shall divide the country into three zones, corresponding to these three seasons, and call them the frigid, temperate, and torrid. The high level plateau, three thousand feet above the sea, supplies the first field; the deep ravines which cleave it include the other two. The level of the Mediterranean may be taken as the division between the second and third.

What I have called the frigid zone yielded, during the months of February and March, twenty plants in flower, the temperate eighty-three, and the torrid one hundred and forty-seven—just reversing the ratio of time, and giving one plant a day to the plateau and sixteen to the shores of the sea and its gullies.

1. The great plateau of Moab is chiefly grass south of the Arnon and west of Heshbon; the turf is turned over once in some three or four years by the plow; the rest is virgin grazing land. There is fine grass in the western section, but it grows gradually poorer and thinner as you advance eastward, till it begins to give way to a low scrub of *Artemisia*. This, not yet in flower in March, gave out aromatic scent as it was bruised by our horses' feet; and among it masses of whitened snail-shells and armies of caterpillars betokened the past, and formed the present food of myriads of larks. This wormwood, in turn, gives way to patches of sandy soil and a white lichen, as the low range of desert hills which bounds the plain is approached.

No trees, not even any shrubs or bushes, exist over the whole of this great plateau, except the summit of Jebel Attarus. This, for some miles, is studded with old trees, after the fashion of a scattered park. There were almonds in blossom, and the larger ones seemed terebinths, by guess; but not even leaves were out when I was there.

To deal with this zone slightly more in detail. At Kerak and its neighborhood there was absolutely nothing out; my only observations were *Ceterach officinarum* in the walls of the Western Castle, and leafless figs and pomegranates in the valleys below it: olives and oleanders alone kept their gray and sombre foliage. Considering the frosts at nights, it was rather marvelous than otherwise that there should be any thing in flower beyond a few diminutive Geraniaceæ and Cruciferæ, and *Asperugo procumbens*, among the shelter of the ruins of Khan Zebib, and other places. Yet a white *Pancratium* had chosen the richest soil of the plains near Dibon, to drive its roots beyond the reach of any thing but a spade, and was starring the ground in February. Even near Ziza, where it was the coldest, *Leontice leontopetalum* was preparing to pave the ground with gold, its spreading yellow spikes and peony-like leaves bursting from among the grass in masses. In the more sheltered hollows of the plain, farther west, was already spread a scarlet carpet of anemones (*A. coronaria*) bordered and patterned with the brilliant blue of the lovely *Veronica syriaca*. It was not, however, until the middle of March that the dull orange spikes of *Asphodelus luteus* were in full flower among the ruins of Ma'in, and *Geranium tuberosum* out on the plowed lands of Nebo.

2. Leaving the plateau, and descending to the valleys and slopes tending toward the Dead Sea, we at once reached a rich spring flora. Its chief feature was the immense variety of leguminous plants: out of thirty-five species of this order, collected in the country, twenty-five were in flower in this division. The upper valleys of the Arnon and the Zerka Ma'in, the slopes and nooks of Attarus and Nebo, were the chief fields of this temperate zone. On the southern side of the Arnon Valley the almond-tree was in full flower, and the white asphodel (*A. ramosus*) bursting into bloom on the 15th of February, while a little golden *Gagea* studded the slopes. Clumps of oleander grew about the stream, not yet showing signs of flower. I saw it in its glory a month later, fringing the shores of Gennesareth.

On the northern and more sunny side of the Arnon the flowers were much more numerous. Here we first met with four plants which soon became very familiar friends—*Echium violaceum*, the purple Bugloss of our Channel Islands, which is one of the commonest plants throughout the whole of Palestine; and of which I afterward saw, literally, miles covering the basaltic boulders of Galilee, on the descent from Tabor to Tiberias; *Astragalus hamosus*, or a species very nearly allied to it; *Salvia horminum*, with a tuft of bright lilac bracts crowning its spike; and *Lathyrus cicera*, rather pinker and much larger flowered than our *L. nissolia*. Numbers of little crucifers and the diminutive *Ceratocephalus falcatus* grew higher up. Among the crucifers was *Capsella bursa-pastoris*, as a pendant to which *Draba verna* grew abundantly at Dibon.

So much for Arnon. A fortnight later we dropped down into the valley of the Zerka Ma'in. Grateful to man and beast were the rich, rank herbage and abundant water after the cold bare plains. Our old friends of the Arnon Valley re-appeared—*Astragalus hamosus*, *Echium violaceum*, and *Lathyrus cicera;* others, that were equally conspicuous, were a dwarf blue iris (*I. sisyrinchium*), which covered the open ground after twelve o'clock, and which appeared everywhere afterward, from Moab to Lebanon; and the Retem-bush of Scripture (*Re-*

tama retem), with its white flowers and purple calyx. Here and there a gorgeous tulip (*Tulipa gesneriana*) was in flower, and two rock cistuses (*Helianthemum guttatum* and *H. ægyptiacum*).

Leguminosæ, as I said before, were profusely represented; three species of Astragali, besides the one already referred to; *Hippocrepis ciliata*, with its bizarre pods, already formed; *Vicia lutea*, two kinds of *Lotus*, and several others. It was early for Labiates, which must form a large proportion of the summer flora of this zone of Moab, as they do that of the rest of Palestine. A few deliciously-scented ones were in flower, a yellow ajuga (*A. Chamæpitys?*), in the crannies of the rocks; *Salvia commentata*, and the superb *Eremostachys laciniata*, with its large, deeply-cut leaves, giving out the most refined scent of musk. A month after, I walked up to my ears through a bed of it in the borders of the plain of Esdraelon. Another fortnight, and the valley under Nebo, by the Wells of Moses, added a number of leguminous plants and *Rhagadiolus stellatus* to my list of this zone; and the cave under the water-fall at the latter place furnished the finest maiden-hair (*Adiantum capillus-veneris*) I ever gathered, except the three-foot fronds of Engedi.

3. By far the most interesting of the three fields was, of course, the Dead Sea basin. Seven years ago, Dr. Tristram worked the natural history of the Holy Land during a period of nine months, and Mr. B. T. Lowne accompanied him as botanist of his party. Passing along the whole of the western shores of the Dead Sea, and round the south end as far as the Ghor es Sáfieh, he had every opportunity of seeing the flora of the basin on its western side. His collection, kindly put at my disposal by Dr. Tristram, has materially aided me in naming my own, and also in giving me data for a comparison between the east and west shores of the sea.

This comparison leads me to the conclusion that there is no essential difference between the flora of the two shores. Most of the more conspicuous of Mr. Lowne's species, peculiar to the Dead Sea basin, I gathered, or observed, on the eastern side. A considerable number of his plants are wanting in my list; but they are either not the most typical, or their place is supplied by species allied in character and geographical distribution.

One remarkable fact, however, became patent by our visit, and that is the dependence of the different oases round the shores of the Dead Sea upon the partial rain-falls of the winter. It so happened that we were in the Wady Zuweirah and the Ghor es Sáfieh, situated, respectively, at the south-west and south-east corners of the sea, in exactly the same week as Dr. Tristram and Mr. Lowne had been seven years ago. That year every thing was in full flower; this, hardly a plant showed even signs of budding. *Ruta tuberculata* and a little *Spergularia* were the only plants I gathered in flower at the Wady Zuweirah, while Mr. Lowne collected eighty-two. Similarly, on the Ghor es Sáfieh, *Ricinus communis*, *Salvadora persica*, *Loranthus acaciæ*, and *Solanum sanctum* made up the total of two days' observation. Corn was but just springing. The canebrakes had not begun to shoot, and the ground was hard and dry. The more settled Arabs of the districts, who till the ground, complained of the lateness of the rains, and so explained the phenomena, which had appeared the more curious to us as at Engedi every thing was much farther advanced, and a very short distance north of the Sáfieh we came across a spring vegetation the following day.

Mr. Lowne remarks in his paper ("Journal Linn. Soc.," vol. ix., p. 201, 1865) that the curious asclepiad, *Calotropis procera*, is not nearly so abundant on the Ghor es Sáfieh as at Engedi. Had the force of circumstances allowed him to cross the chief Seil, or torrent, which divides the oasis into two nearly equal halves, he would have found that the district to the north of it consists of a perfect miniature forest of this odd tree, far exceeding any thing that Engedi can show.

Thus this oasis of the Sáfieh consists, first, of a park-like district, with thorny trees, such as *Zizyphus* and *Acacia seyal*, growing among the corn and grass; second, of a scattered wood of *Calotropis procera*; third, of an open belt studded with rushes, running parallel with these two parks on the sea-side; and, lastly, of a dense jungle of canebrake, which, growing in water, bars the passage to the edge of the sea, and forms a secure retreat for the wild boar.

Leaving the park and working northward, flowers covered the ground as we approached the open shore of the Dead Sea, near Bey Nmeirah; no less than nine species of crucifers were in flower, a dwarf stock (*Matthiola oxyceras*) studded the ground, while the Rose of Jericho (*Anastatica hierochuntica*) was in flower and leaf; whereas

APPENDIX. 405

at the Wadi Zuweirah, two days before, nothing was to be seen of it but the dry contracted bunches of last year. At the Wady Dra'a we left the tropics.

It was three weeks later when we descended to the remarkable gorge, or hot springs, of Callirrhoe, the lower portion of the wady now known as the Zerka Ma'in. The sides of the gorge were covered, on the 1st of March, by the summer flowers of the more temperate zone above—*Ranunculus syriacus*, which had already succeeded to *Anemone coronaria*, several *Allia*, and a large *Fœniculum*. *Iris sisyrinchium* was still in flower, and much more luxuriant than up above. The course of the hot river is marked by a jungle of canebrake and tamarisks, with bushes of *Atriplex halimus* scattered just above. The oleanders, which fringe the cold stream higher up, cease as soon as the first hot spring comes in, as do also, if I mistake not, the willows and the water-cress. There is a perfect paradise of flowers in the neighborhood of the hot springs themselves, which, although some seven miles east of the Dead Sea, is more nearly allied to the flora of the Wady Zuweirah than any locality on the west coast, or, in fact, than any other yet worked, except the shore just north and south of the outfall of its waters.

A very considerable proportion of the conspicuous Asiatic and African plants found by Mr. Lowne in the Mahawat and Zuweirah flats, occur either in the Callirrhoe gorge near the sulphur springs, or among the embouchures of the similar springs at Zara, a mile or two south of its mouth. For example, the curious asclepiad, *Dæmia cordata*, with its habit of throttling itself by climbing on the stiff but withering branches of the previous year, was fairly abundant just on the sulphur deposited by the springs. *Cleome trinervia* flourished in the same locality, growing almost in bushes, and giving out when bruised a nauseous smell resembling the sulphur on which it grew. Bushes of *Zygophyllum album* cling to the rocks. *Fagonia sinaitica*, and another more shrubby and more spiny species, with large pink flowers, were there. *Trichodesma africana* and a *Forskahlea* attached themselves to one's clothes by their viscous hairs, as one forced one's way along-side the stream. Two heliotropes also occurred, one by the baths, the other at Zara; and *Statice pruinosa*, as well as *S. Thouini*, at one or both places. All these, or their congeners, were found by

Mr. Lowne at the Wady Zuweirah. The composites, too, correspond, as far as I have been able to identify them; five of the more marked *Anvillea garcini*, two *Asterisci* (*pygmæus* and another), *Senecio Decaisnei*, and *Pulicaria undulata*, occur in both our lists. Mr. Lowne got eleven species from Zuweirah; I, twelve from Callirrhoe and Zara together. Of these, five have been shown identical; a few belong to the temperate zone, and the remainder are difficult to determine. This order, it will be observed, was as largely represented in this locality in March as Cruciferæ had been three weeks before at N'meirah, and nearly as largely as Leguminosæ was in the more temperate regions. Out of twenty-six composites, twenty-one come from this zone, and twelve from Zara and Callirrhoe. Of less abundant orders, we have *Ærua javanica*, *Boerhaavia verticillata*, *Atriplex halimus*, and *Rumex vesicarius*, which belong, also, either to Zuweirah or Engedi; and the same grasses, an *Andropogon* and two *Aristidæ*, were also found. The chief additions to Mr. Lowne's Wady Zuweirah list, as regards plants inhabiting the eastern and southern deserts, are—*Helianthemum kahiricum*, a shrubby rock-cistus; *Astragalus timidus*, with its bladder-like calyx; *Acanthodium spicatum*, and the odd *Pteranthus echinatus*, found by others already in the neighborhood of Jericho; the lovely geranium (*Erodium hirtum*), the distribution of which is from the deserts of Algeria to those of Palmyria, and which, with *Trigonella pecten*, was very abundant just above the baths. Two Orobanches of most gorgeous hue I have been unable to identify; they grow to the height of two or three feet, and even more, the one a deep purple, the other a deep chrome-yellow, apparently parasitic on *Atriplex halimus;* they occurred both at Callirrhoe, on the shore, and in the Seisaban. *Rœmeria orientalis* grew on the basalt going down to Zara. Of other additions, *Freirea alsinæfolia*, a *Callipeltis*, and an *Epipactis*, the latter, from within a yard or two of the water of the Dead Sea, are instances of the commingling of the European with the tropical flora, as also *Notholæna lanuginosa* on a detached basaltic boulder at Zara. *Ceterach officinarum*, growing at Kerak, and *Adiantum capillus-veneris*, wherever it could find a moist place, whether in the mouths of old store-wells among the ruined cities of the high level plateau or at the very exit of Callirrhoe, make up the Moab ferns.

As for the trees in the neighborhood of the baths, the palm *Phœnix* was by far the largest and most abundant, growing, however, only on clumps, just about the sources of the hot streams. The Arabs, either through ignorance or indifference, make no attempt to fructify them: on the contrary, they ruin both their health and their appearance by setting fire to the canebrakes among which they grow, for the sake of burning the tangled thickets and providing a fresh supply of cane-shoots, which are a favorite food for their camels at a certain time of the year, when they are said to stand in need of purgatives. In consequence of this, the stems of the palms are left blackened and charred, and their lower branches dead and drooping. The ever-accumulating deposit from the sulphur springs is another enemy to the palm-tree; some stumps remain, not petrified, but, if I may be allowed the expression, "*sulphurized*," the formation of the wood still quite visible, but soft, and gray, and crumbling, so that you can cut it out with a pocket-knife, in blocks like cheese. The only other tree beside the tamarisk, at the water-side, which hardly deserves the name, was the curious and abnormal *Moringa aptera*, observed both by Mr. Lowne and myself at Engedi.

It only remains for me now to say a few words about the plains of Shittim and the north-east shores of the Dead Sea, between that and the mouth of Callirrhoe. It was the middle of March by the time we visited these districts, and the grasses were in much greater force than before: a third of the twenty-three *Gramina* were collected in the Seisaban. This oasis is of much greater extent than any of the others which border on the Dead Sea; the trees are much scattered: but otherwise it resembles the Sâfieh and Jericho. I observed the osher-tree again, but not in great profusion; in which, however, it may well be, as it was impossible to explore the whole district. At the time we were there the place seemed already suffering from lack of rain, and the ripe grasses had quite an autumnal look in March, while the sirocco blowing dried every thing to tinder.

Riding from the Seisaban south toward the mouth of Callirrhoe, the stony shores of the Dead Sea were covered with masses of color, the winged bracts of *Statice Thouini* and the large membraneous petals of *Rumex vesicarius* alternating in acres of lavender and pink. By far the commonest plant next to these was a little dwarf campanula (*C. dichotoma*), its deep blue bells dotted among the stones.

The borders of the streams which come down from the mountains every few miles were fringed with deciduous trees, whose bright light-green foliage formed a refreshing contrast to the dull olive-green line of the more usual shrubs of the country, such as *Atriplex halimus, Zizyphus, Lotus, Retama retem,* and *Moringa aptera.* Large bushes of a hawthorn (*Cratægus*), not yet in flower, still more pleasantly reminded one of English verdure; our old friends of Callirrhoe, *Dæmia cordata* and *Cleome trinervia,* occurred again here not far from the north-east shore of the sea, apparently only on a line of mordine detached from some sulphurous vein in the mountains; an asclepiadeous shrub, which I have not been able to identify, was also found; a *Cuscuta* was parasitic on *Rumex vesicarius,* and oleanders (*Nerium oleander*), reached down the streams nearly to the shore, while maiden-hair (*Adiantum*), flourished in a water-fall not more than twenty yards from the sea. The most unexpected botanical feature in the landscape, however, was the comparative abundance of the palm close to the water's edge, the trees growing on the cliffs overhanging the water, clinging in the clefts of rocks where a miniature gorge brings down a trickling fall of water, and dotted right up the mountain side, in some places, as far as one could see.

This feature is one of the most conspicuous in the present difference between the two sides of the sea. On the west not a trace of the palm exists, save one little clump found by Dr. Tristram in a sequestered nook of Mons Quarantania, the sole remnant of the trees of Jericho, once the city of palms, and at Hazezon-tamar, or Engedi, petrified in the rocks above the stream. On the east it still obtains at the Wady Dra'a, Callirrhoe, all along the north-east shore, and up the Wady Heshban. To draw out further the contrast between the two shores may be worth a few words. Owing partly to a much larger supply of water, partly to the almost entire absence of the marl deposit, which is nearly always absolutely bare of vegetation where it occurs, the whole of the east side is comparatively fertile, and abounds not only in smaller plants, but has a fair allowance of trees and larger shrubs; nowhere is the eye pained by the frightful desolation of the western shore, where a solitary tamarisk or salicornia looks like a signal of distress hung out at a distance of a mile or two from its next neighbors. Even the oases on the west, as Engedi and Zuweirah, are sparse, barren, and sandy, compared with Zara and the Sáfieh, to which they exactly correspond in point of position. This well-watered and fertile condition, speaking comparatively, of the eastern side, results in a much greater commingling of the flora of more temperate regions with that of the desert, which needs such special conditions of soil and climate as the Dead Sea affords, than occurs on the western side.

The 250 plants found in Moab from the beginning of February to the middle of March belong to fifty-eight natural orders, of which by far the best represented are *Leguminosæ*, with thirty-five species, *Compositæ* and *Cruciferæ*, each twenty-six; and *Gramina*, twenty-three. After these follow *Liliaceæ*, twelve; *Scrophulariaceæ*, nine; *Caryophyllaceæ*, *Geraniaceæ*, *Labiatæ*, and *Boragineæ*, eight apiece. Umbellifers were remarkably scarce, although I took particular pains to remark them. I have only five in flower; and of these hardly any are in fruit. *Ranunculaceæ* and *Zygophylleæ* had also five representatives; but no other order had more than four—*Cistineæ*, *Orobancheæ*, *Euphorbiaceæ*, and *Cyperaceæ*, having each that number. These statistics bring me two results. I think we have sufficiency of data to establish three:

1. The flora is remarkable for a small average number of species distributed through a large number of orders—an average of four and a half species to each of the fifty-eight orders. This fact was previously remarked by Mr. Lowne, and is not unnatural in a country which forms the border-land of Europe, Asia, and Africa, the more hardy and accommodating plants of each of these geographical divisions holding their own, while those more readily affected by variation of soil or climate disappear.

2. The east shore of the Dead Sea differs widely from the west, in its general character; yet, notwithstanding the said differences, as to soil and water, the flora of the two shores is identical in character, and, as far as our experience yet goes, nearly coincident in detail.

3. The *desert* flora of the Dead Sea is not confined so exclusively to its southern extremity as an examination of the western shore alone might lead one to conclude; its peculiarities extend nearly to its northern limits; and not only so, but also obtain, under similar conditions, in one spot, six or seven miles removed from the sea, and

one thousand feet above it. The hot baths of Callirrhoe, where the heat locally generated by the outburst of five or ten springs of water at 145° Fahr., and the chemical properties of the soil and water, tend, within a limited area, to produce a result similar to that of the Dead Sea itself. This result is not produced except in the immediate neighborhood of the said springs, and does not extend the whole way down the gorge to the sea.

INDEX.

Abou da Houk, 31.
Abou Endi, 319.
Aboul Hayad, Wady, 40.
Aboul Obeidah, 226.
Abou Sheebeh, Jebel, 297.
Acoustic properties of the climate, 49.
Adwân, the, 20, 351.
Agriculture, Arab, 136, 320.
Ah'la, Kirbet el, 230.
Ahsa, Wady el, 64.
Ain Jidy, 43.
Ajermeh Arabs, 169, 175, 177, 351.
Alukhi-kasr, 155.
Alexander, son of Hyrcanus, 275.
Ammonites, battle with Joab, 321.
Anazeh, 366.
'Anizeh, raid of, 206.
Ar of Moab, 121, 124, 133.
Ara'ar, Aroer, 144, 147.
Arab sacrifice, 262.
Areopolis, 124.
Aretas, 278.
Areyeh, Wady, 42.
Arnon, Pass of, 140.
Arrest at Kerak, 98.
Artillery, Turkish, 173.
Asabaia, 240.
Asal, Wady, 73.
Ashteroth Karnaim, 134.
'Atabeiyeh, Wady, 313.
Atargatis Carnion, 134.
Ataroth, 118, 283.
Atiyeh-beni, 33.
——, attack by, 58.
Atroth Shophan, 290.
Attarus, 283, 318.
——, *Jebel,* not Pisgah, 287.
——, trees on, 285.
——, view from, 286.

Aurora borealis, remarkable, 49.
Ayun Moussa, Wady, 332, 339, 347.
Azubarah, 240.
Azizah, Kirbet, 116.

Baal-meon, 316, 317.
Baaras, root, 277.
Balaam and Balak, 318.
Bal'hua, 139, 145.
Baris, 290.
Basalt blocks, 126, 137.
Bassus, L., 278.
Baths, natural hot, 254.
——, Arab hot, 261.
Beggars, Arab, 178.
Beiram, 172, 178.
Beit-harran, 360.
Beit el Kurm, 133.
Belka, the, 238, 333.
Beni Hamideh, 130, 245.
Beni Na'ur, 36.
Beni Sakk'r, 109, 351; character of, 156; migrations, 238, 293; pride of, 293.
Betan el Bareil, 243.
Bethany, 375.
Beth-haran, 360.
Beth-jeshimuth, 362.
Bethlehem, 23.
Beth-meon, 318.
Birch, Dr., 181.
Black country, 182.
Botany of Moab, 357; of Callirrhoe, 263.
Botany:
  Artemisium, 163, 184.
  Atriplex halimus, 264.
  Baaras, gigantic rue, 277.
  Crucifer, 264.
  Dæmia cordata, 263.

BOTANY, continued:
   Geranium, 269.
   Lonicera indica, 43.
   Maiden-hair fern, 45.
   Mistletoe, Oriental, 286.
   Orobanches, 264.
   Poterium spinosum, 144.
   Statice, 364.
   Tulipa gesneriana, 248.
Burials, primeval, 315.
Burckhardt, 85, 143.
Burrhoughat, 332, 334.
Bushariyeh, Kasr el, 63.
Butm, Wady, 165.
Butterflies of Callirrhoe, 264.
—— of Zara, 298.
Buxton, 19, 88, 110, 371.

CAIRNS, ancient, 189, 315, 359.
Caled, 220.
Callirrhoe, 248, 257, 368; botany of, 263; butterflies, 264; geology, 252, 258; legends on, 262; mouth of, 300; sacrifice at, 262; springs of, 256.
Camels, 170.
Camping in darkness, 144.
Carnaim, 134.
Castle of Kerak, 91.
Cat, wild, 156.
Cattle, only found in the Hamideh, 266.
——, breed of, 266.
Cemetery, Arab, 64.
Chapel, Crusading, 91.
Chaplin, Dr., 255.
Characmoab, 257.
Chedorlaomer's expedition, 134, 335.
Chosroes II., 224; history of, 223.
Churches, Christian, 159, 326, 342.
Circles of stones, primeval, 283, 359.
Coffee-making, Arab, 38, 177.
Cold, intense, of the plains, 232.
Crusading remains at Kerak, 90.

Dal'al, Wady, 41.
Daoud, our dragoman, 58, 101, 127.
Dead Sea, view of, 82; appearance, 369.
Deib, Wady ed, 332, 365.
Delaiyat, 243.
Dhiban, 146.

Dhra'a, 190.
Dibon, 146; vineyards of, 154.
Dimnah, 120, *n*.
Dimon, 120, *n*.
Diplomacy, Arab, 31.
Dodge, Rev. D. S., 180.
Dolmens, 283, 314, 358.
Dra'a, Wady, 79.
Drake, Mr. Tyrwhitt, 18, 130, 183, 218.
Duweineh, 124.

EDOM, ancient boundary of, 64.
El 'Ahl, 352.
Elealeh, 352.
Engedi, 43.
Es Salt, 174.
Essenes, the, 256.
Eusebius, 77, 151, 290, 322, 340.

FANTASIA, Arab, described, 44.
Feifeh, Wady, 64.
Fendi y Faiz, 241.
Fergusson, Mr., 88, 223, 378–395.
Fishing in Callirrhoe, 249.
Flora of Judean wilderness, 60.
Ford of the Dead Sea, 51.
Fox, sagacity of, 207.
Fulco, King, 92.

GAZELLE, 316.
Geology of Moab, 74–80, 252; of Callirrhoe, 252, 258; of Jebel Usdum, 55; of the highlands, 212.
Gerahi, Seil, 65.
Ghar, Wady el, 36, 40.
Ghawarineh tribe, 60, 359.
Ghedeid, Wady, 363.
Ghedeimeh, Wady, 332, 364.
Ghor es Sâfieh, 61, 67, 70.
Ghurrah, Wady, 136.
Ghurundel, Wady, 57, 65.
Ghuweir, Wady, 332.
Goblan, Sheik, 21, 329, 352, 353, 356.
Godfrey of Boulogne, 92.
Gra'hhi, 71.
Grove, Mr. G., 347.
Gypsies, 179.

Habis, Wady, 241.

INDEX.

Haditha, Jebel, 82.
Hadj road, 185, 212.
Hakim, expectations from, 265, 306.
Ham, Hameitát, Ham-mat, 132.
Hamad, 120, *n.*
Hamídeh, the, 130; character of, 246, 308.
——, Sheik, 245, 319; cattle of, 266; hospitality, 280.
Hammad, Wady, 86.
Hamman, el, 284.
Hamzi, Sheik, 27, 49, 58.
Hawizir, 71.
Haroun, Jebel, 51.
Hashib, Um el, 71.
Hatrura, Wady, 51.
Hattin, battle of, 81.
Hawara, Wady, 332, 366.
Hayne, Mr. W. A., 20, 110, 239, 292, 376.
Hebron, 28.
Hemta, 132.
Heraclius, 225.
Herod visits Callirrhoe, 255; fortifies Machærus, 276.
Herri, Kasr el, 192.
Heshban, Wady, 355.
Heshbon, 351; fish-pools of, 353.
Hhoweiyeh, 116.
Hhurreh, el, 182.
Hish, ras, 52.
Hor, Mount, 51.
Horse-hunting, 100, 283, 289.
Humeh, Jebel, 310.
Husasah, el, 41.

IBEX, 264, 305.
Ibex-hunter, 206.
Ibn Tarif, 130, 140.
Ibrahim Pasha, 92, 113, 205.
Irby and Mangles, 85, 143, 255.
Irrigation, ancient, 200.

JAHAZ, 139.
Jazel, 332.
Jedeid, Kirbet, 337; *Wady*, 332.
Jehalin, the, 67.
Jeib, Wady, 57.
Jelamet es Subhha, 114.
Jeljul, 118.

Jelul, Jebel, 240.
Jemeel, 329, 370.
Jephthah, 155.
Jericho, 374.
Jerifeh, Wady, 332, 339, 363.
Jeruel, wilderness of, 41.
Jerome, 124, 134, 151.
Jerusalem, destroyed by Chosroes, 224.
Jiahl, Jebel, 184.
Jiddreh, Wady, 167.
John Baptist, place of imprisonment and martyrdom, 278.
Johnson, R. C., 20, 110.
Jordan, ford of, 372.
Josephus, 137; description of Callirrhoe, 255; history of Machærus, 275, 276.

KA'ABINEH, the, 37.
Kefeir, 332.
Kerak, ascent to, 79, 84; entrance of, 84, 87; description of, 85, *seqq.*; wells of, 93; mosque of, 93; houses, 96; Roman baths at, 97; Christians of, 95, 106; Christian church at, 97; our arrest at, 99; Mudjelli of, 103; view from, 107; relations to Beni Sakk'r, 109; identity with Kir-moab, 120; visit to Sanhedrim of, 121.
Kerioth, 289.
Khazal, Sfayet, 165.
Kir-haraseth, 120.
Kirjath-huzoth, 318.
Kir-moab, 120.
Kiriathaim, 114, 289, 318.
Klein, Mr., 20, 68, 94, 97, 99, 100, 102, 103, 104, 106, 108, 110, 111, 120, 127, 128, 129, 136, 145, 255.
K'nif, Wady, 284.
Kobeisheh, Wady, 86.
Korcha, 71, 149.
Kubboh, el, 80.
Kureitun, 114.
Kureiyat, 289.
Kureiyeh, 289.
Kurm Dhiban, 154.
Kurmul, 35.
Kuseib, Wady, 57.
Kustul, 232.

414   INDEX.

Lasha, 132.
Legend of the Christian lady, 160.
Lejum, Seil, 153.
Letter-carrier robbed, 128, 308.
Lisan, features of, 73, 74; panorama of, 78.
Luynes, Duc de, 255.

Maccabæus, John, 322.
Maccabees, the, 275.
Machærus, ride to, 268; description of, 271.
Machpelah, cave of, 28.
Mâdin, 119.
Mahk'henah, 117.
Ma'in, 316.
Mammals:
   Canis niloticus, 211.
   Cheetah, 179.
   Felis caligata, 156.
   Gazelle, 215, 316.
   Ibex, 264, 305.
   Melio melanurus, 160.
   Spalax typhlus, 139, 327.
   Vulpes variegatus, 207.
   Wolf, 334.
Marl, deposition of, 75.
Marriage, Arab, 356.
Mars, temple of, 133.
Masada, 46.
Mâshitâ, discovery of, 212; sculpture of, 214; history of, 222; chapter on, by Mr. Fergusson, F.R.S., 378-395.
M'Deineh, 167.
Medeba, 319, 322, etc.; reservoir of, 326.
Mejd, Wady, 51.
Mejdelein, 136.
Mckhersit, 124.
Menjah, 155.
Mersed, 51.
Mesha, 117, 148, 149.
Mesh'had, 119.
Mezra'ah, 75.
M'Heiyat, 337.
M'hheileh, Wady, 116.
Mile-stones, Roman, 118, 131, 142, 358.
Minnith, 155.
Mirage, 185.

Mishor, or plain of Moab, geology of, 140, 153, 163.
Missdehh, 132.
M'khaur, 271; wells of, 272; citadel, 272; history of, 275.
Mkharrhas, Wady, 145, n.
Moab, towns of, 114.
Moabite Stone, 148.
Mochrath, 82, 118.
Modeh, 118.
Mole-rat, 139.
Moore, Mr. Noel, 134.
Mouriyeh, 120.
M'Seitbeh, 163, 164.
M'Shuggar, 350, 358.
Mudjelli, the, of Kerak, 104, 122; manœuvres of, 123, 128.
M thatet el Haj, 139.
Muleteers, artifices of, 22; prejudices of, 268.
Murwhashah, Nahr, 71.
Muslubeiyeh, 334, 385; view from, 335.

Nachal, 120.
Naturalist, Arab, 339, 370.
Na'ur, Wady, 156, 382, 340.
Nebo, 318, 338; view from, 338; identity of ancient site, 340.
Nebuchadnezzar, 150.
Nejd, Wady, 52.
Nekad, 116.
Nemriyeh, gorge of, 49.
Nim'r, 328.
Nimrim, waters of, 72.
Night affray, 77.
N'meirah, Wady, 71, 72.
"Notitia," the, 181, 197, 240.
N'ssour, Wady, 167.
Nubian slave-girl, 253.

Orak, Jebel, 72.
Oil-press, 151.
Ornithology:
   Ammoperdix heyi, 144.
   Aquila nævia, 248.
   Bimaculated duck, 233.
   Caccabis saxatilis, 144, 159.
   Corvus affinis, 264, 282, 307, 366.
   Cuckoo, spotted, 370.

INDEX.

ORNITHOLOGY, continued:
   Cypselus melba, 248, 366.
   Dotterell, 169.
   Griffons feeding, 239.
   Gypaëtus barbatus, 146.
   Imperial eagle, 232.
   Launer, 241.
   Passer moabiticus, 307.
   Sakk'r falcon, 207, 241, 366.
   Sand-grouse, 169.
   Saxicola monacha, 49.
   Sun-bird, 307.
   Sylvia melanothorax, 45.
   Tristram's grakle, 282, 307.
   Turtur risorius, 66.

PALMER, Professor, 18, 19, 64, 130, 161, 181, 322, 344.
Pasha, reception by the, 170.
Peor, 318.
Peutinger tables, 181.
Phocas, Emperor, 223.
Pisgah, 287, 318, 339.
Plain of Moab, 154, 163.
Pliny, description of Callirrhoe, 256; description of Machærus, 275.
Population, decay of, 201.
Porter, Dr., 18.
Ptolemy, description of Callirrhoe, 256.

QUARANTANIA, Mount, 374.

Rabba, 121; ruins of, 125; temple near, 132, 133.
Raid, Arab, 206.
Rain, effect of, in the wilderness, 39.
Rakim, 124.
Rashâyideh Arabs, 43.
R'mail, 191.
Reservoir, ancient, 198, 326.
Reuben, tribe of, 244.
Raynald of Chatillon, story of, 81.
Riha, er, 135.
Robbers, alarm of, 311.
Roman mile-stones, 118, 131, 142, 358.
Roman roads, 124, 131, 136, 142, 193, 271, 284, 286, 293, 313, 315.
R'seir, Wady, 83.

Rubt el Jamus, 51.
Ruins, how caused, 227.
Rujum Hamam, 237.
Rujum Selim, 155.

SACRIFICE, Arab, 262.
Sâfich, the, described, 61, 66, 70.
Safsaf, Wady, 51, 73.
Sahan, 112, 207, 243, 328.
Salt cave, 54.
—— Mountain, geology of, 54.
Samak, 175.
Sandstone, formation of Moab, 62.
Sassanian kings, 223.
School-master, Greek, at Kerak, 94.
Sebbeh, 46.
Seetzen, 151.
Seideh, Wady, 146.
Seisaban, the, 345, 360.
Selameh, Sheik, 31, 51, 58.
Selami, Mr., 171.
Senin, Wady, 51.
Seyal, Wady, 45.
Sheik 'Aisa, ruins of, 62.
Shihan, Jebel, 135, 136; ruins of, 138.
Shittim, Plain of, 336.
Shobek, Wady, 167.
Siddiyeh, Wady, 65.
Sihon, battle-field of, 137.
Skirmish, Arab, 58.
Sodom, site of, 344.
Solomon, Pools of, 24.
Solomon's Servant, legend of, 262.
Stones, custom of piling, 51.
——, written, search for, 180.
Stone circles, 283, 293, 359.
Store-houses, under-ground, 196.
Strabo on Machærus, 275.
Suaga, Jebel, 184.
Sudeir, Wady, 42, 45.
Sugar-mills, 76.
Suhl, 120.
Sulphur deposits, 258, 366.
Sum'hra, Kirbet es, 139.
Sumia, Castle of, 355.
Sunday observance, 207.
Suwaineh, Ain, 363.
Suweiniyeh, 124.
Synagogue, ancient, 48.

TA'AMIRAH, 22, 24, 35.
Teim, et, 290, 330.
Temples, Doric, 188, 195; Corinthian, 235.
Tents, Arab, description of, 37.
Terebinth-tree, 133.
—— of Attarus, 287.
Thamathæ, 181.
Thief-catching, 100.
Themed, Wady, 167, 179.
Thenib, 236.
Theniyeh, 120.
Trees on Attarus, 285.
Trotter, M., 20, 160, 168, 189, 232, 249.
Tufileh, Wady, 57, 64.
Turkish camp, 169.
Tziatin, 113.

Um Baghek, Wady, 51.
Um el Bedân, Wady, 51.
Um Halassah, 36.
Um el Kuscir, 197.
Um Rasas, 156; its churches, 158; tower of, 160.
Um Weleed, 193; khan, forum, and temple, 194, 195.
Usdum, Jebel, 52; geology of, 54, 55.

VINEYARDS, ancient, 155.

Waleh, Kirbet, el, 243.
Warren, Captain, 229.
Watch-towers of vineyards, 25.
Watering fields, system of, in Sâfieh, 61.
Weideh, Wady, 73.
Wells, 115, 119.

Wilderness of Judah, 39.
Willows, brook of, 72, 82.
Wilson, Captain, R. E., 49.
Wind, gale of, 371.
Wine-press, ancient, 116.
Wolf, 334.

Yakin, 36.

ZADAM, 20; rescues us, 103; courtesy of, 109, 243, 294, 356, 375, 376; at home, 167; marriage of, 356.
Zadoud, Kirbet, 36.
Zafaran, 191, 192.
Zamzummim, 132.
Zara, 270, 291; descent to, 293; oasis of, 295; to Callirrhoe from, 298.
Zared or Zered, brook, 64.
Zareth-shahar, 270, 291.
Zatum, 243.
Zebib, Khan, 185; caves and temples at, 187, 188.
Zerka Ma'in, Wady, or Callirrhoe, 249, 262, 287; mouth of, 300; clamber up the, 301.
Zi'ara, 338, 341; view from, 342; identity with Zoar, 343.
Ziph, wilderness of, 35, 36.
Ziz, cliff and pass of, 41.
Ziza, 197; tank of, 198; sculpture at, 204.
Zoar, conjectured, 76; bishop of, 76; identity with Zi'ara, 343.
Zophim, field of, 339.
Zuweirah, Wady, 52.
Zuzim, 132.

THE END.

VALUABLE AND INTERESTING

WORKS OF TRAVEL

PUBLISHED BY

HARPER & BROTHERS, New York.

☞ HARPER & BROTHERS *will send either of the following works by mail, postage prepaid, to any part of the United States, on receipt of the price.*

PIKE'S SUB-TROPICAL RAMBLES. Sub-Tropical Rambles in the Land of the Aphanapteryx. By NICHOLAS PIKE, U. S. Consul, Port Louis, Mauritius. Profusely Illustrated from the Author's own Sketches; containing also Maps and valuable Meteorological Charts. Crown 8vo, Cloth, $3 50.

THE LAND OF MOAB. The Result of Travels and Discoveries on the East Side of the Dead Sea and the Jordan. By H. B. TRISTRAM, M.A., LL.D., F.R.S., Master of the Greatham Hospital, and Honorary Canon of Durham. With New Map and Illustrations. Crown 8vo, Cloth, $2 50.

THE DESERT OF THE EXODUS. Journeys on Foot in the Wilderness of the Forty Years' Wanderings; undertaken in connection with the Ordnance Survey of Sinai and the Palestine Exploration Fund. By E. H. PALMER, M.A., Lord Almoner's Professor of Arabic, and Fellow of St. John's College, Cambridge. With Maps and numerous Illustrations from Photographs and Drawings taken on the spot by the Sinai Survey Expedition and C. F. Tyrwhitt Drake. Crown 8vo, Cloth, $3 00.

NORDHOFF'S CALIFORNIA. California: for Health, Pleasure, and Residence. A Book for Travellers and Settlers. Illustrated. 8vo, Paper, $2 00; Cloth, $2 50.

SANTO DOMINGO, Past and Present, with a Glance at Hayti. By SAMUEL HAZARD. Maps and Illustrations. Crown 8vo, Cloth, $3 50.

AROUND THE WORLD. By EDWARD D. G. PRIME, D.D. With numerous Illustrations. Crown 8vo, Cloth, $3 00.

ALCOCK'S JAPAN. The Capital of the Tycoon: a Narrative of a Three Years' Residence in Japan. By Sir RUTHERFORD ALCOCK, K.C.B., Her Majesty's Envoy Extraordinary and Minister Plenipotentiary in Japan. With Maps and Engravings. 2 vols., 12mo, Cloth, $3 50.

ANDERSSON'S OKAVANGO RIVER. The Okavango River: a Narrative of Travel, Exploration, and Adventure. By CHARLES JOHN ANDERSSON. With Steel Portrait of the Author, numerous Woodcuts, and a Map showing the Regions explored by Andersson, Cumming, Livingstone, and Du Chaillu. 8vo, Cloth, $3 25.

ANDERSSON'S LAKE NGAMI. Lake Ngami; or, Explorations and Discoveries during Four Years' Wanderings in the Wilds of Southwestern Africa. By CHARLES JOHN ANDERSSON. With numerous Illustrations, representing Sporting Adventures, Subjects of Natural History, Devices for Destroying Wild Animals, &c. 12mo, Cloth, $1 75.

ATKINSON'S AMOOR REGIONS. Travels in the Regions of the Upper and Lower Amoor, and the Russian Acquisitions on the Confines of India and China. With Adventures among the Mountain Kirghis; and the Manjours, Manyargs, Toungous, Touzempts, Goldi, and Gelyaks; the Hunting and Pastoral Tribes. By THOMAS WITLAM ATKINSON, F.G.S., F.R.G.S. With a Map and numerous Illustrations. 8vo, Cloth, $3 50.

c

Valuable and Interesting Works of Travel.

ATKINSON'S SIBERIA. Oriental and Western Siberia: a Narrative of Seven Years' Explorations and Adventures in Siberia, Mongolia, the Kirghis Steppes, Chinese Tartary, and Part of Central Asia. By THOMAS WITLAM ATKINSON. With a Map and numerous Illustrations. 8vo, Cloth, $3 50.

BARTH'S NORTH AND CENTRAL AFRICA. Travels and Discoveries in North and Central Africa. Being a Journal of an Expedition undertaken under the Auspices of H.B.M.'s Government, in the Years 1849–1855. By HENRY BARTH, Ph.D., D.C.L. Illustrated. 3 vols., 8vo, Cloth, $12 00·

BALDWIN'S AFRICAN HUNTING. African Hunting, from Natal to the Zambesi, including Lake Ngami, the Kalahari Desert, &c., from 1852 to 1860. By WILLIAM CHARLES BALDWIN, Esq., F.R.G.S. With Map, Fifty Illustrations by Wolf and Zwecker, and a Portrait. 12mo, Cloth, $1 50.

BURTON'S LAKE REGIONS OF CENTRAL AFRICA. The Lake Regions of Central Africa. A Picture of Exploration. By RICHARD F. BURTON, Captain H. M.'s Indian Army, Fellow and Gold Medalist of the Royal Geographical Society. With Maps and Engravings on Wood. 8vo, Cloth, $3 50.

BURTON'S CITY OF THE SAINTS. The City of the Saints; and Across the Rocky Mountains to California. By Captain RICHARD F. BURTON, Fellow and Gold Medalist of the Royal Geographical Societies of France and England, H. M.'s Consul in West Africa. With Maps and numerous Illustrations. 8vo, Cloth, $3 50.

BELLOWS'S TRAVELS. The Old World in its New Face: Impressions of Europe in 1867, 1868. By HENRY W. BELLOWS. 2 vols., 12mo, Cloth, $3 50.

CURTIS'S THE HOWADJI IN SYRIA. By GEORGE WILLIAM CURTIS. 12mo, Cloth, $1 50.

CURTIS'S NILE NOTES OF A HOWADJI. By GEORGE WILLIAM CURTIS. 12mo, Cloth, $1 50.

CUMMING'S HUNTER'S LIFE IN AFRICA. Five Years of a Hunter's Life in the far Interior of South Africa. With Notices of the Native Tribes, and Anecdotes of the Chase of the Lion, Elephant, Hippopotamus, Giraffe, Rhinoceros, &c. With Illustrations. By R. GORDON CUMMING. 2 vols., 12mo, Cloth, $3 00.

DAVIS'S CARTHAGE. Carthage and her Remains: being an Account of the Excavations and Researches on the Site of the Phœnician Metropolis in Africa and other Adjacent Places. Conducted under the Auspices of Her Majesty's Government. By Dr. N. DAVIS, F.R.G.S. Profusely Illustrated with Maps, Woodcuts, Chromo-Lithographs, &c. 8vo, Cloth, $4 00.

DILKE'S GREATER BRITAIN. Greater Britain: a Record of Travel in English-speaking Countries during 1866 and 1867. By CHARLES WENTWORTH DILKE. With Maps and Illustrations. 12mo, Cloth, $1 00.

DOOLITTLE'S CHINA. Social Life of the Chinese; with some Account of their Religious, Governmental, Educational, and Business Customs and Opinions. With special but not exclusive Reference to Fuhchau. By Rev. JUSTUS DOOLITTLE, Fourteen Years Member of the Fuhchau Mission of the American Board. Illustrated with more than 150 characteristic Engravings on Wood. 2 vols., 12mo, Cloth, $5 00.

DU CHAILLU'S AFRICA. Explorations and Adventures in Equatorial Africa; with Accounts of the Manners and Customs of the People, and of the Chase of the Gorilla, the Crocodile, Leopard, Elephant, Hippopotamus, and other Animals. By PAUL B. DU CHAILLU, Corresponding Member of the American Ethnological Society, of the Geographical and Statistical Society of New York, and of the Boston Society of Natural History. With numerous Illustrations. 8vo, Cloth, $5 00.

DU CHAILLU'S ASHANGO LAND. A Journey to Ashango Land, and Further Penetration into Equatorial Africa. By PAUL B. DU CHAILLU. New Edition. Handsomely Illustrated. 8vo, Cloth, $5 00.

Valuable and Interesting Works of Travel. 3

ELLIS'S MADAGASCAR. Three Visits to Madagascar, during the Years 1853, 1854, 1856. Including a Journey to the Capital, with Notices of the Natural History of the Country, and of the Present Civilization of the People. By the Rev. WILLIAM ELLIS, F.H.S. Illustrated by a Map and Woodcuts from Photographs, &c. 8vo, Cloth, $3 50.

HALL'S ARCTIC RESEARCHES. Arctic Researches and Life among the Esquimaux: being the Narrative of an Expedition in Search of Sir John Franklin, in the Years 1860, 1861, and 1862. By CHARLES FRANCIS HALL. With Maps and 100 Illustrations. 8vo, Cloth, Beveled, $5 00.

HOLTON'S NEW GRANADA. Twenty Months in the Andes. By I. F. HOLTON. Illustrations and Maps. 8vo, Cloth, $3 00.

KINGSLEY'S WEST INDIES. At Last: A Christmas in the West Indies. By CHARLES KINGSLEY, Author of "Alton Locke," "Yeast," &c., &c. Illustrated. 12mo, Cloth, $1 50.

LIVINGSTONE'S SOUTH AFRICA. Missionary Travels and Researches in South Africa; including a Sketch of Sixteen Years' Residence in the Interior of Africa, and a Journey from the Cape of Good Hope to Loando on the West Coast; thence across the Continent, down the River Zambesi, to the Eastern Ocean. By DAVID LIVINGSTONE, LL.D., D.C.L. With Portrait, Maps by Arrowsmith, and numerous Illustrations. 8vo, Cloth, $4 50.

LIVINGSTONE'S EXPEDITION TO THE ZAMBESI. Narrative of an Expedition to the Zambesi and its Tributaries; and of the Discovery of the Lakes Shirwa and Nyassa. 1858–1864. By DAVID and CHARLES LIVINGSTONE. With Map and Illustrations. 8vo, Cloth, $5 00.

LAYARD'S NINEVEH. A Popular Account of the Discoveries at Nineveh. By AUSTEN HENRY LAYARD. Abridged by him from his larger Work. With numerous Wood Engravings. 12mo, Cloth, $1 75.

LAYARD'S FRESH DISCOVERIES AT NINEVEH. Fresh Discoveries at Nineveh and Babylon; with Travels in Armenia, Kurdistan, and the Desert. Being the Result of a Second Expedition undertaken for the Trustees of the British Museum. By AUSTEN HENRY LAYARD, M.P. With all the Maps and Engravings in the English Edition. 8vo, Cloth, $4 00.

MACGREGOR'S ROB ROY ON THE JORDAN. The Rob Roy on the Jordan, Nile, Red Sea, and Gennesareth, &c. A Canoe Cruise in Palestine and Egypt, and the Waters of Damascus. By J. MACGREGOR, M.A. With Maps and Illustrations. Crown 8vo, Cloth, $2 50.

NEVIUS'S CHINA. China and the Chinese: a General Description of the Country and its Inhabitants; its Civilization and Form of Government; its Religious and Social Institutions; its Intercourse with other Nations; and its Present Condition and Prospects. By the Rev. JOHN L. NEVIUS, Ten Years a Missionary in China. With a Map and Illustrations. 12mo, Cloth, $1 75.

OLIPHANT'S CHINA AND JAPAN. Narrative of the Earl of Elgin's Mission to China and Japan, in the Years 1857, '58, '59. By LAURENCE OLIPHANT, Private Secretary to Lord Elgin. Illustrations. 8vo, Cloth, $3 50.

ORTON'S ANDES AND THE AMAZON. The Andes and the Amazon; or, Across the Continent of South America. By JAMES ORTON, M.A., Professor of Natural History in Vassar College, Poughkeepsie, N. Y., and Corresponding Member of the Academy of Natural Sciences, Philadelphia. With a New Map of Equatorial America and numerous Illustrations. Crown 8vo, Cloth, $2 00.

PAGE'S LA PLATA. La Plata, the Argentine Confederation, and Paraguay. Being a Narrative of the Exploration of the Tributaries of the River La Plata and Adjacent Countries during the Years 1853, '54, '55, and '56, under the Orders of the United States Government. New Edition, containing Farther Explorations in La Plata during 1859 and 1860. By THOMAS J. PAGE, U. S. N., Commander of the Expeditions. With Map and numerous Engravings. 8vo, Cloth, $5 00.

Valuable and Interesting Works of Travel.

PRIME'S (S. I.) TRAVELS IN EUROPE AND THE EAST. Travels in Europe and the East. A Year in England, Scotland, Ireland, Wales, France, Belgium, Holland, Germany, Austria, Italy, Greece, Turkey, Syria, Palestine, and Egypt. By Rev. SAMUEL IRENÆUS PRIME, D.D. Engravings. 2 vols., large 12mo, Cloth, $3 00.

REINDEER, DOGS, AND SNOW-SHOES. A Journal of Siberian Travel and Explorations made in the Years 1865-'67. By RICHARD J. BUSH, late of the Russo-American Telegraph Expedition. Illustrated. Crown 8vo, Cloth, $3 00.

PRIME'S (W. C.) BOAT-LIFE IN EGYPT. Boat-Life in Egypt and Nubia. By WILLIAM C. PRIME. Illustrations. 12mo, Cloth, $2 00.

PRIME'S (W. C.) TENT-LIFE IN THE HOLY LAND. By WILLIAM C. PRIME. Illustrations. 12mo, Cloth, $2 00.

SQUIER'S NICARAGUA. Nicaragua: its People, Scenery, Monuments, Resources, Condition, and Proposed Canal. With One Hundred Maps and Illustrations. By E. G. SQUIER. 8vo, Cloth, $4 00.

SQUIER'S WAIKNA. Waikna; or, Adventures on the Mosquito Shore. By E. G. SQUIER. With a Map and upward of 60 Illustrations. 12mo, Cloth, $1 50.

SPEKE'S AFRICA. Journal of the Discovery of the Source of the Nile. By Captain JOHN HANNING SPEKE, Captain H. M.'s Indian Army, Fellow and Gold Medalist of the Royal Geographical Society, Hon. Corresponding Member and Gold Medalist of the French Geographical Society, &c. With Maps and Portraits and numerous Illustrations, chiefly from Drawings by Captain Grant. 8vo, Cloth, $4 00.

STEPHENS'S TRAVELS IN CENTRAL AMERICA. Travels in Central America, Chiapas, and Yucatan. By J. L. STEPHENS. With a Map and 88 Engravings. 2 vols., 8vo, Cloth, $6 00.

STEPHENS'S TRAVELS IN YUCATAN. Incidents of Travel in Yucatan. By J. L. STEPHENS. 120 Engravings, from Drawings by F. Catherwood. 2 vols., 8vo, Cloth, $6 00.

STEPHENS'S TRAVELS IN EGYPT. Travels in Egypt, Arabia Petræa, and the Holy Land. By J. L. STEPHENS. Engravings. 2 vols., 12mo, Cloth, $3 00.

STEPHENS'S TRAVELS IN GREECE. Travels in Greece, Turkey, Russia and Poland. By J. L. STEPHENS. Engravings. 2 vols., 12mo, Cloth, $3 00.

THOMSON'S LAND AND BOOK. The Land and the Book; or, Biblical Illustrations drawn from the Manners and Customs, the Scenes and the Scenery of the Holy Land. By W. M. THOMSON, D.D., Twenty-five Years a Missionary of the A.B.C.F.M. in Syria and Palestine. With Two elaborate Maps of Palestine, an accurate Plan of Jerusalem, and *Several Hundred Engravings*, representing the Scenery, Topography, and Productions of the Holy Land, and the Costumes, Manners, and Habits of the People. Two large 12mo Volumes, Cloth, $5 00.

WALLACE'S MALAY ARCHIPELAGO. The Malay Archipelago: the Land of the Orang-Utan and the Bird of Paradise. A Narrative of Travel, 1854-'62. With Studies of Man and Nature. By ALFRED RUSSEL WALLACE. With Maps and numerous Illustrations. Crown 8vo, Cloth, $2 50.

WELLS'S EXPLORATIONS IN HONDURAS. Explorations and Adventures in Honduras; comprising Sketches of Travel in the Gold Regions of Olancho, and a Review of the History and General Resources of Central America. By WILLIAM V. WELLS. With Original Maps and numerous Illustrations. 8vo, Cloth, $3 50.

WHYMPER'S ALASKA. Travel and Adventure in the Territory of Alaska, formerly Russian America—now ceded to the United States—and in various other Parts of the North Pacific. By FREDERICK WHYMPER. With Map and Illustrations. Crown 8vo, Cloth, $2 50.

WILKINSON'S ANCIENT EGYPTIANS. A Popular Account of the Ancient Egyptians. Revised and abridged from his larger Work. By Sir J. GARDNER WILKINSON, D.C.L., F.R.S., &c. Illustrated with 500 Woodcuts. 2 vols., 12mo, Cloth, $3 50.

www.ingramcontent.com/pod-product-compliance
Lightning Source LLC
Chambersburg PA
CBHW020533300426
44111CB00008B/641